REVISITING HERSTORIES

The Young Lords Party

ALSO BY IRIS MORALES

BOOKS
Through the Eyes of Rebel Women: The Young Lords, 1969-1976
(2016)

Latinas: Struggles and Protests in 21st Century USA, Anthology
Editor and Author (2018)

Voices from Puerto Rico: Post Hurricane María/
Voces desde Puerto Rico: Pos-Huracán María
Anthology Editor (2019)

Vicki: A Summer of Change! / ¡Un verano de cambio!
Children's book co-authored with Dr. Raquel M. Ortiz (2020)

ESSAYS ABOUT THE YOUNG LORDS
"Power to the People!"
Palante: Voices and Photographs of the Young Lords, 1969-1971 (2011)

"¡Palante, Siempre Palante!" Interview with Richie Pérez
Centro Journal, Volume xxi Number 2. (Fall 2009)

"¡Palante, Siempre Palante! The Young Lords"
The Puerto Rican Movement: Voices from the Diaspora (1998)

DOCUMENTARY
¡Palante, Siempre Palante! The Young Lords
Producer, writer and codirector (1996)
Distributed by Third World Newsreel. www.twn.org

REVISITING HERSTORIES

The Young Lords Party

IRIS MORALES

Red Sugarcane Press, Inc.
New York, New York

Revisiting Herstories: The Young Lords Party
Copyright © 2023 Iris Morales

Red Sugarcane Press, Inc.
534 West 112th Street #250404
New York, New York 10025
www.RedSugarcanePress.com

Book cover and interior design: Iris Morales

ISBN: 978-1-7340271-9-8
Library of Congress Control Number: 2022922406

Printed in the United States of America

Dedicated to my mother Almida Roldán
and the women of her generation who
migrated from Puerto Rico and created
opportunities for their daughters to have
more liberated lives.

To the human rights organizers and activists
who hold our hopes and dreams in their actions.

CONTENTS

Illustrations

ABBREVIATIONS

BPP	Black Panther Party
BWA	Black Women's Alliance
BWLC	Black Women's Liberation Caucus
CESA	Committee to End Sterilization Abuse
CCNY	City College of New York
CUNY	City University of New York
DRUM	Detroit Revolutionary Unity Movement
FBI	Federal Bureau of Investigation
GLC	Gay and Lesbian Caucus
GLF	Gay Liberation Front
HRUM	Health Revolutionary Unity Movement
IWK	I Wor Kuen
LGBTQ	Lesbian, gay, bisexual, transgender, and questioning
MPI	Movimiento Pro Independencia
PRNP	Puerto Rican Nationalist Party
PRRWO	Puerto Rican Revolutionary Workers Organization
PSP	Partido Socialista Puertorriqueño (Puerto Rican Socialist Party)
PRSU	Puerto Rican Student Union
SNCC	Student Nonviolent Coordinating Committee
STAR	Street Transvestite Action Revolutionaries
TLC	Think Lincoln Committee
TWGR	Third World Gay Revolution
TWWA	Third World Women's Alliance
UPR	University of Puerto Rico
WC	Women's Caucus
WU	Women's Union
YWAF	Youth Against War and Fascism
YLO	Young Lords Organization
YLP	Young Lords Party

PREFACE

Extraordinary political events erupted in Puerto Rico in the summer of 2019. Over five hundred thousand people streamed into the streets and highways of the capital, San Juan, demanding that Governor Ricardo Rosselló resign.[1] Marchers carried Puerto Rican flags of all sizes and huge banners that read, #Ricky Renuncia. (Ricky Resign.) The immediate spark was an exposé of hundreds of pages of chats between the governor and his closest advisers. Their messages revealed pervasive abuse of power and contained sexist, racist, misogynist, homophobic, and other offensive content. The officials made derogatory and insulting remarks about women and LGBTQ individuals. They even mocked victims of hurricane disasters. Outraged by their absolute disdain for the people, Puerto Ricans from all walks of life joined the demonstrations. The chats were yet another transgression heaped on decades of government corruption and severe austerity politics. Marchers shouted "*¡Somos más, y no tenemos miedo!*" ("We are more, and we are not afraid"). It was a *leaderful* movement. At the forefront were feminists,[2] Afro-Boricuas,[3] queer activists, young people, and artists. In New York City, Puerto Ricans rallied at Columbus Circle, echoing protesters' demands that the governor resign. I was among them.

As Governor Rosselló made one excuse after another about the chats, more and more people joined the protests, bringing renewed international attention to US colonialism in Puerto Rico. Rosselló insisted he would not resign, but after twelve days of the massive demonstrations, he was compelled to do so. The power of the people achieved this collective victory. Though it soon became apparent that another colonial puppet would replace Rosselló, his ouster was a victory, nonetheless, and cause for celebration. Jubilant Puerto Ricans of all ages gathered, singing, playing drums, and dancing in front of San Juan's capitol building, and in town plazas across the country. They expressed joy and happiness to be rid of this agent of colonialism and corruption. As the people of Puerto Rico celebrated, so did Puerto Ricans across the diaspora.

When news about these events broke, former members of the Young Lords Organization were preparing for the commemoration of the group's founding in New York. The victory in Puerto Rico energized the fiftieth anniversary celebration and inspired the writing of this book.

On July 26, 1969, the Young Lords Organization formed a chapter in New York City, demanding "self-determination for Puerto Ricans on the island and inside the United States."[4] By engaging in people-to-people organizing, bold acts of civil disobedience, and mass protests, the Young Lords sparked a grassroots movement against poverty, racism, government neglect, and corporate exploitation. Thousands joined the movement—high school and college students, young mothers, retail and service workers, former gang members, Vietnam War veterans, artists, and community organizers. Most were first-generation Puerto Ricans, born or raised in the United States. Other Latinx and African American young people also enlisted. The diversity of experiences grounded the organization in the realities, sufferings, and triumphs of low-income and working-class Puerto Ricans.

I joined the Young Lords Organization in New York in 1969, later renamed the Young Lords Party, then the Puerto Rican Revolutionary Workers Organization, and was a member for over five years. I've documented these experiences in the award-winning film *¡Palante, Siempre Palante! The Young Lords*, the book *Through the Eyes of Rebel Women: The Young Lords, 1969–1976*, and many articles. Building on this work, *Revisiting Herstories: The Young Lords Party* is an in-depth examination of the rise and decline of revolutionary feminist ideals and campaigns from 1969 through 1972. In this seminal period for US feminists of color, the women in the Young Lords brought a focus to gender justice and played an important role in shaping the organization's liberatory politics and practices. The focus on the activism and contributions of women members, necessarily reviews theories of US feminists of color and ideologies of revolutionary nationalist movements, among other topics. Our activism paralleled that of Black, Latinx, Asian, and Indigenous feminists with whom we shared interconnected struggles for racial, economic, and social justice.

Revisiting Herstories: The Young Lords Party is about women's activism. It is also about the battle of ideas. I write about these experiences as "part of a larger process, as one voice in a dialogue among people who have been silenced."[5] What follows is a multifaceted account of the contributions of women members and a more nuanced history of the Young Lords Organization.

The activism of Puerto Rican women in the United States was not new. From the earliest migrations, women trailblazers fought for justice in workplaces, neighborhoods, schools, and society at large. Among them were activists such as labor organizer and feminist Luisa Capetillo; poet, journalist, and nationalist Julia de Burgos; and education rights and community organizer Evelina López Antonetty, to name a few. The women in the Young Lords ushered in "another cycle of militancy"[6] determined to fight poverty, racism, sexism, and other societal ills. We brought attention to the concerns of Puerto Ricans in low-income communities and believed that wherever women faced injustice, it was a woman's issue. As Black "woman warrior poet" Audre Lorde so insightfully wrote, "There is no such thing as a single-issue struggle because we do not live single-issue lives."[7]

Our political ideas flowed from several historical rivers. We identified as socialists and nationalists. Our central demand was self-determination. As "revolutionary nationalists," we were inspired by and allied with the Black Panther Party to fight poverty and white supremacy. As Puerto Rican nationalists, the Nationalist Party of Puerto Rico was our main inspiration. We organized to end Puerto Rico's colonial status and policies that orchestrated the post–World War II mass migration and displacement of Puerto Ricans to US ghettos. As children of this migration, we saw ourselves as "colonial subjects" intimately familiar with US imperialism and connected with anticolonial movements around the world.

Long before we knew the words "feminist" or "patriarchy," we experienced gender discrimination. We yearned for something different—for economic, social, cultural, and political freedom. Our aspirations birthed a women's agenda grounded in our lived experiences and political analysis. We allied with Black feminists who rejected prioritizing women's oppression over racism, and vice versa. The feminism we "defended was radically anti-racist, anti-capitalist, and anti-imperialist, therefore anti-patriarchal."[8] We understood that the inequities we lived as women of color were not solely the result of gender but the outcome of intersecting social locations, class and economic interests, race and national origin, and the legacy of history.

From the outset, the nationalist ideology of the Young Lords Organization, led by an all-male Central Committee, conflicted with feminist ideals. Male supremacy promoted gendered and inferior roles for women. In 1970, the women in the New York chapter formed a caucus to challenge the organization's patriarchal structure and beliefs and successfully ended blatant gender discrimination. In 1971, a Young Lords' "people's organization," the Women's Union, formed to address the concerns of women in the community and created a platform that combined socialist, feminist, and nationalist beliefs. It called for full employment, an end to rape and gender violence, the liberation of Puerto Rico, and a socialist society, among other demands. At a high point, the activities and ideas of women members gained the Young Lords Party a reputation as a leading feminist voice in the New Left. The momentum ended, however, when the Central Committee members pronounced gender and racial justice struggles were of secondary importance.

The herstories and contributions of women in the Young Lords Party are absent from the literature of the women's liberation and social justice movements. Even chronicles and histories of the Young Lords Organization ignore revolutionary feminist ideas and activism in favor of male-centered narratives that dominate most academic and popular renderings. *Revisiting Herstories: The Young Lords Party* opens new avenues of study for activists and scholars. The words of historian and women's studies scholar Edna Acosta-Belén have special resonance. She observes:

> Building a historical memory, however, is always a rugged and convoluted terrain of contesting claims, but more so for those populations that have endured the coloniality of being silenced and are seeking to voice their untold stories, and in this way, contribute to the production of new decolonial knowledge.[9]

"Contesting claims" is not only about historical erasure; it also addresses issues of individual and collective representation. How are women of color represented? Are women portrayed as social change agents and revolutionaries? And what ideas, actions, and strategies advanced by women of color are documented as worthy of passing on to future generations? At stake is not only how we interpret the past "but also the most effective action for the future."[10]

In recounting this herstory, I took notes from *Silencing the Past: Power and the Production of History* by Michel-Rolph Trouillot, the renowned Haitian anthropologist and scholar. Trouillot reminds us: "[T]he past does not exist independently from the present."[11] Guided by the link between "past" and "present," I combed through many different sources, familiar narratives, and silences, probing and minutely studying fragments of overlooked stories. Chicanx and women's studies scholar Maylei Blackwell describes the practice as "retrofitted memory." She writes:

> [S]ocial actors read the interstices, gaps, and silences of existing historical narratives in order to retrofit, rework, and refashion older narratives to create new historical openings, political possibilities, and genealogies of resistance.[12]

Using this lens to discover discarded or forgotten herstories brought new life and vitality to existing accounts of the Young Lords Party.

Despite limited materials about the activism of Puerto Rican feminists in the diaspora in the 1969 to 1972 period, the tremendous development in gender studies since then offered a wealth of resources to supplement my interpretations and conclusions. I'm thankful for the availability of research and scholarship that allowed a wider and more detailed examination of the 1960s and 1970s movements. It gave language to concepts and practices we explored intuitively as Young Lords but for which we had no words. Hence, a more accurate and complex portrayal emerges about the role and contributions of revolutionary feminists in the organization.

Revisiting Herstories: The Young Lords Party is an insider-outsider perspective, combining primary sources and research with lived experiences. It reflects my analysis and interpretation, including my assessment of the organization's strengths, mistakes, and lessons learned. Trouillot emphasizes: "Historical actors are also narrators, and vice versa."[13] Reexamining these histories, I was acutely aware that social justice movements look different from a distance than they do when living the intensity of the day-to-day organizing. To anchor the narrative, I began with a chronology of events, relying on the organization's primary source documents—letters, retreat reports, position papers, essays, speeches, and newspaper articles. Interviews with and articles written by women members add crucial experiences. Research about the philosophies of feminists of color, histories of Puerto Rico, African American liberation struggles, texts from the queer movement, and readings regarding the relation between nationalism and feminism provide context and political analysis. Intertwined are my reflections inspired by Lucille Clifton's poem, "Why Some People Be Mad at Me Sometimes." She writes,

> they ask me to remember
> but they want me to remember
> their memories
> and i keep on remembering
> mine[14]

Note that I use both "I" and "we." "I" refers to my views. "We" indicates beliefs and actions developed and shared collectively. Primarily, I use the political terms of the period.

Revisiting Herstories: The Young Lords Party is organized in five sections. References to "Young Lords" or "Young Lords Organization" indicates the timeframe from 1969 through 1972. "Young Lords Party" is specific to the period from May 1970 to July 1972. Important events already described in *Through the Eyes of Rebel Women: The Young Lords 1969-1976* are referenced but not detailed in this book.

Part I, "Another Cycle of Grassroots Militancy," sets the historical context. The first chapter introduces the emergence of the Young Lords Organization in New York City in 1969. Chapter 2 provides an overview of early activities and the main tenets of the Young Lords' revolutionary nationalist ideology. Chapter 3 focuses on the rise of the Women's Caucus.

Part II, "Feminists of Color and Gender Justice Movements," reviews herstories that inspired women in the Young Lords Organization. Reproductive rights and the battle against involuntary and coerced sterilization were principal concerns. Chapter 4 reviews population control politics implemented in Puerto Rico and the United States and surveys reproductive justice campaigns led by feminists of color. Chapter 5 discusses the influence of the Black and Chicana feminists' movements. It describes relationships between women in the Young Lords and other feminists of color and the ascendency of feminist ideas in the organization. Chapter 6 focuses on ten demands the Women's Caucus presented to the Central Committee and the gains achieved. In May 1970, the New York YLO becomes the Young Lords Party and organizational changes advance the status of women. Chapter 7 examines the relationship between the YLP and LGBTQ movements.

The chapters in Part III, "We Do Not Live Single-Issue Lives," focus on campaigns during 1970 in which women members of the Young Lords Party played key roles. Chapter 8 details several protests at Lincoln Hospital, demanding health care as a human right. It emphasizes the leading role of Puerto Rican and African American women hospital workers and the intersectionality of feminism, workplace, and community organizing. Chapter 9 reviews a series of New York City jail rebellions and community protests directed against the criminal justice system. It recaps inside/outside organizing strategies and efforts implemented at the Women's House of Detention. Chapter 10 summarizes collaborations between the Puerto Rican Student Union and the Young Lords Party that mobilized thousands in the United States to support Puerto Rico's pro-independence movement and launched Free Puerto Rico Now! committees in high schools and colleges.

Part IV, "Nationalisms and Feminisms," analyzes the ascent of narrow nationalist ideas and practices and their impact on feminist organizing. Chapter 11 focuses on the debate among Central Committee members regarding the role of the Young Lords Party in Puerto Rico. They decide the organization's main political priority was Puerto Rico's anticolonial struggle and open two branches in the archipelago. In the United States, the work shifted to creating "people's organizations." Chapter 12 details the formation of the Women's Union, its organizing activities and intersectional feminist, nationalist, and socialist agenda. Chapter 13 details the rise of nationalist ideas that abandoned the Women's Union's agenda and feminist organizing. Narrow nationalist ideas ascend but fail. By mid-1972, the YLP branches in Puerto Rico were compelled to close. Back in the United States, the Young Lords Party morphed into the Puerto Rican Revolutionary Workers Organization, continuing to its demise in 1976.

Part V, "Reckoning with the Past," sums up recurring themes and challenges. Chapter 14 reviews the role of the FBI and New York City police in the organization's disintegration and decline. Chapter 15 sums up the struggles of the Women's Caucus and Women's Union toward a socialist feminist agenda and analyzes the factors that advanced and derailed it. Today, feminist organizing must reckon with the impact of COVID-19 and the intensification of poverty and inequalities for women across and within countries. The pandemic has created new challenges.

In the 1960s and 1970s, US feminists of color fought patriarchy, male privilege, classism, and racism to bring about systemic changes and a just society for everyone. Local struggles linked with and supported international "Third World" feminist movements. Puerto Rican, Black, Indigenous, Asian, and other women of color took to the streets and organized movements for economic, gender, and racial justice in neighborhoods, workplaces, and schools. The socialist feminist activism of women in the Young Lords Party charted new ground in the Puerto Rican diaspora. In the following pages, *Revisiting Herstories: The Young Lords Party* grapples with a past whose concerns are still very much present.

Iris Morales
2022

PART I.
ANOTHER CYCLE OF GRASSROOTS MILITANCY

Revolution is a great act of imagination and creativity where we fight for a future that does not yet exist.[1]

—Zuleica Romay Guerra, Director of Afro-American Studies at Casa de las Américas, Havana, 2021.

Fig 1. The Young Lords Party. New York City. June 1970.
(Courtesy: Michael Abramson)

1.
HUMAN RIGHTS, NOT JUST CIVIL RIGHTS

> No one person starts, let alone sustains, a movement.
> A movement is only made possible when there is a
> collective vision, mission, strategy, working hands,
> walking feet, listening ears, and resources. A movement
> is not spontaneous; it is a cumulative set of human
> circumstances over a period of time when a critical
> mass of people in one accord say, "enough is enough,"
> and we are not going to take disrespect anymore.[1]
>
> —Gwendolyn Patton, From letter on the sixtieth anniversary
> of the Montgomery Bus Boycott, 2015

The Young Lords emerged in East Harlem, New York in the summer of 1969. Garbage was piled high and strewn throughout the streets because the sanitation department did not haul it away. Neighborhood residents were sick and tired of the vermin, the putrid smells, and the respiratory health problems it bred. A group of Puerto Rican activists, the Young Lords, began sweeping the streets, putting the garbage in trash bags, and demanding that it be cleared. But government officials did nothing. In response to their silence, local people joined the activists. They pushed the trash to the middle of the street and set it on fire. The garbage cleanup turned into a confrontation with the police, and all traffic through the area came to a halt. Police cars and fire engines raced in, sirens blasting. New York City sanitation trucks, trailing behind, began to pick up the garbage.[2] Television news reporters and camera crews rushed uptown to get the story about young Puerto Rican New Yorkers, burning trash and demanding that the city clean the streets. The dramatic story aired on the evening news. Audiences watched with curiosity. Who were the Young Lords?

On July 26th, the activists announced the formation of the New York State chapter of the Young Lords Organization at a public event in Tompkins Square Park. The group consisted of students from the State University of New York at Old Westbury and youth activists from the

Lower East Side and East Harlem. They had been meeting since early 1969 and read in the Black Panther Party's newspaper an article about the Chicago Young Lords. The former street gang had transformed into a human-rights organization in 1968 with the objective of fighting for the rights of Puerto Ricans. Several New York activists drove to Chicago to meet the Young Lords and returned with authorization to open a chapter.

Women joined the Young Lords Organization in New York from the start. Poverty, racism, migration, and gender discrimination shaped our activism. We grew up in the city's most destitute neighborhoods. Most of us were Puerto Rican, born or raised in the United States in Spanish-speaking, working-class homes. African American, Cuban, Dominican, Mexican, and Panamanian women, as well as women of Puerto Rican–Filipino and Puerto Rican–South Asian backgrounds, also joined. We were young—sixteen to twenty-six years old. In our ranks were mothers with young children, high school and college students, service and retail workers, homemakers, survivors of domestic violence and alcohol and drug addiction, artists, and community organizers. English was our primary language, although most of us spoke Spanish and/or Spanglish, a mix of Spanish and English. At the high point, women made up one-third to 40 percent of the membership.[3] On our blouses and scarfs, we pinned a button that read, "Tengo Puerto Rico en mi corazón," "I have Puerto Rico in my heart," exclaiming our love for Puerto Rico and our yearning for home. We wore purple berets but no other uniform. The berets were a symbol, linking us to social justice activists and revolutionaries around the world.

THE GREAT PUERTO RICAN MIGRATION AFTER WORLD WAR II

The story of the Young Lords begins in the Caribbean. On July 25, 1898, the United States invaded and began the colonization of Puerto Rico. Puerto Ricans were made US citizens in 1917 and as such did not require a passport to enter the United States. After World War II, Puerto Rico experienced a mass exodus as a direct result of colonial conditions. About 470,000 Puerto Ricans arrived in the United States during a ten-year-period.[4] They came from the poor and working-class sectors—uprooted farmers and sugarcane workers, domestics, Afro-Boricuas, and the unemployed. Like most immigrants, they left home for the promise of economic opportunity. The constant migration back-and-forth to Puerto Rico kept strong connections between families living in the United States and those back home. This bilateral flow of people became known as "circular" or "commuter" migration.

In *Puerto Ricans in the United States: A Contemporary Portrait,* the distinguished scholars Edna Acosta-Belén and Carlos E. Santiago detail the reasons for the migration.[5] The US invasion of Puerto Rico caused extreme poverty as large absentee American corporations destroyed the agriculture and sugar industries. They seized ownership of the land and forced farmers into migrant labor, low-wage jobs, unemployment, and scarcity.[6] Officials attributed the devastating poverty to "overpopulation" and accused Puerto Ricans of having too high fertility rates.[7] This led to the mass sterilization of Puerto Rican women, begun in the 1930s, which reached among the highest rates of this procedure in the world.[8] In 1947, the Puerto Rican government launched the "Operation Bootstrap" industrialization program as a proposed solution to poverty. It gave US companies access to low-cost labor and generous tax breaks and promoted the emigration of the poorest people from the archipelago.[9]

Most Puerto Ricans settled in large US cities—New York, Chicago, and Philadelphia—but also in smaller towns throughout the Northeast.[10] They were met with xenophobia and lack of economic opportunities. The geographer Matthew Gandy describes the conditions in "Between Borinquen and the *Barrio*: Environmental Justice and New York City's Puerto Rican Community, 1969-1972."

> The new arrivals found that they were restricted to menial, poorly paid work—if they worked at all—in combination with overcrowded, dilapidated housing and inadequate access to basic services such as education and health care.[11]

Puerto Ricans also confronted language barriers for speaking Spanish and racism and ethnic discrimination as a mixed-race people.[12]

In New York City's low-income communities, Puerto Ricans lived side by side with African Americans who had arrived from the South. We shared migration stories and learned about Jim Crow racism and discrimination. Between 1964 and 1968, uprisings in low-income neighborhoods, including in Harlem, rocked the United States.[13] They were caused by glaring poverty, enduring Jim Crow segregation, and rampant police brutality and murders. Many young Puerto Ricans raised in the United States joined African Americans in the fight against white supremacy and racism. Malcolm X expressed the essential principle of Black liberation and the humanist aspirations of the movement, asserting:

> We declare our right on this earth to be a man, to be respected as a human being, to be given the rights of a human being in this society, on this earth, in this day, which we intend to bring into existence by any means necessary.[14]

For many young Puerto Rican activists, like myself, Malcolm X was our hero.

In 1966, the Student Nonviolent Coordinating Committee (SNCC), a leading civil rights organization in the US South, led the call for "Black Power." Among its leaders were Ella Baker, Stokely Carmichael, and Jamil Abdullah Al-Amin (H. Rap Brown). The call for Black Power reflected a new militancy. SNCC had experienced "a profound transformation, not simply an escalation in militancy but also a shift in vision, philosophy, and structure."[15] Historian and activist Barbara Ransby explains that the civil rights fight for integration with white America had given way to the goal of revolutionary societal transformation.[16] In California, the Black Panther Party for Self-Defense popularized a 10-Point Program demanding employment, land, housing, justice for African Americans, and an immediate end to police brutality.[17] When Martin Luther King Jr. was assassinated in 1968, an outpouring of grief, frustration, and anger led to uprisings in more than one hundred US cities.[18] Many people had lost faith that the United States could be reformed via elections or legislation.

Deepening poverty and state violence accelerated grassroots organizing in communities of color. In 1968, José "Cha-Cha" Jiménez formed the Young Lords Organization,[19] inspired by the Black Panther Party and Fred Hampton, chairman of the Panthers' Chicago chapter. Jiménez and Hampton met in prison and continued their relationship as community organizers. The YLO united with the Black Panthers and the Young Patriots (poor whites from Appalachia) in an alliance called the Rainbow Coalition. Their rallying cry was "Black Power, Brown Power, and White

Power."[20] In a 1970 interview, YLO field marshal Cosmoe Torres, explains the group's evolution:

> It's not that we were a gang one minute and the next we were all Communists. What we had to realize was that it wasn't no good fightin' each other, but that what we were doing as a gang had to be against the capitalist institutions that are oppressing us.[21]

Torres goes on to describe the Young Lords' commitment to "human rights, not just civil rights."[22]

Human rights are fundamental, universal, and inherent to human beings. They include the right to life and liberty, freedom from slavery and torture, and the right to food, work, and housing. Civil rights, on the other hand, refer to legal protections granted by a particular nation. They vary from country to country, such as the right to vote or the right to an attorney. The first legal document to set out basic human rights was the United Nations' Declaration of Human Rights in 1948.[23]

NIXON'S LAW AND ORDER POLITICS

Four months after the Young Lords Organization formed in Chicago, Richard M. Nixon became the thirty-seventh president of the United States on January 20, 1969 and was in office during the height of the Young Lords' activism. Though he gained the popular vote by a slim victory, Nixon won the electoral college by a comfortable margin, directing his message to white Americans eager to return to pre–civil rights norms. His election showed that these voters rejected appeals for racial, economic, and social justice. Nixon professed to speak for the "Silent Majority," for "those who were not out in the streets."[24] He vowed to enforce a program of "law and order" to safeguard the system of white supremacy that kept African Americans and other people of color in subservience. In 1971, Nixon made good on his promise when he launched the "War on Drugs." His policies flipped the national conversation from that of eliminating the causes of crime to one of punishment and criminalization of Black and Brown communities.[25] Nixon whipped up fear to justify the mass incarceration of African American and Latinx people, laying the foundation to position the United States as the world's most carceral nation.[26]

On the international front, Nixon expanded and escalated the Vietnam War into Laos and Cambodia. From 1969 to 1970, he ordered a secret massive bombing offensive that dropped 2.7 million tons of bombs over Cambodia, killing more than half a million people.[27] In Laos, where bombing had begun as early as 1964, per capita tonnage of bombardment was at an even higher rate.[28] The escalation galvanized worldwide protests, including in the United States.

In 1974, the House Judiciary Committee recommended Nixon's impeachment; however, it cited neither the War on Drugs nor the genocidal bombing of Cambodia and Laos as reasons for his removal. Instead, Nixon's term ended with the Watergate scandal related to his involvement in burglarizing and wiretapping the Democratic Party's national headquarters and attempting to destroy tapes that proved his crimes.[29] Facing impeachment for his activities, Nixon resigned, declaring, "I am not a crook."[30]

THE YOUNG LORDS FORM A NEW YORK CHAPTER

By the late 1960s, 815,000 Puerto Ricans lived in New York City, the largest Puerto Rican community in the United States at the time.[31] The city's Republican mayor John V. Lindsay was elected in 1966 and held office until 1973. Unlike Nixon, Lindsay identified as "a liberal" because he opposed the war in Vietnam.[32] Nonetheless, progressives and social justice activists clashed with his administration, which was marked by poverty, labor, racial strife, and increased "white flight."[33] Historian Stephen Brier comments on the city's changing population:

> Totaling nearly 8 million residents, New York City experienced a major demographic transformation in the postwar era, with nearly one million African Americans and Puerto Ricans replacing an equal number of white New Yorkers who had moved out of the city to nearby suburbs during the 1950s and 1960s.[34]

By the sixties, the city's demographics were transformed.

Among New Yorkers, Puerto Ricans had the lowest income, level of education, and housing quality, and the highest percentage of people in poverty.[35] Puerto Rican women, like my mother and aunts, were a major labor source for New York City's garment industry and other factory work, which paid starvation wages.[36] Jobs were precarious in a fluctuating labor market as factories left the city looking for even cheaper labor costs and bigger profits elsewhere.[37]

The disappearance of garment factory jobs displaced Puerto Rican women, who since the 1950s had provided labor for the struggling industry. Sociologist Alice Colón-Warren explains that the loss of these jobs was at "the structural roots of the declining labor force participation of Puerto Rican women throughout the 1960s."[38] A small segment of Puerto Rican women at the time, those who spoke English and had some formal education, might be hired as store clerks, administrative assistants, nurses' aides, and other nonprofessional jobs. Unemployed women fell into deep poverty, and single mothers had no choice but to seek public assistance to support their families. Single-women-headed families were prevalent in Puerto Rican communities before the term "feminization of poverty" came into use. According to Colón-Warren, the problem lay in the societal discrimination that considered women secondary and nonessential workers. Yet, gendered roles held Puerto Rican women responsible for their children's survival and compelled them "to become heads of household."[39] All working mothers struggled to find affordable childcare. Without employment opportunities or access to childcare, Puerto Rican working-class women and their children were trapped in a cycle of poverty.

A new generation of Puerto Ricans coming of age in New York City in the 1960s was eager to fight the poverty conditions facing our parents, communities, and future. Inspired by the goals of social justice movements, we joined campaigns across the city and gained organizing experience. Among numerous examples, Puerto Ricans marched for civil rights and against the war in Vietnam. Puerto Rican workers joined picket lines, protesting unfair hiring practices, and demanding decent working conditions. In 1964, Puerto Rican parents, students, and educators joined 450,000 participants, in the largest New York school boycott to end de facto segregation.[40] In 1967, Puerto Ricans responded to the police killing of an East Harlem youth by protesting in the streets for three days.[41] Across the city's public university system, Puerto Rican students united with African Americans, occupied buildings and demanded access and opportunities for students of color.[42] Puerto Rican writers, poets, artists, and muralists shaped the "neorican" and "nuyorican" identities and launched a literary and cultural movement. It merged *New York* and *Rican* and gave voice to the oppressive social, political, and economic realities of Puerto Ricans in the United States.

In March 1969, the Crusade for Justice invited activists to the National Chicano Youth Conference in Denver, Colorado. Over 1,500 youth attended,[43] including a busload of Nuyorican and African American youth from New York City. The Real Great Society, an East Harlem organization founded by former gang leaders and young professionals, sponsored the bus.[44] During the conference, the New Yorkers met with members of the Chicago Young Lords Organization and José "Cha Cha" Jiménez, its chairman. Carlito Rovira and myself were part of the New York group. Little did we know that a Young Lords' chapter would form in New York later that year, and we would become members.

About four months later on July 26, 1969, the Young Lords established the New York chapter. Like the Black Panther Party and other revolutionary nationalist groups of the era, the YLO was structured as a paramilitary hierarchy with a strict chain of command and rules of discipline. The structure responded, in part, to the belief that the US government had declared war against progressive organizations. FBI director J. Edgar Hoover declared the Black Panther Party "the greatest threat to the internal security" of the United States in 1969. Information among the different levels of the YLO flowed on a "need-to-know basis" from top to bottom. The hierarchal structure intended to keep information secure and out of the hands of FBI and police infiltrators likely in our ranks.

The Young Lords' governing, and final decision-making, body was the Central Committee. In New York, the initial group consisted of Felipe Luciano as deputy chairman, Juan González as deputy minister of education and health, Pablo "Yoruba" Guzmán as deputy minister of information, David Pérez as deputy minister of defense, and Juan "Fi" Ortiz as deputy minister of finance. Sixteen-year-old Ortiz was the youngest. At twenty-two, González was the oldest. The men selected each other as the leaders; there were no elections. They were the public representatives of the organization. As spokespersons, they interacted with the press, handled negotiations with officials, and met with other political leaders. Each Central Committee member oversaw a ministry that consisted of "captains," "lieutenants," and rank-and-file members called the cadre. They were the backbone of the organization, running "serve the people" programs, conducting day-to-day organizing, attending protests, and selling newspapers.

The Central Committee adopted "democratic centralism" as the YLO's governing principle. In theory, it provided a balance of power between the Central Committee and the rank-and-file. "Democratic" referred to the participation of the cadres in the organization's affairs. Through discussion and debate at general membership meetings, cadres took part in decision making. All members committed to follow the majority decision reached at the meetings, whether or not they voted for it. "Centralism" referred to the Central Committee's role to ensure "unity in action," implementing the majority consensus. However, during the YLO's evolution, the Central Committee members abused and corrupted the practice of democratic centralism.

The 13-Point Program and Platform written by the Young Lords' New York chapter in October 1969 was the group's most important and unifying document, articulating its philosophy, beliefs, and demands. The platform points are introduced here briefly and discussed further in subsequent chapters. Point 1 expressed the Young Lords' main goals and dual commitment: "We want self-determination for Puerto Ricans: liberation on the Island and inside the United States." It denounced the colonial status of Puerto Rico. The program also identified the "Latin, Black, Indian, and Asian people inside the u.s." as internal colonies, pointing to the "experiences of ghettoization, police brutality, and racialized oppression under US capitalism" as comparable "to colonialism elsewhere."[45] The platform suggested the concept of "settler colonialism," although the term was not used. Activist scholar Roxanne Dunbar-Ortiz describes it as "the founding of a state based on the ideology of white supremacy, the widespread practice of African slavery, and a policy of genocide and land theft."[46] When Europeans first arrived in the Americas, they proceeded to remove and kill the Indigenous inhabitants, claimed the land as their own, and used enslaved Africans to extract its value.

Point 3 demanded "self-determination for all Latinos and the liberation of all Third World people." The term "Third World" conveyed unity with the exploited peoples of Asia, Africa, and Latin America and their descendants. It expressed internationalism.

Denouncing US military domination around the world, the 13-Point Program called for the withdrawal of US military bases from Puerto Rico and all oppressed nations and communities. It demanded the freedom of political prisoners and prisoners of war.

Like the Black Panther Party, the Young Lords identified as "revolutionary nationalists" committed to racial justice. The Young Lords' program called for community control of police, health services, churches, schools, housing, and transportation.

Unlike other nationalist organizations, the YLO's 13-Point Program stated, "We want equality for women" but endorsed the notion of "revolutionary machismo." This idea showed ambivalence about ending power over women and male supremacy. It did not demand or advocate for ending patriarchy or systems of male exploitation and oppression against women.

The final points of the YLO's platform articulated beliefs aligned with other US revolutionary groups. Point 11 declared, "We believe armed self-defense and armed struggle are the only means to liberation."

Point 13 concluded:

> We want a socialist society. We want a society where the needs of the people come first and where we give solidarity and aid to the people of the world.

In *The Case for Socialism*, author Alan Maass writes:

> At its heart, socialism is about the creation of a new society, built from the bottom up, through the struggles of ordinary working people against exploitation, oppression, and injustice—one that eliminates profit and power as the prime goals of life, and instead organizes our world around the principles of equality, democracy, and freedom.[47]

The final lines of the 13-Point Program pledged: "Hasta la victoria siempre"—always until victory.

Fig 2. "We Want a Socialist Society." East Harlem. 1970.
(Courtesy: Michael Abramson.)

POWER TO THE PEOPLE: THE NEW LEFT

The Young Lords were part of the "New Left," consisting of activist or-ganizations that opposed US government policies and committed to changing the status quo. In *Rethinking the New Left: An Interpretative History,* historian Van Gosse summarizes:

> From the 1950s through the 1970s, a series of social move-ments surged across America, changing the relationship between white people and people of color, how the US gov-ernment conducts foreign policy, and the popular consen-sus regarding gender and sexuality. Together, these move-ments redefined the meaning of democracy, and "power to the people" is what linked them together. They constituted a "movement of movements" that was considerably greater than the sum of its parts.[48]

Under the New Left umbrella, many groups organized diverse popula-tions around a multitude of issues, using varied strategies and tactics.

Within the New Left, the Third World Left included African American, Latinx, Asian, and Native peoples. While the meaning of "Third World" varied, the groups under this banner acknowledged the influence of worldwide liberation movements against colonialism as well as the US civil rights struggle, the Cuban Revolution, and opposition to the Vietnam War. Committed to fighting racism, colonialism, and imperialism, they "embraced the idea that lasting social change" required pressure and movement building "from below"—from the most disenfranchised communities and sectors.[49] At the forefront were African American activists and communities, and the Black Panther Party and other Black liberation organizations. The Puerto Rican Left focused on ending colonialism in Puerto Rico and organizing for the rights of Puerto Ricans in the United States. Feminists of color introduced emancipating theories and practices, organized caucuses, created autonomous women-led organizations and committees, led campaigns to fight male domination and supremacy in the movement, and battled for the rights of women of color in society.

The New Left groups were not isolated from each other. Collaborations and coalitions promoted movement building and advanced social justice goals. Learning from each other's successes and mistakes enhanced each group's effectiveness to mobilize within the rapidly fluctuating US social justice movements in the late 1960s and early 1970s.

2.
SERVING THE PEOPLE. WE ARE
REVOLUTIONARY NATIONALISTS[1]

> Great transformations do not begin from above
> nor with monumental and epic deeds, but with
> movements small in size and that appear irrelevant
> to politicians and analysts from above. History is
> not transformed by packed squares or enraged crowds,
> but … by the organized conscience of groups and
> collectives that know and recognize one another,
> below and to the left, and build another politics.[2]
>
> —Insurgent Subcommander Marcos, Chiapas, México, 2018

In the fall of 1969, the Young Lords Organization opened a storefront office at 1678 Madison Avenue between 110th and 111th Streets in El Barrio. It was the main hub of Young Lords' activities through April 1970, when a second storefront opened in the Bronx. The East Harlem site attracted self-sacrificing and loyal members from low-income backgrounds and neighborhoods who were not afraid, but eager, to go to the people, knocking on doors, to spread the word of revolution. Women joined to fight racism and economic inequality. Through community organizing and "serve the people" programs, the Young Lords advanced the idea of socialism, emphasizing the US government's refusal to meet the basic needs of Puerto Rican, Latinx, and African American communities. This chapter describes early YLO activities, and the organization's version of revolutionary nationalism and ideas about women's liberation.

All members reported to the East Harlem office to attend meetings, receive assignments, and meet with neighborhood residents. At the front desk sat the "officer of the day," who greeted visitors, answered the telephone, and assigned members to community programs. Many YLO initiatives responded to the needs of mothers and children, such as the free breakfast programs, clothing giveaways, and preventative health screenings. Inspired by the Black Panther Party, the breakfast program was a priority. During weekday mornings, Young Lords cooked and served breakfast to children and escorted them to school. Other Young Lords arranged free clothing drives and health screenings. Education ministry cadre planned and facilitated weekly political education classes for Young Lords and for the public. Young Lords also assisted residents who stopped by the office with a housing or workplace problem or a police brutality complaint. Often, these contacts led to campaigns that lasted for months. The information ministry cadre scheduled press conferences with English- and Spanish-language media to get our message out widely. Young Lords responded to incidents that erupted spontaneously in East Harlem, especially involving the police. All Young Lords took part in citywide protests and demonstrations.

Fig 3. Officer of the Day. Connie Morales. East Harlem. 1970.
(Courtesy: Michael Abramson)

Among the initial community organizers in the East Harlem branch were women. Sonia Ivany, who took part in the 1969 garbage offensive, was the first woman to join the YLO in New York. She was Cuban, a New

York University student, and a new mother of a baby girl. Mirta González, Puerto Rican, was also a mother with a young daughter. González,
Iris Benítez, and Denise Oliver were among the members setting up
"serve the people" programs, a name adopted from the *Quotations of
Chairman Mao Tse-Tung*, the "little red book" we studied for political
guidance. Benítez was Afro–Puerto Rican; Oliver was African American.
In addition to their community organizing responsibilities, González,
Benítez, and Oliver were cadres in the information ministry and wrote
news pieces for the Chicago Y.L.O. newspaper.

LEAD POISONING CAMPAIGN

After the summer garbage offensive, the Young Lords turned to address
the lead-poisoning crisis in El Barrio. Landlords applied cheap lead-
based paint on tenement walls that easily peeled and crumbled to the
floor. In the hands of small children, the paint chips were lethal. If in-
gested, the lead caused brain injury, seizures, and even death. Though
aware of the problem, politicians had not responded.[3] Hence, a group of
Young Lords along with workers and medical students from East Harlem's Metropolitan Hospital tackled the problem. On the morning of
November 24, 1969, about thirty people sat-in at the city's Department
of Health in the deputy commissioner's office[4] and demanded access to
available lead-testing kits in the city's possession that were not being
used. The government officials surrendered more than two hundred uri-
nary lead detection kits.[5]

The Young Lords put the testing kits to immediate use. For several
Saturdays, Young Lords, hospital workers, and medical students gathered outside the East Harlem storefront. Teams prepped to go door to
door to collect urine samples and educate residents about the lead-poisoning danger. Women played key roles, persuading mothers to open
their doors and allow their children to be tested. When the results arrived, they showed that 30 percent of the children tested positive.[6] It was
an outrage—Puerto Rican and African American children poisoned inside their homes due to the negligence and greed of politicians, health
officials, and landlords. Jack Newfield, a well-known journalist from the
Village Voice, helped expose the scandal. Reforms followed. The city's
Department of Health created a bureau to order housing repairs in lead-

poisoning cases and launched a prevention program, including lead screening of preschool children in Head Start programs and day-care centers.[7] It was an example of the Young Lords' grassroots activism, bringing life-saving services and reforms to low-income communities.

THE PEOPLE'S CHURCH

The Young Lords' revolutionary project included free breakfast programs for needy children. The first program in East Harlem served thirty children at the Emmaus House on East 116th Street. Another opened at the Theater Arts Center on East 110th Street. A third opened in the Lower East Side at St. Mark's Church. Neighborhood merchants donated the food. Mothers enthusiastically welcomed the programs. By October 1969, the Young Lords were scrambling for additional space to feed the number of children requesting breakfast. The First Spanish United Methodist Church on 111th Street and Lexington Avenue looked like a potential site. It was centrally located and largely unused during weekdays. Several Young Lords went to speak with the church's pastor and asked for space to offer a free breakfast program and free day-care center for mothers in the community. But Reverend Humberto Carranza said "no." He was a Cuban exile vehemently opposed to the Young Lords' socialist politics.

On December 7, 1969, a testimonial Sunday when any person could address congregants, a group of Young Lords returned to the First Spanish United Methodist Church. As soon as deputy chairman, Felipe Luciano, stood up to speak, several policemen, waiting inside, jumped him and broke his arm. In the ensuing brawl, police arrested thirteen persons, among them five women, including YLO members Sonia Ivany, Elena González, Mirta González, and Denise Oliver, and a journalist, Erika Sezonov.[8] They were charged with disruption of church services, felonious assault, and riot. Iris Benítez from the Information Ministry described the arrests in the Chicago Y.L.O. newspaper, observing that "the highest bail was set ... on Mirta González, lieutenant of information, and Daoud Velásquez, captain of information."[9] The Young Lords raised the bail, and all members were released in twenty-four hours.

Three days after Christmas, the Young Lords returned to the church, calling attention to the dire need for social programs in East Harlem. In a dramatic appeal, the Young Lords barricaded the doors and hung a sign from a side window announcing, "la iglesia de la gente," the People's Church. When police arrived, a spirited press conference was in progress with Iris Benítez, Pablo "Yoruba" Guzmán, and Juan González speaking to reporters. They emphasized the church's isolation from the community. "The church is supposed to serve the people, help them, and work with them. This is a public building in *El Barrio* that does not pay taxes," they explained.[10] Later, Benítez gave a further detailed account about events leading up to the takeover on the Young Lords' *Palante* radio show.[11] News traveled at warp speed and attracted thousands to the church. Militant speeches by young Puerto Ricans, Afro-Boricua leaders, and women of color, and the working-class character of the group, made a distinct impression. Luciano delivered a speech, asserting, "What we are doing is showing the contradictions of how organized religion oppresses our people."[12] The urgency with which the Young Lords spoke was a clarion call, amplifying conflicting interests between the poor working-class Puerto Ricans of El Barrio and powerful church and government elites. As the takeover began, the Young Lords opened the church doors, welcoming neighborhood residents, activists, and other supporters.

The Young Lords offered free "serve the people" programs, including breakfast and clothing distribution, a day-care center, health services, a liberation school, community dinners, poetry and theatrical performances, film screenings, and speakers. During the next eleven days, frequent performers included nuyorican poets Pedro Pietri and José Angel Figueroa, the guerrilla theater group Third World Revelationists, and Puerto Rican folkloric musicians Pepe and Flora. One evening, a group of young children put on a play, showcasing the theme, "no one wants to be poor." Activists, artists, and community supporters all contributed to the revolutionary effort and joy at the People's Church.

On New Year's Eve, people arrived to celebrate the coming "decade of the people." "Yoruba" Guzmán, the deputy minister of information, spoke to a lively and animated crowd. "The People's Church is part of a global struggle," and US imperial power is "the common enemy of the peoples of the world, even those who live within its borders,"[13] he said. He emphasized the importance of fighting from within the "belly of the beast."[14]

On January 8, 1970, the police invaded the church, and they arrested 106 Young Lords and supporters. Fists raised and singing, "Qué Bonita Bandera," "What a Beautiful Flag," protesters loaded into police vans. The dramatic end to the People's Church occupation signaled a new cycle of grassroots militancy among Puerto Ricans in the United States. The Young Lords showed an alternative for community voices in the public discourse, counter to the passive top-down let's-wait-and-see antipoverty approach adopted by many reformers at the time.

"WE ARE REVOLUTIONARY NATIONALISTS"

The Young Lords' activities in New York attracted far-reaching interest and excitement. The defiant young Puerto Ricans challenging the government's neglect and disdain were like a burst of sunlight, reviving faith in the power of ordinary people to spark social change. The fight against poverty and injustice was urgent and unifying. "We are revolutionary nationalists," declared the Young Lords, "committed to the liberation of Puerto Ricans in the United States and Puerto Rico." The Young Lords' revolutionary nationalism reflected a mix of ideas, strategies, and practices derived from socialist philosophies, the African American liberation struggle, and the anticolonial struggles in Puerto Rico and across the world. These ideas were not static. Rather, they took on different meanings and roles during the organization's evolution.

According to historian and women's studies scholar Edna Acosta-Belén, the Young Lords Organization was one of the groups redefining what it meant to be Puerto Rican in the diaspora in the late 1960s and early 1970s. What was the relationship of US Puerto Ricans to Puerto Rico? And what connected Puerto Ricans in the United States to each other?

In the May 1970 issue of the Young Lords' *Palante* newspaper, deputy chairman, Felipe Luciano writes:

> Puerto Ricans, wherever they are, whether in the united states or *Borinquen* (Puerto Rico), constitute a colony and their oppression is that of a colonial people.[15]

The Young Lords saw colonialism as core to the Puerto Rican experience and identity, and it shaped the organization's version of revolutionary nationalism.

Traveling back and forth from the United States to Puerto Rico to visit family and friends and sharing migration stories across generations gave Puerto Ricans a strong sense of being one people. Historian Jorge Duany explains that transnational migrants like Puerto Ricans develop separate loyalties, creating imagined communities in their new countries and participating actively in both places.[16] The Young Lords' "imagined community" connected all persons of Puerto Rican ancestry, whether or not born in Puerto Rico, even if they had never visited Puerto Rico or did not speak Spanish. Acosta-Belén observes that the Young Lords affirmed *la puertorriqueñidad,* "Puerto Ricanness," and popularized the use of the Puerto Rican flag on T-shirts, berets, pins, posters, and other paraphernalia. Importantly, the Young Lords made a distinction between revolutionary and cultural nationalism, asserting that the promotion of culture alone would not liberate the Puerto Rican people. For the Young Lords, culture was integral to, not separate from, political goals. The Young Lords' *puertorriqueñidad* affirmed a shared culture, collective history, and legacy of struggle against colonialism. As Acosta-Belén observes, the Young Lords advanced Puerto Rican national identity and pride, including Afro–Puerto Ricanness, suppressed in Puerto Rico by colonial authorities. She explains that being a nationalist or pro-independence supporter in the archipelago at the time was an invitation to "being *fichado* as a *subversive*" (marked as a subversive) and subjected to police repression.[17]

Luciano further describes the YLO's outlook on the Puerto Rican struggle:

> Puerto Ricans have suffered as a group, racially and culturally, not as individuals. Therefore, the fight against amerikkanism must be as a group struggle, a nation struggle.[18]

He reiterates the YLO's goals: self-determination for Puerto Ricans in the United States and the liberation of Puerto Rico from US colonial rule.

The Black Panther Party profoundly influenced the founding ideology of the Young Lords Organization. Both organizations identified as nationalist and socialist. As Huey P. Newton, BPP cofounder, proclaimed in a 1968 interview, "[T]o be a revolutionary nationalist you would by necessity have to be a socialist."[19] Combining community-based organizing with a critique of capitalism as the root cause of the exploitation and oppression of poor people, the Panthers and Young Lords believed that liberation could not be achieved within the existing capitalist economic and political system. Like the Panthers, the Young Lords believed that societal change required active participation of oppressed people across races, nationalities, and ethnic groups. The YLO's 13-Point Program explained, "We each organize our people, but our fights are the same against oppression, and we will defeat it together." The Black Panthers and the Young Lords also expressed unity with anticolonial and anticapitalist movements around the world.

El Partido Nacionalista Puertorriqueño, the Puerto Rican Nationalist Party (PRNP), was also a main influence. Unlike the Black Panther Party and the Young Lords Organization, the PRNP was not socialist.[20] It was an anti-imperialist organization. Under the leadership of Pedro Albizu Campos, the PRNP led a fervent anticolonial struggle against the United States from 1930 to 1965 to establish Puerto Rico as a free and sovereign nation. The history recapped here contextualizes why we declared, "The Young Lords are the children of the Nationalist Party."

In 1935, Colonel Francis Riggs was the US-appointed police commander in Puerto Rico. When police killed four students at the University of Puerto Rico,[21] two young Nationalists, Hiram Rosado and Elias Beauchamp, assassinated Riggs in retaliation.[22] Immediately, the police arrested and executed them in police headquarters.[23] The authorities charged Albizu Campos and other PRNP leaders with seditious conspiracy against the United States. Albizu Campos was convicted and sentenced to six to ten years in federal prison.[24] On March 21, 1937, people assembled in the town of Ponce, Puerto Rico to call for the release of the Nationalists still in prison and to commemorate the end of slavery in Puerto Rico. The US-appointed governor, Blanton Winship, ordered police to fire into the peaceful gathering. They killed twenty-one persons and seriously wounded two hundred others.[25] The date is remembered in Puerto Rican history as La Masacre de Ponce, (the Ponce Massacre).

Growing demands for Puerto Rico's independence, as well as international pressure from the United Nations regarding non-self-governing territories like Puerto Rico, led the US Congress to pass Public Law 600 on July 3, 1950. President Harry Truman signed the law, which allowed Puerto Rico to draft a local constitution to govern its internal affairs, subject to congressional limitations.[26] It proposed no change in Puerto Rico's colonial status; the United States retained political, economic, and social control.

The Nationalist Party launched a campaign against Public Law 600. Albizu Campos, who had returned to Puerto Rico in 1947 after ten years in prison,[27] denounced the law as a continuation of US colonialism. On October 30, 1950, Blanca Canales Torresola, a leading Nationalist Party member, led a revolt in the town of Jayuya.[28] The US government declared martial law, sending in National Guard troops along with P-47 fighter bombers, which conducted air strikes.[29] Four hundred people were arrested.[30] To bring international attention to the repression and mass arrests in Puerto Rico, two Nationalists, Oscar Collazo and Griselio Torresola, went to Washington D.C. on November 1, 1950 and attacked the Blair House where President Truman was staying during White House renovations. During the assassination attempt, Torresola was killed. Collazo was imprisoned for twenty-nine years.[31] Albizu Campos was arrested again in a roundup of nationalists and communists and sentenced to 80 years in prison.[32] In 1954, Lolita Lebrón Soto, Rafael Cancel Miranda, Irvin Flores Rodríguez, and Andrés Figueroa Cordero entered the House of Representatives Chamber in the US Capitol Building. Lebrón unfurled the Puerto Rican flag and shouted "¡Viva Puerto Rico Libre!" They shot into the chamber, wounding five US representatives. The Nationalists were imprisoned with sentences from seventy to eighty-five years.[33]

In 1964, Albizu Campos was still in prison and seriously ill; he contended that he was being poisoned with radiation, which officials denied. On April 21, 1965, Albizu Campos died of radiation-induced cancer in Puerto Rico, shortly after his release from prison.[34] In 1994, the US Department of Energy confirmed that radiation experiments had been conducted on prisoners without their consent.[35]

Historian Manuel Maldonado-Denis describes the Nationalists' battle as "the highest expression of rebelliousness" against imperialism,"[36] noting that the PRNP remained "a profound symbol of resistance among the people and in the revolutionary national consciousness."[37] In unity with the nationalist legacy, the Young Lords organized for self-determination, believing Puerto Ricans were affected by the economic, psychological, cultural, and racial exploitation of US colonialism whether living in Puerto Rico or in the diaspora.[38]

The Young Lords Organization, Black Panther Party, and Puerto Rican Nationalist Party shared similar views regarding armed revolution. They believed that when political methods failed to achieve justice or social change, and when people's rights and lives no longer progressed under the rule of those in power, then armed revolution was justified.

POINT 4. "... WE OPPOSE RACISM."

"We are revolutionary nationalists and *oppose racism*," declared the Young Lords' 13-Point Program. The emphasis reflected the deep effect of the civil rights and Black Liberation movements on Puerto Rican consciousness. African Americans and Puerto Ricans collaborated in many fights against racist institutions. Many Young Lords had participated in these struggles and maintained close relationships with African American activists. The fight to end racism was a priority for the organization, including African Americans who made up approximately 20 percent of the membership. The YLO fought many manifestations of racism—systemic and anti-Black racism, racialized discrimination, and internalized racism.

In the daily political work, the Young Lords organized with Puerto Ricans and African Americans in low-income communities to battle institutionalized racism—lack of jobs, inadequate housing, police brutality, inferior education, and horrendous public health care. Like the Black Panther Party, the YLO believed racism was inherent to capitalism. In the 1968 interview cited earlier, Black Panther cofounder Huey Newton explains:

> We realize that this country became very rich upon slavery and that slavery is capitalism in the extreme. We have two

evils to fight, capitalism and racism. We must destroy both racism and capitalism.[39]

Newton underscores the link between the accumulation of capitalist wealth and the enslavement of Black people. He concludes that the fights to end racism and capitalism are inseparable. White supremacy is the undergirding system.

Scholar activist Loretta Ross develops this idea further, describing how racism intersects with class, gender, religion, and other classifications. "Racism is a fundamental feature of white supremacy, but not its totality," she asserts.[40] Activist Elizabeth "Betita" Martínez adds that white supremacy is "a system of exploitation and oppression of continents, nations, and peoples of color ... for the purpose of maintaining and defending a system of wealth, power, and privilege."[41] They highlight that white supremacy is an interconnected global system of many oppressive ideologies and practices.

To the discourse about anti-Black racism, the Young Lords brought the experiences of Afro-Boricuas. Hundreds of thousands of Puerto Ricans arrived in the United States after World War II from the poorest economic strata. Dark-skinned and Black Boricuas made up the largest numbers. Pablo "Yoruba" Guzmán, minister of information and a second-generation Afro-Boricua-Cubano, emphasizes that Puerto Ricans also confronted anti-black racism. He exclaims, "[B]efore people called me a 'spic,' they called me a 'nigger.'"[42] Guzmán insists that the experience of Black Puerto Ricans is part of Black history. He writes:

> It is important for us to study the history of Blacks in the Americas, because it is part of Puerto Rican history, in terms of Black slaves in Puerto Rico and how they came into the culture, and in terms of our better understanding the development of Blacks in the United States, who are the major force in the Amerikkkan revolution. ... To study Black history is to complete the study of Puerto Rican history and vice versa.[43]

Guzmán connects African American and Afro–Puerto Rican histories to a broader, global, Afro-diasporic transnational community.[44]

In addition to institutional racism, the Young Lords brought to the community discussions about racism in the Puerto Rican and Latinx culture, language, and history and laid bare the myth of racial equality. The organization tackled the issue of racism "between Puerto Ricans and Blacks, and between light-skinned and dark Puerto Ricans" as contradictions among the people, distinct from the antagonistic contradictions with the ruling class. "Puerto Ricans don't like to talk about racism or admit that it exists among Puerto Ricans," I wrote in the article "Puerto Rican Racism" (Racismo Borinqueño), published in *Palante* in 1970.[45] Puerto Rico's racial hierarchy, originating with the Spanish colonizers, promoted the "one drop of white blood" rule, defining whiteness along a gradation of classifications that stipulated "the whiter the better." The notion of bettering the race, or "mejorar la raza," urged individuals to marry lighter-skinned people "to whiten" the population, relegating enslaved Africans, their offspring, and descendants to the bottom rung of society. With the US invasion of Puerto Rico in 1898, the imposed racial hierarchy deemed that any traceable amount of Black blood rendered a person Black.[46] Anti-Black racism deepened, and whiteness was further elevated as a desired value and tool of oppression.

As "aids in resisting the silence around Blackness,"[47] the Young Lords Party popularized the Afro-Boricua and Afro-Puertorriqueño identities, lifting up African history and culture. A likely forerunner of the terms was "Afro-Borincano," appearing in the 1930s in the writings of Arturo Alfonso Schomburg, the Afro-Boricua who built a vast collection of documents related to Black history and the African diaspora.[48] *The Ideology of the Young Lords Party*, a pamphlet published by the Young Lords in 1971, highlighted the Afro-Boricua identity.[49] So did the *Palante* newspaper in articles such as "Loiza Aldea," about slavery in Puerto Rico and the African contributions to Puerto Rican culture and history.[50] Given the rarity of information about Black Puerto Ricans at the time, the Young Lords' materials offered a resource and foregrounded the discourse about Black Puerto Rican history and anti-Black racism among Puerto Ricans.

The Young Lords also fought racialized discriminatory policies and practices that pushed Puerto Ricans and other people of color into unemployment, poverty wages, substandard housing, inferior schools, and horrible public health care. Puerto Ricans as a group, especially the poor and working class, whether light- or dark-skinned, faced systemic discrimination based on class, nationality, ethnicity, and language. Moreover, as a mixed-race people, Puerto Ricans did not fit neatly into the white/Black binary categorization dominant in the United States,[51] and were classified and treated as "colored" or "other." The Young Lords identified systemic discrimination as another form of racism. From 1969 to mid-1971, the Young Lords fought for racial justice as a principal goal. When the Central Committee reframed the political priorities in July 1971, the organization took another direction detailed in Part IV.

THE 13-POINT PROGRAM AND "EQUALITY FOR WOMEN"

The Young Lords embraced the 13-Point Program and Platform, inspired by its principles of independence, revolution, and socialism. As revolutionary nationalists, the Young Lords identified as warriors, protectors, and liberators of the Puerto Rican people and nation. The YLO declared itself "a revolutionary party, fighting for the liberation of all oppressed people" but did not regard men and women as equals. Men were positioned as leaders, spokespersons, and strategists heading the struggle for self-determination and national liberation. Women were relegated to subservient roles as bearers of children, mothers, caretakers, wives, assistants, and mere shadows of men. From the very beginning, revolutionary nationalism was a "gendered discourse."[52] Feminist scholar and historian Anne McClintock observes, nationalism produces gendered relationships and preserves traditional structures and practices that limit women's rights.[53]

The 13-Point Program showed slight understanding of the gender oppression and exploitation of Puerto Rican and other women of color. Written by an all-male Central Committee, the program was woefully inadequate in reflecting concerns and aspirations of women of color. This was disappointing to young women activists eager to take part in imagining and building a just society for all. Women welcomed the statement, "We want equality for women," but point 10 also stated, "machismo must be revolutionary, not oppressive,"[54] as if machismo could be made revolutionary. This idea reflected reluctance to call for the end of male supremacy. The authors explained men use "the doctrine of machismo to take out their frustrations against their wives, sisters, mothers, and children." However, they did not explain machismo as a system of beliefs, behaviors, and institutions passed from generation to generation that insisted on male power and supremacy and condoned violence to dominate women. The Central Committee fixated on individual male chauvinist attitudes and behavior, not on ending the system of male domination. While the 13-Point Program demanded an end to capitalism, racism, colonialism, and imperialism, it did not demand an end to patriarchy or sexism. This failing was a recurring theme in the Young Lords' history and reflected underlying beliefs about women and the role of women in the revolutionary struggle and new society.

Early in 1970, women in the New York Young Lords Organization formed a caucus to challenge male supremacist views and to infuse feminist ideas into revolutionary nationalism. Daily offensive conduct and ideas such as "revolutionary machismo" minimized the liberatory struggles of women of color. The Central Committee members also introduced the idea of "male chauvinism-female passivity." They admitted that men were male chauvinist, but they blamed women for "permitting" this behavior.[55] It was a form of victim blaming that created a false power equivalency between men and women and diminished male accountability. The Women's Caucus had to contest the macho culture and its outdated views about women, if women were to stay members. As McClintock observes, "[F]eminism is a political response to gender conflict, not its cause."[56]

The struggle to advance the liberation of women of color was energizing and empowering. The Women's Caucus advocated and campaigned for *women's issues*, such as reproductive rights, ending gender violence, equal pay for women of color, and childcare, among others. Emphasizing the struggle for gender justice as ongoing, we adopted the phrase "the revolution within the revolution." The caucus organized for both gender justice and revolutionary nationalist goals. We saw no contradiction in fighting for women's liberation and Puerto Rico's national liberation.

Feminists of color across the US revolutionary nationalist movement analyzed the "triple oppression" of women by class, race, and gender and advocated for including feminist ideas and concerns in the social justice agenda. But nationalist leaders argued that women's issues could wait until after the revolution. They accused women of being divisive and causing disunity in the movement by raising these issues. Feminists of color refused to put aside women's concerns and believed the treatment of women in the revolutionary struggle forecast the status of women after the revolution. Throughout the social justice movement, women formed caucuses or split off from nationalist groups to form women-led autonomous organizations to pursue revolutionary feminist goals. We fought for gender justice though we did not use the term "feminist," which we associated with white middle-class women whose liberation movement did not include the fight against poverty, racism, and colonialism.

In June 1970, the New York Young Lords became the Young Lords Party. Because of the activism of the Women's Caucus, revolutionary socialist feminist perspectives ascended. The YLP published a Position Paper on Women, presenting a socialist feminist analysis and acknowledging the "deadly" systems of capitalism, racism, and machismo. Women led campaigns and mass mobilizations. In 1971, the Women's Union formed as a people's organization and developed a 12-Point Program, an intersectional socialist, feminist, and nationalist agenda focused on issues affecting working poor and disenfranchised women in communities of color. Also in 1971, the Central Committee members reframed the political priorities of the Young Lords Party, declaring the national liberation of Puerto Rico as the organization's main mission. They declared gender and racial justice struggles secondary and halted the revolutionary feminist momentum.

Feminists in the Young Lords Organization organized to end gender injustice and to elevate the revolutionary struggle of women. The battle of ideas produced real-life consequences, advances, and setbacks for women. The exchange and interplay between nationalist goals and the liberatory aspirations of revolutionary feminists of color played a critical role in the Young Lords' political arc. It shaped the rise and decline of socialist feminism and is a major theme in the Young Lords' story, detailed in subsequent chapters.

3.
THE RISE OF THE WOMEN'S CAUCUS

The sky is a conga drum stretched tight
for a bembe of the gods.[1]

—Ana Lydia Vega, "Cloud Cover Caribbean"

The militancy of young Puerto Ricans fighting poverty and racism drew thousands of supporters to the People's Church. Puerto Rican and other women of color of all ages arrived in solidarity with the families and children of El Barrio. Details of the December 7, 1969 police attack on the Young Lords and arrests inside the First Spanish United Methodist Church circulated widely. The public took note of the activism of women. Among the thirteen arrests were Young Lords Sonia Ivany, Elena González, Mirta González, and Denise Oliver.[2] At the church steps, women delivered passionate speeches on bullhorns. Inside, Iris Benítez, a young Afro-Boricua, was one of the spokespersons, explaining to reporters the reasons for the takeover. Other women coordinated serve the people programs. The visibility of young women of color activists inspired Puerto Rican, Latinx, and African American women to join. The direct-action advocacy attracted new members and resulted in an exponential increase in women recruits. Though personal histories and motivations varied, many women activists of color saw their emancipation closely linked to the social justice movements. This chapter describes early activities of women in the Young Lords Organization, the launch of the Women's Caucus, and the growth of feminist ideas and programs.

In those days, David Pérez, then the deputy minister of defense, met new recruits at the Young Lords' East Harlem storefront to provide an orientation. Pérez reviewed the 13-Point Program and rules of discipline, pointing out that attendance at general membership meetings and political education classes was mandatory. All members committed to distribute flyers, sell newspapers, take part in protests, and engage in local organizing campaigns. The orientation and intake procedures evolved over time, but the core membership requirements remained the same.

Because of the exceptional role of women members at the People's Church, new female recruits imagined receiving substantive assignments. But this was not the case. Most women were relegated to behind-the-scenes work assisting men and doing clerical and administrative tasks, cleaning duties, and housekeeping chores. Despite the increase in women members, the Central Committee did not show interest in or concern for feminist issues. Several YLO leaders openly mocked the "women's liberation movement," claiming their activism stemmed from sexual frustration.[3] Although most women in the Young Lords Organization, myself included, were not, nor had ever been, activists in the white women's liberation movement, we did not condone the contempt men showed them. We recognized that their disdain also extended to the liberatory aspirations of women of color. "How can YLO leaders claim to be for the liberation of all oppressed people when they demean half of humanity? Do they want liberation only for men?" we asked.

THE WOMEN'S CAUCUS DEVELOPS COLLECTIVE CONSCIOUSNESS

Shortly after the People's Church takeover, the masculine toxicity rampant in the Young Lords motivated several "old-timers"—women who joined before the church occupation—to call a women's meeting. We saw the need for a collective women's voice in a paramilitary male-led organization. Caucus participants expressed similar reactions to the macho and male chauvinist culture. "We joined to fight for the rights of Puerto Ricans not to perpetuate machismo, parading under the guise of a Puerto Rican revolution." Women aimed to gain equality in the Young Lords Organization and raise awareness about the societal oppression of women of color. Certainly, we would have more influence together than as individuals. The first caucus participants included Iris Benítez, Denise Oliver, Lulu Carreras, Connie Morales, Martha Duarte (Arguello), Nydia Mercado, Olguie Robles, Doleza Miah, Cookie, Emma, Olgita, myself, and others whose names I do not now recall. We were young, fourteen to twenty-six years old. Several mothers with young children unable to attend the Sunday meetings nonetheless supported us, stayed informed, and provided feedback that aided our collective development.

Fig 4. Mirta González, Connie Morales, and Iris Benítez. 1970.
(Courtesy: Michael Abramson.)

For most participants, the caucus sessions were the first experience with women-led discussions regarding gender oppression and women's liberation. We had no blueprint and were learning from each other. Each woman could propose a topic or bring a reading. Our free-flowing conversations touched on the manifestations of oppression, racism, and exploitation women faced in society. We discussed realities that shaped our lives related to work, reproductive rights, and as caretakers in the home. Women spoke eagerly about the possibility of organizing in the community to address institutionalized gender discrimination and advance demands for reproductive rights, childcare, and an end to sexual violence. Some caucus members focused on the second-class status of women in the home, doing the cooking and cleaning while taking care of children, husbands, and other family members. Others gave examples of male domination in the Young Lords Organization.

During initial meetings, we shared our reasons for joining the organization. Some women had been active in the civil rights and Black Liberation movements, student and workplace struggles, and organizations such as ASPIRA and the United Bronx Parents. We spoke about influential women in our lives—our mothers, *tías*, *abuelas*, *primas*, and other family members—as well as iconic revolutionary women such as Sojourner Truth and Lolita Lebrón. All caucus members were encouraged to share their views. We made decisions by consensus. After everyone spoke, someone would say, "It looks like we're all in agreement." When there was a hot topic with mixed opinions, we voted by a show of hands. Every voice was heard. Our decision-making was more inclusive and democratic than that practiced in other YLO venues.

The Women's Caucus focused on the circumstances of Puerto Rican women, but members also included Latinas and African American women. We identified as *women of color*, recognizing similar struggles and distinct ways systems of exploitation, violence, and separation affected us.[4] "Women of color" was a coalitional term,[5] embracing the possibility of a larger "we" and the interconnectedness of our herstories.[6] In the words of the Santa Cruz Feminist of Color Collective:

> "[W]omen of color" enables a way of seeing the world through a lens that refracts light in many ways to reveal a world full of possibilities, a world that is constantly shifting and in motion.[7]

Migration and familiarity with displacement gave us a transnational and anti-imperialist outlook. Connecting the experiences of "women marginalized in the United States and outside of it,"[8] we expressed unity with "Third World women," referring to women in Africa, Asia, and Latin America and their descendants in the United States and throughout the world. Note that, at the time, we used the words "sex," "women," and "gender" interchangeably. We did not have the nuanced meanings of gender or concepts such as gender fluidity, gender nonconformity, cisgender and non-binary identities, among others, that are known today. Nevertheless, the Women's Caucus committed to ending gender-based oppression.

The caucus was a safe space to break the silence about women's oppression. Like the *testimonio* tradition in Latin America and throughout the Third World, we sought "to bring to light a wrong, a point of view, or an urgent call for action."[9] Women described the sacrifices they made to take part in political activism. Working mothers juggled jobs and childcare. They brought their children to the Young Lords' storefront office when they had no babysitter or could not afford one. Women with full-time jobs devoted their evenings and weekends to doing the political work of the organization. Several members were their family's financial providers, allowing their partners to be the "full-time revolutionaries." Although the women held jobs, paid the bills, cared for the children and the home, and took part in political activities, their work was undervalued and unrecognized. Their partners and others frequently criticized them for not engaging in enough "real political work."

During caucus sessions, members examined beliefs inherited from society, families, schools, and media that fostered powerlessness, self-hatred, and inferiority regarding our abilities, physical appearance, and skin color. We explored the meaning of "colonized mentality," "internalized oppression," and "nonconscious" ideology. We read sections of Frantz Fanon's *The Wretched of the Earth* and *Black Skin, White Masks* and discussed how colonizers imposed their culture and ideas, ingraining them in the people they oppress.

Violence against women of color was so common that each member had a story to tell, recounting incidents of verbal assault, beatings, rapes, and other violence. Several women reported their partners warned them, "What happens between a man and a woman is private and not to be talked about with anyone." It was an implicit threat. Refusal to obey could provoke a punch in the face or worse. By labeling actions "private," men signaled women to cover up the emotional and physical abuse and the misery they inflicted. Caucus members exchanged strategies to fend off sexual advances, including from men in the social justice movement.

Sharing confidences and knowledge, members of the Women's Caucus developed a feminist consciousness,[10] a collective identity as Puerto Rican, Latina, and African American women with similar hopes, dreams, and politics. We were eager to bring feminist ideas to the organization and the Puerto Rican community. As comrades and friends, we were ready to transform the dominant social order. Women and gender studies scholar Kristie Soares observes that the Women's Caucus provided

> a model for decolonial feminist praxis that creates alternate forms of kinship, prioritizes care of self and community, and claims public space for nontraditional performances of femininity and masculinity.[11]

Fig 5. Women's Caucus Meeting. Early 1970.
(Courtesy of Michael Abramson.)

Though we did not use the term "feminist" at the time, the idea that Isabel Allende expresses in *The Soul of a Woman* describes how we felt. Allende writes:

> Feminism, like the ocean, is fluid, powerful, deep, and encompasses the infinite complexity of life; it moves in waves, currents, tides, and sometimes in storms. Like the ocean, feminism never stays quiet.[12]

The members of the Women's Caucus aspired for equality and new ways of being.

CHALLENGES TO MACHISMO AND MALE CHAUVINISM

As the Young Lords' membership grew during 1970, the Women's Caucus welcomed new recruits to the Sunday meetings. We studied the 13-Point Program and Platform and were proud that it expressed "equality for women." We were told that no other nationalist group included a similar public statement. Still, women faced discrimination and male supremacy in the organization, and we were determined to end these practices. To be clear, we opposed male supremacist ideology, but we did not consider Puerto Rican and "Third World" oppressed men to be "the enemy." We understood that male chauvinism and machismo were systemic political problems, not biological or character defects.

Point 10 of the 13-Point Program described the relationship between machismo and capitalism, as follows:

> Under capitalism, our people have been oppressed by both the society and our own men. The doctrine of machismo has been used by our men to take out their frustrations against *their* wives, sisters, mothers, and children.[13]

The description was superficial, concluding that "Machismo must be revolutionary... not oppressive." The idea that machismo could be revolutionary was absurd. Imagine anyone, declaring that "racism must be revolutionary and not oppressive." What point 10 revealed was an unwillingness to let go of the system that gave men power and privilege.

Initially, the Women's Caucus did not challenge the concept of "revolutionary machismo." But as we deepened our analysis about the exploitation and oppression of women of color under capitalism, we understood machismo" was more than male "frustrations." It was more than men misbehaving or acting badly against the women in their lives, making them objects of their disappointments, rage, and violence. The subjugation of women was systemic, as well as a problem of individual attitudes and bias. We concluded that the "revolutionary machismo" concept should be removed from the 13-Point Program. We added it to a list of recommendations to make the Young Lords Organization more advanced and forward-thinking. Our goal was both societal and personal transformation.

Caucus members opposed male supremacist ideas with a zeal beyond what most men wanted to hear. We questioned every manifestation of male supremacy and privilege, big and small. We called out the inferior treatment of women in the home, the workplace, in political organizations, and society. Men tired of our enthusiasm. The Central Committee members—Felipe Luciano, Juan González, Pablo "Yoruba" Guzmán, David Pérez, and Juan "Fi" Ortiz—accused us of taking time away from "real political work." They ordered the Women's Caucus to stop meeting. Several of us talked among ourselves and concluded, "They can't tell us what to do in our free time," and the Women's Caucus met as usual.

When the Central Committee members learned that we continued to meet, they were furious. How dare the women disobey the Central Committee? They charged the caucus with violating a direct command, a serious indictment under the organization's rules that mandated obedience to Central Committee directives. In those days, all Young Lords took martial arts self-defense classes run by the all-male Defense Ministry. At the end of the next session, the sensei called the caucus members to the center of the room and motioned us to line up in rows. The men fanned out to the edges of the large room to watch. Then a loud commanding voice barked at us, "You have violated a direct Central Committee order for which you are being disciplined. Give me one hundred pushups." He caught us by surprise. We glanced at one another and followed his instructions. Then he shouted a second order. "Give me one hundred sit-ups." Again, we darted looks to each other, asking with our eyes, should we comply? Should we refuse? Silently, we obeyed. We felt humiliated. But we got through the workout, winded, and bodies aching. Our anger was the energy source that Audre Lorde described when she spoke about using anger against racism for growth and "corrective surgery."[14] Some men, standing on the side, hung their heads in embarrassment, avoiding eye contact with us. They were uncomfortable with the naked display of male ego and power. In contrast, we held our heads high, feeling we had taken a collective step forward for women's independence. Justice was on our side.

After that, the Women's Caucus continued to meet, even more unified than before. The episode opened the floodgates to discuss our grievances and emboldened us to take bigger actions. We scrutinized all male chauvinist behavior from disrespectful language to physical assault and abuse of power. Sexual objectification and harassment were huge problems. Men commented on women's bodies and acted like we should thank them for their "compliments." On the other hand, we expected revolutionary men to treat us as comrades, not as walking body parts or mindless bodies. Most caucus members criticized the hypocrisy of men who claimed to be "for the people" but flaunted their Young Lords membership, trying to persuade young women to have sex with them.

Some men spoke as if it were no big deal to lie to women about their male chauvinistic activities. They wore their lies as badges of manhood. "You dishonor the purple beret," some of us said. Many women in the community also commented. They said, "Some men join the Young Lords to get into women's pants." The macho behavior dissuaded potential recruits from joining. "These men are not serious about revolution," they insisted. Some men in the movement approached women as if we were automatically interested in having sex with them. A woman who refused a sexual advance might be called a "butch" or "lesbian" or "cold fish," intended as an insult. Not all male Young Lords engaged in this behavior, although onlookers, both men and women, often defended the offenders, saying, "Oh, it's just part of the Latin culture." The justification was infuriating. "If the *culture* degrades women, it has to change," many of us shouted. "If you claim to be a revolutionary, you have to 'walk the talk.'" "What type of society do we want to create?" many of us asked.

Our concerns were like those of women today. How do we end gender abuse and violence? "Without consequences, our principles mean nothing," we argued. Long before the #MeToo movement, the Women's Caucus insisted that men take responsibility for their actions and face consequences for abusing women. Some women threatened to resign if the Central Committee did not address these issues. "Why should a woman risk her life in an organization that did not respect women?" Men unwilling to accept the liberation of half of humanity were not revolutionaries. They were pretenders, fakers, and opportunists.

THE EMERGENCE OF AN INTERSECTIONAL ANALYSIS

Across the US revolutionary nationalist movements, feminists of color organized to promote liberatory ideas and practices. Arguments in the Young Lords Organization about the treatment of women prompted questions about the relationship of the women's struggles to the revolutionary nationalist and Puerto Rican independence movements. A debate surfaced about whether women's issues should be addressed as part of the social justice movements or wait until after the revolutionary struggles were won. In a *Palante* radio show titled *Women in the Colonies* that aired in March 1970, several caucus members tackled the topic.[15] Iris Benítez, Myrna Martínez, Denise Oliver, and I were the participants. Benítez said, "We are first revolutionaries, second, Puerto Ricans, and thirdly women." I added: "It's not to say that one comes before the other. Both national and gender oppressions work together." Underlying the exchange were discussions taking place in the Women's Caucus. We had no group agreement yet. However, the radio program previewed nascent ideas about the interaction between feminism and nationalism that would be fiercely debated in the year ahead. However, at the time, caucus members were focused on challenging male chauvinism and discriminatory practices in the Young Lords Organization, determined to defeat the idea that women of color were inferior and to end practices flowing from this belief.

THE MALE CHAUVINISM–FEMALE PASSIVITY IDEA

A couple of months later in May, the Central Committee—Felipe Luciano, Juan González, Pablo "Yoruba" Guzmán, David Pérez, and Juan "Fi" Ortiz—went into a leadership retreat. The meeting agenda was full of weighty topics such as the Young Lords' political philosophy and organizing priorities, and the relationship with the Chicago Young Lords. Nevertheless, Guzmán describes that the retreat also involved substantial discussions about male chauvinism. He recaps their conclusion:

> The attitudes of superiority that brothers had toward sisters would have to change, as would the passivity of sisters toward brothers (allowing brothers to come out of a macho or chauvinist, superior bag).[16]

The Central Committee members admitted men had to change their attitudes of superiority toward women, but they introduced the idea of "female passivity" as an equivalent problem. They blamed women for "allowing" men to behave as machos and chauvinists, diminishing men's responsibility for male supremacist ideas and behavior. In effect, the "male-chauvinism-female passivity" notion accused women of being complicit in their own oppression. It was a form of victim blaming. "Look what you made me do!" Yet, when women stood up for themselves, they were criticized as being too aggressive or too opinionated. "Male-chauvinism-female passivity," like the idea of "revolutionary machismo," reflected reluctance to dismantling the system of male supremacy.

However, the members of the Women's Caucus interpreted "female passivity" differently. What the Central Committee called "passivity," we understood as the manifestation of "internalized oppression," the result of historical legacies, systems of exploitation, and oppressive ideologies. Colonialism, racism, poverty, and gender discrimination instilled and perpetuated inferiority complexes in women. Hence, the struggle against "female passivity" was to eliminate and replace oppressive ideas with new ways of thinking and practices that encouraged women to feel capable and confident. We viewed the struggle against passivity as an opportunity for personal growth and transformation to become more empowered revolutionaries.

Despite the opposition to "revolutionary machismo," it remained in the 13-Point Program until December 1970. The revised version read: "We want Equality for Women. Down with Machismo and Male Chauvinism!" The description was also rewritten. "Men must fight *along with* sisters in the struggle for economic and social equality." However, the edited version still did not reference patriarchy, the systemic exploitation of women, or the personal transformation required for gender justice.

CHAINS ON OUR MIND: THE POWER OF WORDS

The Women's Caucus explored many strategies to transform the political, cultural, and power dynamics of the organization. One was to change language. We came to understand that transforming capitalist thinking and behavior required a conscious and intentional struggle to "a new way of being"[17] for both men and women. New ways of thinking required words other than the sexist, racist, misogynist, and exploitative ones inherited from a society that subjugated and exploited women. Committed to personal transformation, we stopped using words and phrases that perpetuated inequality or demeaned women. We rejected being called "girls," a term that infantilized adult women. Patriarchal identifiers such as "so-and-so's wife" reduced woman to men's property and exhibited ignorance regarding a women's desire for independence and freedom. Instead, we advocated for what today is referred to as gender-inclusive and gender-neutral language. New words became part of our daily vocabulary, such as "people power" for "manpower" and "humanity" for "mankind." We used inclusive terms such as "brothers and sisters," "hermanos y hermanas," and "compañeros y compañeras." We also introduced concepts such as triple oppression, sexism, sexual fascism, and "the revolution within the revolution," to name a few.

In the struggle for new language, the Women's Caucus had male allies. Richie Pérez, then Information Ministry captain and a highly regarded officer, wrote an essay in 1971, criticizing the words "chicks" and "broads" as negative terms that take away women's humanity.[18] "Words do show an attitude; and, if you want to change that attitude, you have to begin by changing the words that you're using," Pérez explained. Huey Newton, Black Panther chairman, also addressed this issue in his "Letter to the Revolutionary Brothers and Sisters about the Women's Liberation and Gay Liberation Movements."[19] Acknowledging the widespread use of derogatory language against gay people, Newton called upon activists to eliminate the words "faggot" and "punk" from their language, calling these words obstacles to building solidarity.[20]

The Women's Caucus also replaced racist Spanish words and phrases. In the essay, "Colonized Mentality and Non-Conscious Ideology," Denise Oliver, minister of finance, wrote about racism inherent in labeling kinky hair *pelo malo* (bad hair) and criticized other terms. She wrote, "We call Black Puerto Ricans names like *prieto*, *molleto*, and *cocolo* … we 'non-consciously' reject the Blackness we are all a part of." Oliver concludes, "We should not be afraid to criticize ourselves about racism. … We will never have socialism until we are free of these chains on our mind."[21] The push for nonracist and nonsexist language gained momentum as a tool to advance revolutionary practice.

POLITICAL EDUCATION INSPIRES NEW WAYS OF BEING

In addition to our informal study in the Women's Caucus, all members took part in required weekly political education classes. Juan González headed the Education Ministry until September 1970, when he became minister of defense. In March 1970, Iris Benítez was the first woman officer appointed to the Education Ministry. I was among the first education cadre in the East Harlem branch and was subsequently joined by Olguie Robles and Gloria Colón. The ministry was responsible for preparing curricula, compiling reading lists, and facilitating weekly classes for members and for the public. Political education, which we called "P.E.," was empowering and highly valued. Our goal was to nurture a love of learning and political analysis. We encouraged Young Lords to read newspapers, articles, and books beyond those required. The organization's rules of discipline highlighted this point: "Political Education classes are mandatory. All members must read at least one political book a month, and at least two hours a day on contemporary matters." Most Young Lords had attended public schools where our intelligence was undermined. Hence, we welcomed political education as a tool for understanding and analyzing policies and ideologies affecting our lives. We viewed theory as a guide to action. Because study was so valued, every Young Lord, no matter his or her formal education, carried a book or article around, to always have something to read. Through study, we enhanced our critical thinking skills and developed a common language.

Ignorance about women's activities in the Young Lords Organization has led to the incorrect conclusion that the early political education program did not include women-related studies. This is not true. Copies of class outlines show that the Young Lords' education program covered all themes in the 13-Point Program in sequential order in recurring cycles. We studied Point 10, "We want equality for women," in the tenth week of each cycle. Despite an absence of books about the activism of women of color, the first P.E. rotation focused on inspirational herstories about anticolonialists and abolitionists in Puerto Rico, including Lola Rodríguez de Tió and Mariana Bracetti, fighters in the struggle against the Spanish colonizers. Rodríguez de Tió wrote the patriotic lyrics to "La Borinqueña," Puerto Rico's national anthem. Bracetti helped organize the insurrection against the Spanish in 1868 known as El Grito de Lares (the Cry of Lares) and created the original Lares flag. We learned about the twentieth-century labor organizer and women's rights advocate Luisa Capetillo, who organized workers and unions and wrote the first feminist manifesto in Puerto Rico in 1911.[22] Juana Colón, a descendant of slaves and also a labor organizer, cofounded the first Socialist Party in Puerto Rico and was active in the tobacco workers' movement.[23] Ana Roqué de Duprey was a feminist suffragette leader who published *La Mujer*, Puerto Rico's first women's newspaper.[24] We studied the activities of Nationalist Party militants, including Lolita Lebrón and Blanca Canales, imprisoned for armed actions against US colonialism. We read the poetry of Julia de Burgos and learned about her work with the Nationalist Party. We learned about the contributions of African American activists and feminists such as Harriet Tubman, who led hundreds of enslaved people to freedom, and Sojourner Truth, widely known for her "Ain't I a Woman?" speech.[25] We claimed these feminist foremothers and identified with the fight for women's rights as part of our legacy.

The second and third P.E. cycles in 1970 increased readings about activist women and feminist ideas, including selections from *The Black Woman* edited by Toni Cade Bambara, who proclaimed that the role of the artist was to make the revolution irresistible. We read the pamphlet "Enter Fighting: Today's Woman, A Marxist-Leninist View" by Clara Colón. These cycles introduced Frances Beal's essay, "Double Jeopardy: To Be Black and Female." We also studied articles about early societies where women were the equals of men, and how over thousands of years with the development of private property, women were made subordinate to men. By the summer of 1970, the Education Ministry assigned readings from "The Woman Question" and Friedrich Engels's *The Origin of the Family, Private Property, and the State*. Engels wrote that the rise of class society brought with it increasing inequality between men and women. The YLP Position Paper on Women, published in September 1970, synthesized ideas from these writings. The last P.E. cycle that year added "The Black Woman's Manifesto," published by the Third World Women's Alliance. From 1969 through the end of 1970, P.E. classes helped to educate members about women's oppression and contributions. The fight to advance women's liberation was part of the struggle for socialism.

Political education classes also covered the histories of African Americans, Indigenous Americans, and other people of color in the United States. *The Autobiography of Malcolm X* sparked discussions about self-determination. In January 1970, *Puerto Rico: A Profile* by Kal Wagenheim was published, and we quickly assigned it as required reading. At that time there were few books in English about Puerto Rican history. The Center for Puerto Rican Studies (El Centro de Estudios Puertorriqueños) was not established until 1973. *History of the Indians of Puerto Rico* by cultural anthropologist and archaeologist Ricardo E. Alegría was a favorite reading about Taínos and Taínas. We had the most difficulty finding books about Blacks in Puerto Rico. *Historia de la esclavitud negra en Puerto Rico* by Luis M. Díaz Soler was one source but was less accessible to us because not all members could read Spanish. Our studies of Afro-Boricua history came primarily from pamphlets, talks with individuals knowledgeable about the legacy of slavery and African history in Puerto Rico, and the *Palante* newspaper.

We also studied works about capitalism and imperialism, the philosophy of dialectical materialism, writings by Marx, Lenin, and Engels, and *The Little Red Book* and others by Mao Zedong. Required readings included *Introduction to Socialism* by Leo Huberman and Paul Sweezy and *Labor's Untold Story* by Richard O. Boyer. We studied international revolutionary movements and the writings of anticolonial leaders and thinkers such as Amílcar Cabral, Kwame Nkrumah, Patrice Lumumba, Ho Chi Minh, and Che Guevara. Frantz Fanon's writings provided insight into the traumas of oppression and provoked discussions about how we carry the oppressor's ideas.

Political education opened our minds and hearts to new ways of knowing ourselves and the world. It inspired our political outlook and guided our work. We studied every article we could find about the activism of women of color, assessing models and strategies that might apply. Organizing activities and programs in East Harlem grounded us in the realities facing Puerto Rican women. These experiences empowered us to envision more liberated roles for ourselves, our families, and our community. The Women's Caucus flourished.

PART II.
FEMINISTS OF COLOR AND GENDER JUSTICE MOVEMENTS

… they are the unsung, unrecognized workhorses who provide cohesion to organization while the men parade their "leadership" at meetings and important functions. The women are tired of playing this role. They want the opportunity to assume organizational, political leadership and responsibility in the movement.[1]

—"Women Who Disagree," *Regeneración*, 1970

"Women can never obtain real independence unless her functions of procreation are under her own control."[1]

—Antoinette Konikow, *Voluntary Motherhood*, 1923 pamphlet

4.
STERILIZATION POLITICS AND STRUGGLES FOR REPRODUCTIVE JUSTICE

> Forced sterilization of poor women of color
> is an American tradition.[1]
>
> —Natasha Lennard, *The Intercept*, 2020

At a Women's Caucus meeting in 1970, we read a report issued by Puerto Rico's Department of Health regarding a study conducted in 1965 that found 34 percent of women in Puerto Rico, twenty to forty-nine years old, were sterilized. Given the pervasiveness and permanency of the procedure, we called it genocide. "Sterilization is irreversible and as such the u.s can control the Puerto Rican population," declared the article "Sterilized Puerto Ricans," published in the May 1970 issue of *Palante*.[2] Caucus members believed in a woman's right to control her body, to decide whether to have children, and how many, without coercion or interference. Our list of reproductive freedoms included access to birth control, the right to legal and safe abortions, and the end to involuntary sterilization and experimentation on women's bodies. Historian Jennifer Nelson remarks that the Women's Caucus advanced "an inclusive reproductive rights agenda that influenced (socialist) feminist politics later in the decade."[3]

Historically, individual men, the family, the state, and other institutions have exerted control over women's reproduction. During slavery and colonization in the Americas, white men wielded total power over the bodies of Black and Indigenous women. Slave owners forced enslaved women to bear children, using their bodies as "factories" to reproduce free labor. They experimented on women at will, or allowed others to do so, not as an exception but as the norm.[4] Slave owners used sexual violence and the breakup of families to compel obedience.[5] Rape was everyday terrorism.[6] White women rarely opposed the violence performed by their husbands and actively participated in the system as brutally as men, which is documented by historian Stephanie E. Jones-Rogers in *They*

Were Her Property: White Women as Slave Owners in the American South.[7]

During the early 1900s in the United States, the eugenics movement surged in popularity. Eugenicists argued that humanity could be improved by promoting the reproduction of humans who had what they regarded as desirable qualities and purging from the population traits labeled as "undesirable." Generally, nonwhite people and the lower economic strata were those identified as "unfit" and objectionable. Historian Isabel Wilkerson writes that the German Third Reich, in debating "how to institutionalize racism, ... began by asking how the Americans did it."[8] Eugenics was popular in the United States years before the rise of Nazi Germany.

STERILIZATION POLITICS IN PUERTO RICO

In Puerto Rico, eugenics and population control policies surfaced in the discourse among government officials, philanthropists, physicians, journalists, and writers about the causes of poverty in the archipelago. According to historian Laura Briggs in *Reproducing Empire: Race, Sex, Science, and U.S. Imperialism in Puerto Rico*, population control theorists and eugenics proponents identified "overpopulation" as the cause. They insisted that "the working class was reproducing too much" and pointed to the population's "excessive sexuality and fertility."[9] James R. Beverley, the US-appointed governor in Puerto Rico from 1929 to 1933, wrote:

> I have always believed that some method of restricting the birth rate among the lower and more ignorant element of the population is the only salvation for the Island.[10]

Beverley proposed population control policies, arguing that the poor and working class, especially dark-skinned and Black people, were "unfit," the least desirable and most ignorant.

Sterilization politics highlights distinctions among "birth control as reproductive freedom, contraception as technique, and population control as policy."[11] As colonialists pushed for population control, women activists in Puerto Rico advocated for reproductive freedom. They sought to make contraceptive information available and to decriminalize laws that prohibited it.[12] The Puerto Rican Socialist Party,[13] whose members included sugarcane workers and people engaged in needlework,[14] actively organized to provide this information.[15] In 1925, Dr. José Lanauze Rolón, an Afro-Boricua physician and socialist trained at Howard University, founded the Birth Control League of Puerto Rico to educate and disseminate information to poor families.[16] Between 1925 and 1932, Puerto Rican public health officials opened clinics in San Juan, Lares, and Mayagüez,[17] but all were shut down due to lack of funding and the opposition of the Catholic Church.

Puerto Rican women "championed birth control as an unmitigated good thing in the face of ongoing attempts by both colonialists and nationalist men to manipulate women."[18] Puerto Rico's bishops vilified efforts to bring reproductive freedom to Puerto Rican women, calling it "the gateway to immorality."[19] The Puerto Rican Nationalist Party condemned birth control as an imperialist import and "genocidal plot" to end the Puerto Rican population.[20] Nationalists called on Puerto Rican women to have children to save the nation. This view was at odds with demands of Puerto Rican women for reproductive rights and birth control alternatives.[21]

As poverty intensified during the Great Depression of 1929, US president Franklin Delano Roosevelt formed the Puerto Rico Emergency Relief Administration (PRERA). It launched a pilot program in 1934 providing contraceptive information and supplies to low-income families. The subsequent opening of sixty-seven maternal clinics[22] served more than ten thousand women in two years.[23] However, Catholic Action, a group in Ponce, denounced the family planning program and threatened a campaign against Roosevelt if he did not shut it down.[24] Fearing the loss of Catholic support in his upcoming election, Roosevelt closed the clinics.[25] Though short-lived, the success of the PRERA clinics showed that poor and working-class Puerto Rican women were eager to have birth control choices.

After the clinics closed, eugenics proponents took advantage of Puerto Rican women's desire for reproductive options. Clarence Gamble, a Harvard Medical School–educated-eugenicist and heir to the Procter and Gamble fortune, ushered in a decades-long involvement, turning Puerto Rico into a laboratory for human experimentation. Gamble had funded birth control clinics and contraceptive research in poor communities across the world and in the US regions of Appalachia and the South.[26] Declaring that Puerto Ricans living in poverty should make room for more "fit" members of society,[27] he launched twenty-three birth control clinics.[28]

The first clinic opened in 1937 when the local Puerto Rican government passed Public Law 116, legalizing sterilization.[29] Gamble's clinics tested federally unapproved contraceptives on 1,500 women.[30] He dispensed unreliable methods such as foams and jellies but did not make the highly reliable diaphragm available, arguing that it was "too expensive and difficult for Puerto Rican women to use."[31] Instead, Gamble promoted sterilization as the most dependable birth control option.[32] By the end of the 1930s, Gamble was flying Puerto Rican doctors to New York City to learn the latest sterilization techniques.[33]

Sterilization was marketed aggressively. Briggs concludes that "the draconian figuring of the Puerto Rican woman by Gamble ... as a source of danger to the United States laid the foundations for postwar population control policies."[34] Health workers went door to door, pitching US government–subsidized sterilization procedures.[35] The US Agency for International Development funded factories to set up family planning clinics on site that provided free sterilization.[36] By 1949, reports showed postpartum sterilizations in 17.8 percent of all hospital birth deliveries.[37] By the 1950s, they were routine—any mother with two or more children was sterilized after giving birth. According to a 1968 study, over one third of the women did not know that sterilization through tubal ligation was permanent.[38] Practitioners' failure to disclose this critical information undercuts claims that Puerto Rican women "consented."

The film *La operación* documents the extensive undertaking carried out in Puerto Rico during the 1950s and 1960s.[39] In an interview in the film, Dr. Helen Rodríguez Trías, a Puerto Rican pediatrician and women's rights advocate, discusses the importance of birth control options:

> Birth control exists as an individual right, something that should be built into health programming; it should be part and parcel of choices people have. And when birth control is really carried out, people are given information, and there is facility to use different kinds of modalities of birth control.[40]

In Puerto Rico, women did not have "different kinds of modalities of birth control." Neither the US nor Puerto Rico governments invested in alternative, safe, and reversible contraceptive methods to sterilization. Instead, they permitted eugenicists to operate freely, running unregulated birth control centers that dispensed ineffective methods and performed irreversible sterilization techniques on poor and working-class women.

STERILIZATION POLITICS IN THE UNITED STATES

The Women's Caucus moved the Young Lords Party to support campaigns and activities against the mass sterilization of women in Puerto Rico. Caucus members conducted radio interviews, wrote articles, organized educational forums, and protested government and hospital policies and practices. In the course of this work, caucus members learned about the widespread coerced sterilization programs in the United States. During the early twentieth century, more than sixty thousand people were sterilized in thirty-two states under US eugenics laws.[41] Of these, California performed one-third, or twenty thousand, of the operations;[42] Latinas were sterilized at 59 percent higher rates than non-Latinas.[43]

During the 1960s and 1970s, African American, other women of color, and poor women were targets of coerced sterilization. In Mississippi, SNCC leader Fannie Lou Hamer led a campaign against a sterilization bill in 1964.[44] The SNCC pamphlet *Genocide in Mississippi* exposed that "six out of ten women sterilized by tubal ligation in the state were African American."[45] Hamer had personal experience. In 1961, she entered a Mississippi hospital for a cyst removal. While under anesthesia, doctors sterilized her without her consent.[46] In the 1970s, the Indian Health Service targeted Native Americans, claiming they had high birth rates.[47] US doctors sterilized approximately 25 to 42 percent of Native American women of childbearing age, some as young as fifteen.[48] In New York City, hospitals sterilized Puerto Rican women at seven times the rate of white women.[49]

In 1974, Dr. Rodríguez Trías cofounded the Committee to End Sterilization Abuse (CESA), along with Maritza Arrastía, Puerto Rican Socialist Party member, and other women's health activists.[50] Through the late 1970s, CESA won several lawsuits, establishing municipal and federal guidelines to stop sterilization abuse.[51] Chicanas in California also won lawsuits against forced sterilization. The film *No más bebés* (No More Babies) documents a landmark case in the late 1960s and early 1970s when Mexican immigrant women sued doctors, the state of California, and the US government.[52] In 2021, California finally compensated thousands of people sterilized under the state's eugenics laws.[53]

PUERTO RICAN WOMEN AS GUINEA PIGS

Mass sterilization was not the only violation of Puerto Rican women's reproductive rights. During the 1940s and 1950s, all major US pharmaceutical companies conducted research in Puerto Rico.[54] Their focus in the 1950s was the birth control pill. Margaret Sanger, founder of Planned Parenthood, played a key role,[55] raising funds and recruiting Gregory G. Pincus, a former Harvard scientist, to conduct human trials in Puerto Rico.[56] Pincus's background in fertility research and population control[57] included experiments on psychotic patients at a Massachusetts state hospital. John C. Rock, also a Harvard professor and obstetrician, joined Pincus. Sanger introduced them to Clarence Gamble so they could access his clinics.[58] The men targeted women who sought options to avoid both pregnancy and sterilization.[59]

When Pincus and Rock launched human trials in San Juan, Puerto Rico in 1956, little was known about the effects of the birth control pill. Nonetheless, Pincus and Rock tested the pill on approximately 1,500 women, telling them it was medication to prevent pregnancy but withholding information that it was experimental and had side effects.[60] An unknown number of Puerto Rican women suffered from high hormone dosages and reported dizziness, nausea, severe cramping, headaches, stomach pain, and vomiting.[61] The researchers made no effort to identify the cause. Instead, Pincus referred to their symptoms as psychosomatic, the result of emotional super activity.[62] Women participating in the human trials also reported blood clotting, which was the suspected cause of three deaths. But the researchers did not investigate[63] or conduct any autopsies. In fact, Pincus and his team ended the birth control pill study without reporting any problems at all to the Food and Drug Association, and the pill was approved as a contraceptive method on May 9, 1960.[64]

In a 2017 article titled "The Bitter Pill: Harvard and the Dark History of Birth Control," Drew C. Pendergrass and Michelle Y. Raji revisit this history. They conclude:

> For the most part, the popular narrative of the pill is one of celebration. When a 2009 Harvard Gazette story discussed Harvard's role in creating the birth control pill, they did so without referencing the Puerto Rican trials or the asylum testing. Pincus and Rock are largely remembered for their contributions to women's reproductive empowerment, without reference to their troubling methods.[65]

The *Harvard Gazette* has attempted to erase the sacrifices, side effects, and deaths of poor and working-class Puerto Rican women. Its narrative buried the unethical and horrific tactics used. It ignored the fact that US researchers did not secure informed consent or disclose the research's purpose and risks. Yet, no one has been held accountable—not researchers, pharmaceutical companies, or the US or Puerto Rico governments. No reparations have been made to victims or their families. Sanger, widely applauded and acclaimed for bringing birth control to women in the United States, did so at the expense and suffering of Puerto Rican women.

5.
UNITIES WITH BLACK AND CHICANA FEMINISTS

> I rarely talk about feminism in the singular.
> I talk about feminisms. And, even when
> I myself refused to identify with feminism,
> I realized that it was a certain kind of feminism
> … It was a feminism of those women who
> weren't really concerned with equality for all women …[1]

—Angela Davis, August 5, 2019,
Oral History Interview, National Museum
of African American History and Culture

The joy and empowerment we felt as social justice activists and community organizers contrasted sharply with the gender discrimination that pervaded the Young Lords Organization. Across the US revolutionary nationalist movements, feminists of color encountered the same contradiction and mobilized to promote liberatory ideas and practices. We organized against systems of power that put men in the forefront and in control of institutions that subordinated, oppressed, and dominated women.[2] Feminist activists of color formed caucuses and committees and spearheaded autonomous all-women groups. As authors of groundbreaking essays, women of color advanced feminist theory. Black feminists critiqued the racism of white supremacy and the sexism of the Black nationalist movement. Chicana feminists formed organizations, linking gender equality with social justice goals. Exchanges and collaborations with Black, Latinx, Native, and Asian women activists inspired the Women's Caucus. We learned herstories, feminist theories, and strategies that influenced the Young Lords' feminist activities and agendas. This chapter describes unities the Women's Caucus shared with Chicanas and African American women activists.

As mentioned, the Women's Caucus did not use the term "feminist." We associated it with the white middle-class women's movement that was not inclusive of issues important to women of color or poor women. We rejected the assumption that the white women's movement spoke for all women. However, the struggle against a system of power that subordinates and oppresses women resonated with us. Today, "feminisms," in the plural, acknowledges the existence of many perspectives, resulting from different experiences, class interests, beliefs about the root cause of oppression, and strategies to achieve gender justice.

THE BLACK FEMINIST TRADITION

The Women's Caucus studied herstories of women of color in the Americas dating back to slavery and colonization. The Black feminist tradition emerged from the resistance of enslaved women during the time when white people held absolute power and control over Black and Indigenous women's bodies.[3] White men raped with impunity. Black and Native women were not passive victims. "Women resisted and advocated challenges to slavery at every turn," confirms scholar activist Angela Davis in *Women, Race, and Class*.[4] Enslaved women destroyed slaveholders' property and even poisoned them. They planned and took part in uprisings and slave rebellions.[5] Some, driven by despair, committed suicide and infanticide rather than suffer or have their children suffer the sadism and brutality of men.[6] Since slavery, Black feminists were "developing a distinct political tradition based upon a systematic analysis of the intertwining oppressions of race, gender, and class," writes historian Sharon Smith in *Women and Socialism: Class, Race, and Capital*.[7] Sojourner Truth's speech "Ain't I a Woman?," delivered at the Women's Rights Convention in Akron, Ohio, in 1851, was an early expression of an intersectional identity. Truth asserts her right to equality as a woman, emphasizing how race and gender subjected her to different and more severe oppression than white women.

In 1949, Claudia Jones, Trinidad-born journalist, poet, and Communist Party member, explicitly advanced the idea that Black women's oppression was threefold based on race, gender, and class. Jones's groundbreaking essay "An End to the Neglect of the Problems of the Negro Woman!" analyzes the historical role of Black women and identifies their "super exploitation" as workers.[8] She asserts, "Negro women—as workers, as Negroes, and as women—are the most oppressed stratum of the whole population." Jones concludes that the liberation of Black women would mean the liberation of everyone.[9] Historian Erik S.

McDuffie describes Jones as an innovator of "a path-breaking brand of feminist politics that centers working-class women."[10]

In the same essay, Jones demands attention to the long legacy of state-condoned sexual assault against Black women and the criminalization of women who defend themselves. She calls for organizing against the rape and sexual assault of Black women by white men as a systemic issue, and she demands that the perpetrators of sexual violence be held liable for their crimes.[11] Jones details the case of Rosa Lee Ingram, a Georgia sharecropper sentenced to death in 1948 by an all-white jury for defending herself from armed attack by a white landowner. Her two teenage sons were also sentenced to death for defending their mother. After many legal campaigns and appeals, the sentences were reduced to life in prison. In all, the Ingram family members were imprisoned for ten years.

Ideas about the multiple and intertwining oppressions that Black women face evolved into the concept of intersectionality, a term coined by scholar and attorney Kimberlé Crenshaw in 1989. In an interview at the African American Policy Forum years later, Crenshaw elaborated:

> Intersectionality is a lens through which you can see where power comes and collides, where it interlocks and intersects. It's not simply that there's a race problem here, a gender problem here, and a class or LBGTQ problem there. Many times, that framework erases what happens to people who are subject to all of these things.[12]

Ashley Bohrer's article "Intersectionality and Marxism: A Critical Historiography" offers a working definition:

> In its most basic form, then, intersectionality is the theory that both structurally and experientially, social systems of domination are linked to one another and that, in order both to understand and to change these systems, they must be considered together.[13]

A key characteristic of Black feminism is its orientation toward action agendas that underline the interconnectedness of systems of oppression and the importance of addressing them together.[14]

In *Living for the Revolution*, historian Kimberly Springer summarizes how Black feminists expanded the women's liberation movement

by challenging Eurocentric and classist interpretations of women's issues.[15] Black feminists traced the resistance of Black women in the
United States to slavery and colonization and defied the idea of a "singu-
lar" feminism. Black and other feminists of color contested the hegem-
ony of the white women's liberation movement and theories that the
feminist struggle developed in "waves."[16] The "first wave" referred to the
women's suffrage movements from 1848 to 1920. The second identified
the women's movement from 1963 to 1980s, and the third was the period
beyond the 1990s. In the article "Is It Time to Jump Ship? Historians Rethink the Waves Metaphor," Kathleen Laughlin and colleagues no longer
favor the waves analysis because it centers the white women's movement
and excludes women of color.[17] Black, Indigenous, Latinx women and
their descendants in the Americas fought colonization, slavery, and the
terrorism of rape generations before the US women's suffrage movement
began in the 1800s.

THE BLACK WOMEN'S ALLIANCE

In 1968, women in the Student Nonviolent Coordinating Committee,
(SNCC) formed the Black Women's Liberation Caucus (BWLC). The cofounders—Frances Beal, Fay Bellamy, Mae Jackson, Eleanor Holmes
Norton, and Gwendolyn Patton—pursued gender equality and challenged the discourse of masculinity permeating the Black Power movement.[18] Insisting that Black women's issues were of immediate concern,
the BWLC emphasized that how the revolutionary struggle was waged
would forecast how the nation would operate after the revolution. If
women's roles were gendered and restricted to being mothers, caretakers, homemakers, and men's assistants, then women would have these
same duties after.[19] When the BWLC raised these concerns, men in
SNCC accused the women of being divisive of the unity required to fight
racism. They criticized them as "saboteurs" of the Black struggle.[20] In
1970, the BWLC separated from SNCC and became the Black Women's
Alliance (BWA), a Black feminist socialist organization.

The ideas expressed by the BWLC resonated with members of the
Women's Caucus in the Young Lords Organization. We were familiar
with SNCC's political work and the activities of women organizers who
ran freedom schools and voter registration drives in the Deep South. We

admired Ella Baker, the SNCC cofounder and organizer who believed that a leader's role was "to strengthen the group, forge consensus, and negotiate a way forward"[21] through open, democratic, and collaborative structures. Baker hailed women as "the backbone of the movement" and criticized sexist practices.[22]

Several members of the YLO met Gwendolyn Patton, BWLC cofounder, when she was living in New York City. Patton was a SNCC staff member and a community and student organizer in Tuskegee, Alabama for many years. As cofounder of the National Black Antiwar Antidraft Union, she coauthored SNCC's position paper against the Vietnam War.[23] Patton spoke to us about organizing women in the Jim Crow South and shared her thoughts about gendered roles in the nationalist movements.[24] According to historian and activist Patricia Romney, Patton's described SNCC's gendered division of labor as "symbolic of the 'you walk behind us' idea prevalent in the movement."[25] Patton emphasized the importance of the activism of women of color in the fight for revolutionary change.

Frances Beal, BWLC and BWA cofounder, authored "Double Jeopardy: To Be Black and Female" in 1969.[26] Beal critiques capitalism's inhumanity and exploitation of Black women and men. She rejects feminisms that suggests gender as the primary source of women's subordination and Black nationalism that theorizes racism as the only source of Black people's oppression. Beal describes the intersecting identities and struggles of being Black and female in the United States and explains how race and gender work together to super exploit Black women workers, reducing them to "a state of enslavement."[27]

"Double Jeopardy" critiques the Black Liberation movement, challenging men "to be revolutionaries in all aspects."[28] In terms of the white women's liberation movement, Beal concludes, "Any white group that does not have an anti-imperialist and anti-racist ideology has absolutely nothing in common with the Black women's struggle."[29] Beal highlights the differences between the Black women's experience and those of white women—especially the middle-class women who dominated the women's movement. The Young Lords' political education classes studied Beal's article, and it was foundational to the feminist analysis of the Women's Caucus.

THE BLACK PANTHER PARTY

Founded in 1966 in Oakland, California, the Black Panther Party followed an ideology of Black nationalism, socialism, and armed self-defense. Women joined the Black Panther Party for the same reasons as men—to fight for Black liberation. The BPP's 10-Point Program stated, "We want freedom. We want power to determine the destiny of our Black Community."[30] Communications Secretary and Central Committee member Kathleen Cleaver explained that her primary motivation as a Black activist was to participate in the revolutionary struggle to end "the legal, social, psychological, economic, and political restrictions imposed on the human rights of Black people."[31] Cleaver believed that gender concerns should be addressed within the Black Panther Party since women's oppression could not be fought as a stand-alone issue.

Women in the Black Panther Party affected "the internal dialogue about gender."[32] They also did not refer to themselves as feminists because of its association with the white women's liberation movement, as previously discussed. Nonetheless, Black Panther Party leader Ericka Huggins observes:

> I would say that the women who were drawn to the Black Panther Party were all feminists. ... [W]e generally believed in the political, social, economic, and sexual equality of women and girls.[33]

In an interview with historian Mary Phillips in 2010, Huggins identifies as a feminist, declaring, "I'm a strong believer of black feminists or women of color feminists, who believe that we have to uplift our entire community."[34] Huggins' feminism is reflected and rooted in her experiences and political practice. She was the first woman to open a BPP chapter, in New Haven, Connecticut, and was arrested and charged with conspiracy with intent to commit murder in 1969. Huggins was separated from her baby daughter and awaited trial in prison for almost two years before the charges were dropped.[35]

By the early 1970s, women in the Black Panther Party made up nearly two-thirds of the membership.[36] As the FBI and police repression against the BPP escalated, increasing numbers of men were incarcerated. Women members assumed leadership roles and kept the organization functioning. In New York, for example, Janet Cyril ran the "serve the people" programs in Harlem during the two-year imprisonment of twenty-one Black Panthers arrested in 1969.[37] Cyril coordinated the free breakfast programs. Often, at the end of a long day, she stopped by the Young Lords' East Harlem office. Several of us would gather to talk and catch up with her about contemporary political events and movement challenges. We discussed gender struggles and the latest incidents with sexism and male chauvinism. Cyril recounted that the Black Panther Party expelled her four times for refusal to comply with sexist demands, and, by her proud admission, for her generally anti-authoritarian attitude.[38] Nevertheless, she loved the Black Panther Party and always returned to the organization. Like the women in the Black Panther Party, the members of the Women's Caucus felt we were on the correct path, advocating for a revolution side by side with men.[39]

THIRD WORLD WOMEN'S ALLIANCE

By the summer of 1970, the Black Women's Alliance was becoming a new organization under the leadership of Frances Beal. Puerto Rican *independentistas* in New York City approached the BWA wanting to join.[40] Their request triggered an internal debate regarding women's oppression beyond the Black/white paradigm.[41] Some BWA members opposed any change in mission or composition. However, the group decided to form the Third World Women's Alliance, a multiracial, women-led and women-centered socialist organization to struggle against racism, imperialism, and sexism.[42] In her book *We Were There,* former member Patricia Romney documents the formation, activities, and contributions of the organization.[43] Composed mainly of Black and Puerto Rican women activists in New York, the TWWA opened a West Coast branch, expanding the membership to Asian and Pacific Islander women and Chicanas. The TWWA defined "Third World" as people of African, Puerto Rican, Native American, Chicana, and Asian descent.[44] The group developed relationships with women's organizations in other countries and brought attention to the impact of US foreign and military policy on women, linking issues in US communities of color to anti-imperialist movements around the world.

Members of the Women's Caucus in the Young Lords Party attended some of the TWWA's initial formation meetings. Certainly, as

Puerto Ricans and African American socialist feminists, we shared ideologies and practices. During that summer in 1970, the women in the YLP were engaged in major protests and organizing campaigns, discussed in Part III. We opted to remain in the Young Lords Party, believing that we could best advance the struggles of Puerto Rican women through our work in the organization.

INFLUENCE OF CHICANA FEMINISTS

In California and the US Southwest, Chicanx activists were also involved in revolutionary nationalist organizations. An important convening took place in March 1969, referred to chapter 1. The National Chicano Youth Conference in Denver, Colorado proposed to unite various civil rights and social justice movements under one banner, specifically the land-grant movement in New Mexico and Arizona, the farm workers' struggle, the student movement, and urban youth struggles.[45] The five-day convening produced the Plan Espiritual de Aztlán, a political manifesto that identified the "cultural values of life, family, and home" as "a powerful weapon"[46] and nationalism as the common denominator for mass mobilization.

During the conference, a debate took place in a workshop among fifty to seventy Chicanas about the role of women in the nationalist movement.[47] Fed up with cooking and cleaning and handling the administrative duties men assigned women, some Chicanas insisted that "women should walk next to, not behind Chicanos."[48] Others argued that Chicanas "should always stand behind their men." In the report back to the conference, the workshop facilitator said, "It was the consensus of the group that the Chicana woman does not want to be liberated."[49] The statement caused an uproar. Activist Elizabeth "Betita" Martínez, who attended the workshop, later clarified that the facilitator intended her statement as a rejection of the white women's liberation movement, not of liberation politics for Chicanas.[50]

Like other US revolutionary nationalists, activists in the Chicanx movement "maintained patriarchal structures of domination"[51] and followed a predominantly masculinist ideology.[52] The projected ideal of the Chicanx family was a strong male at the head and a submissive woman by his side. Chicanx studies historian Alma García elaborates that the movement exalted subservient gender roles and the stereotype of the suffering Chicana as the backbone of the family and Chicano culture.[53] According to García, some men claimed that machismo was a source of masculine pride and a defense mechanism against society's racism. However, Chicana feminists rejected these views, calling for changing the unequal relations between women and men instead.[54]

Chicana feminism emerged in response to the sexism women experienced in the nationalist movement. Chicanas challenged leaders and activists "who preached 'power to la raza' yet relegated Chicanas to answering phones, making coffee, cooking, and servicing the men with sexual favors."[55] "Chicanas believed that feminism involved more than an analysis of gender because, as women of color, they were affected by both race and class in their everyday lives."[56] They also opposed discrimination in education, the role of the Catholic Church, and all backward ideologies intended to dominate women.[57]

During the entire period of social protest and community mobilization, Chicanas were politically active.[58] They urged Chicano leaders to put women's concerns, such as equal pay for equal work, bicultural and bilingual childcare centers, the right to abortion, and an end to forced sterilization, on the social justice agenda. However, Chicano leaders largely ignored their recommendations.

THE BROWN BERETS

The Brown Berets, formed in 1967 in East Los Angeles, created chapters across the southwestern United States.[59] Like the Young Lords, most members were in their early twenties and from working class homes. The Los Angeles chapter controlled over sixty branches, most in California.[60] Although the Brown Berets promoted nationalism as a call for unity, they vacillated between cultural and revolutionary nationalism, between a struggle to maintain cultural traditions and a struggle of an oppressed nationality to achieve liberation.[61]

In the fall of 1969, several Young Lords from New York, including myself, traveled to California to meet the Brown Berets and discuss possible collaborations. I met with several Chicana members who oversaw the health, social services, and children's breakfast programs. We stayed up late into the night talking about neighborhood projects and community organizing. Inevitably, the conversation turned to the role and treatment of women in the movement. My account of the male chauvinism in the Young Lords Organization was no surprise to them. They described being treated as "invisible labor," working as cooks, secretaries, and janitors when "conferences, symposiums, [and] meetings" took place or when the group published newspapers and magazines.[62] "Although this labor was essential to the actual functioning of the political movement, it was seen as women's work and therefore devalued,"[63] emphasizes women's studies and Chicanx historian Maylei Blackwell.

Despite our experiences with male chauvinism, the Brown Beret sisters and I believed in revolutionary change. We united in our hopes that we could educate and persuade the male leaders about the need to discard backward thinking for the sake of community advancement, social justice, and women's rights.

About six months later, Chicanas in the Brown Berets took bold action against ongoing machismo and gender injustice. Gloria Arellanes, the sole woman on the Central Committee and minister of correspondence and finance in the East Los Angeles chapter, had repeatedly brought grievances from Chicana members to the leadership, but the situation did not improve. Disheartened by the men's refusal to address the problems, Arellanes delivered a letter of resignation on February 25, 1970. According to Chicana studies scholar Dionne Espinoza, Arellanes' letter declared the resignation of "ALL Brown Beret women." They were tired of being treated as "nothings, not as 'revolutionary sisters.'"[64] It was a dramatic and powerful exit. After the stormy resignation, the former Brown Berets formed Las Adelitas de Aztlán. Espinoza explains that "gender consciousness and woman-identified solidarity enabled them to break with the Brown Berets and develop a new political identity."[65] Although the group was short lived, the women marched in the historic Chicano Moratorium against the Vietnam War, wearing black to signify mourning. They presented Chicanas as independent and committed political actors against US imperialism and for social justice.

CHICANA FEMINIST ORGANIZATIONS

By the early 1970s, Chicana activists were disillusioned with the nationalist movement. Blackwell elaborates: "Women throughout the Chicano movement were no longer willing to tolerate internal organizational practices and masculinist political culture, which were exclusionary, undemocratic, and unfair."[66] Feminists rejected continued inferior treatment. *Regeneración,* the first Chicana feminist journal, published a blistering critique in 1970 titled "Women Who Disagree." They criticized the gendered division of political work as male privilege and a complete disregard of Chicanas as activists.[67]

Chicanx nationalists, both men and women, equated feminism with antinationalism. They accused Chicana feminists of divisiveness and retaliated against them. Blackwell details several name-calling "silencing mechanisms."[68] Nationalists accused feminists of being traitors and labeled them *vendidas* (sell-outs) and *malinche* (betrayer/collaborator). Other insults such as *agringadas* (white-identified) and *las Chicanas con pantalones* (pants-wearing Chicanas) alleged "cultural betrayal and assimilation into non-Chicano values and life-style."[69] Lesbianism was classified as extreme feminism. García explains, "Clearly, a cultural nationalist ideology that perpetuated stereotypical images of Chicanas as good wives and mothers found it difficult to accept a Chicana feminist lesbian movement."[70] Even harsher assaults were directed against lesbians.

Facing marginalization, Chicana lesbians pursued various strategies. Some formed separate organizations; others attempted to create lesbian coalitions; still others worked within the Chicana movement to challenge homophobia.[71] Across the movement, Chicanas formed autonomous organizations and caucuses, designed their own political agendas, and disseminated feminist ideas and campaigns. Among the new organizations were the Comisión Femenil Mexicana, formed in 1970, the first of its kind to develop leadership within the Chicanx movement and community. Chicana students founded *Hijas de Cuauhtémo*, a feminist newspaper in 1971. The first national conference of *la raza* women took place in Houston, Texas in 1971, attracting more than six hundred Chicanas from across the country.[72] Chicanas also created outlets for writing. Picking up the pen became a political act.[73]

As with African American feminists, Chicana aspirations and objectives extended beyond the nationalist demands of male-led organizations and the issues of the middle- and upper-class white women's movement. Feminists of color advanced the social justice movement and struggles for gender justice. The Women's Caucus learned from their experiences.

6.
DEMANDS OF THE WOMEN'S CAUCUS

> Sometimes we are blessed with being able to choose
> the time, and the arena, and the manner of our
> revolution, but more usually we must do battle
> where we are standing.[1]

—Audre Lorde, "A Burst of Light"

By March 1970, women in the New York Young Lords were actively engaged in all organizational activities and programs. Yet women's ideas and contributions were undervalued. Despite ongoing discussions and debates about machismo and male chauvinism, women were still treated as inferior. Women's concerns and issues were considered secondary to the overall revolutionary agenda and struggle. So why did women remain members? Like African American and Chicana activists, we asked ourselves, "Where do we best put our efforts to collectively fight the oppression our people face?" As young Puerto Rican activists from working-class backgrounds who were born and/or raised in the United States, we were committed to advancing the rights of US Puerto Ricans. In general, organizational options were limited, and male chauvinism was endemic to all of them. Women who joined the Young Lords believed in the 13-Point Program and the organization's direct-action strategies. At the time, the Movimiento Pro Independencia, Puerto Rico's leading *independentista* organization, focused on building support for the anticolonial struggle in Puerto Rico but was not organizing for the rights of Puerto Ricans in the United States. Notwithstanding the YLO's patriarchal practices, the Women's Caucus imagined changing the Central Committee's backward ideas, policies, and practices. After all, the 13-Point Program stated, "We want equality for women." Most members of the Women's Caucus decided to remain in the organization and demand structural and policy changes. If the leadership did not respond, many of us were prepared to exit, as our Black and Chicana sisters had done in similar situations discussed in the previous chapter.

THE WOMEN'S CAUCUS PRESENTS TEN DEMANDS

The unity of the members in the Women's Caucus gave us confidence to challenge male supremacy and male-centered practices. A major issue was the low number of women in leadership and the lack of female representation on the Central Committee. From the founding of the New York YLO chapter in July 1969 through May 1970, the all-male Central Committee assigned few women to officer positions. The notable exception was the Information Ministry. Mirta González served as information lieutenant as early as December 1969. Iris Benítez was also an information lieutenant from January to March 1970 and then an education lieutenant from March through May 1970. The Women's Caucus sought to increase the number of women in leadership positions, believing that women would best represent our collective interests.

Denise Oliver and I summarized the issues discussed in the Women's Caucus and drafted the following list of demands to submit to the Central Committee:

1) Appoint women to leadership positions, including the Central Committee.

2) Hold men accountable for acts of male chauvinism.

3) Provide childcare for members.

4) Organize campaigns related to issues affecting Puerto Rican and other women of color in the community.

5) Expand political education regarding the history and oppression of women.

6) Increase reporting in the *Palante* newspaper related to women's issues and increase the number of women writers.

7) End the "no women" policy of the Defense Ministry.

8) Assign women as public representatives and spokespersons.

9) Remove "revolutionary machismo" from the 13-Point Program and Platform.

10) Recognize the right of women to caucus.

Caucus members believed that the demands were necessary to advance the organization's revolutionary politics and practices.

When the Central Committee members—Felipe Luciano, Juan González, Pablo "Yoruba" Guzmán, David Pérez, and Juan "Fi" Ortiz — read the demands, several of the men were furious. "We're a revolutionary organization. Our struggle is for the liberation of all Puerto Ricans, not just women," they said condescendingly. "But liberation is not just for men either," some of us shouted. "Now is not the time to deal with this issue," the men claimed. As feminist scholar McClintock notes: "To insist on silence about gender conflict when it already exists, is to cover over, and thereby ratify, women's disempowerment."[2] The Central Committee accused caucus members of "divisiveness and disunity." We were familiar with the criticism, having heard from Black and Chicana feminists how it was hurled at them. Divisiveness was the default comeback across the movement. Some men ridiculed our demands as a "white woman's thing," criticizing us for what they deemed foreign to the Puerto Rican culture, as if women's liberation was only for white women.

Attempting to pacify us, a few Central Committee members conceded that women's issues were important. "They'll be addressed after the revolution," they said matter-of-factly. It was a brushoff, a kicking of the can down the road. We rejected it, insisting that women's issues were of immediate concern. As we pressed our demands, the most open-minded Young Lords agreed and advocated with us, and the Central Committee began to respond. The Women's Caucus advanced changes that gained women's rights and transformed the politics and practices of the Young Lords Party.

"No Women" Policy Defeated

In their self-proclaimed roles of "warriors" and "protectors," the all-male Central Committee instituted an explicit "no women" policy in the Defense Ministry. They viewed females as less physically and mentally capable than males to participate in defense. They ignored the countless examples of Puerto Rican women in history and in the YLO who took life-threatening risks and actions in carrying out political work. However, the men's outdated ideas did not stand scrutiny, and the Defense Ministry's "no-women" policy was defeated quickly. As a result, the Central Committee appointed Connie Morales, a young mother from the Bronx who had joined during the People's Church takeover, as the first woman in the Defense Ministry. Marta Duarte (Arguello), a student activist born in the Dominican Republic and raised in New York, entered the Defense Ministry in East Harlem and was later transferred to the ministry in the Lower East Side branch. Several other women were enlisted, including Myrna Martínez, a student activist and cofounder of UNICA, the Latinx student organization at Lehman College in the Bronx. Minerva Solla, a high school student from Manhattan's Chelsea neighborhood who joined in September 1970, was assigned to defense in the Lower East Side. They broke the gender barrier in the Young Lords Organization. Their commitment and bravery under difficult and perilous conditions earned them the respect of all members.

CHILDCARE POLICY

Initially, the Young Lords considered childcare an individual woman's problem, but we came to understand that it was a societal issue requiring a collective solution. Without childcare, poor and working mothers found it almost impossible to hold a job, attend school, or take part in activities outside the home. Mothers in the YLO faced difficulties balancing parental and political responsibilities. Finding a babysitter was time consuming and expensive. Lacking options, mothers brought their children to the Young Lords' office. But this was not a good arrangement, and the Women's Caucus demanded a better solution. In response, the Central Committee announced a childcare policy in 1970, requiring officers to plan and assign members, both men and women, to take care of children during meetings, demonstrations, and other organizational activities. As an added benefit, the policy advanced the idea that men, too, had a role in rearing and parenting children. Communal childcare became an important practice throughout the Puerto Rican political movement.

US feminists united in the demand for childcare. Many women mobilized for federal legislation to provide national access to quality, affordable day care. However, President Nixon vowed that he would not commit "the vast moral authority of the national Government to the side of communal approaches to childrearing over against the family-centered approach."[3] In 1971, he vetoed a bill to establish a system of comprehensive day care for children and launched conservative attacks on a goal that has left mothers without accessible and affordable childcare to the present day.

SEXUAL OBJECTIFICATION

The sexual objectification of women was a huge problem. Members of the Women Caucus demanded political consequences for demeaning acts against women. It was a highly controversial demand. Arguments erupted as Young Lords wrestled with deeply ingrained beliefs about gender roles, male privilege, and accountability. Some men scoffed when we proposed that men take responsibility for abusing or harming women. Many men refused to acknowledge that structural and power inequities existed. Others declined to give up favored positions and male advantages. Some insisted that the sexual objectification issue was a political distraction or a "white women's thing." Many others complained that women were gaining too much power, though they did not explain what they meant or feared.

Since women were not the majority of members, the Women's Caucus sought allies. The youngest men, the teenagers, were the first to join us. They advocated for the rights of women. In retrospect, they were early feminists. They affirmed that sexual objectification had no place in a revolutionary organization. "Women are comrades," they said. There are several reasons why the youngest men supported the Women's Caucus. First, they worked closely with female members in the day-to-day organizing and were familiar with the political commitments and risks we assumed. Then, they were learning about the history of women's oppression and exploitation in political education classes. Most importantly, they were committed to putting their revolutionary beliefs into practice. Hence, they supported the Women's Caucus and joined the journey of personal transformation. Among the first to join were Mark, Ramón, Benjy, Fi, Adrian, Carl, Ray, and others whose names I regret I do not now remember. With their backing, the Women's Caucus achieved another significant victory. Although not all Young Lords agreed, the general membership reached consensus that sexual objectification and abuse of women were unacceptable and that all members, including the Central Committee members, should be held accountable.

To ensure transparency in handling abuse allegations, the leadership introduced a process. A YLO officer would speak with the concerned parties to investigate and seek resolution. As follow up, a case could be brought to the general membership for discussion and discipline. The most serious findings could result in removal from positions of responsibility or expulsion from the organization. Each situation was decided on its facts. During 1970, the Central Committee disciplined, suspended, or demoted male members for demeaning or abusing women, including Central Committee members Juan González, Pablo "Yoruba" Guzmán, Felipe Luciano,[4] and David Pérez. Juan "Fi" Ortiz, the youngest member, was the sole leader not charged.

PALANTE AND THE WOMEN'S CAUCUS

In April 1970, the Young Lords Organization opened a second storefront in the Bronx. At the time, the borough had the fastest-growing Puerto Rican population in the city. Like in East Harlem, members carried out organizing and "serve the people" programs. The Bronx office also served as the organization's communications center under the direction of Pablo "Yoruba" Guzmán, minister of information. The YLO prioritized publishing an independent newspaper as indispensable to generating political discourse, raising class consciousness, and attracting recruits. *Palante* first appeared as a full-length, bimonthly, bilingual newspaper in May 1970. The masthead's subtitle read, "Latin Revolutionary Service," identifying as Latinx and Puerto Rican. The last page was reserved for the 13-Point Program and Platform. As an educational and organizing tool, *Palante* brought international and local news to the community. Every issue expressed solidarity with international revolutionary movements and reported on events in many countries, including Vietnam, Palestine, Cuba, Uruguay, Cambodia, Brazil, Trinidad, the Dominican Republic, the Basque Nation, Italy, Argentina, Panama, Mexico, Laos, India, Japan, Ceylon (renamed Sri Lanka), Bolivia, the Congo, Guatemala, Haiti, Colombia, Spain, the Philippines, Rhodesia (Zimbabwe), among others.

At its peak, *Palante* sold ten to fifteen thousand copies per issue and was a principal source of YLP income. Every member sold *Palante*, and it sold at selected newsstands, bookstores, bodegas, and other venues across the United States. Given the paper's importance in reaching our communities, the Women's Caucus sought to expand the content of women-related articles and the pool of women writers.

Fig 6. Jenny Figueroa selling *Palante*. 1970.
(Courtesy: Michael Abramson)

Two articles authored by women members, published in *Palante* in 1971, deserve to be highlighted. They are significant for their early intersectional analysis of the corporate media's representation of and impact on women and communities of color. Recognizing the media's critically important role in shaping people's understanding and views of the world and society, *Palante* included articles addressing issues relevant to our communities not addressed elsewhere, especially about women of color. Along these lines, Jenny Figueroa, cadre in the Information Ministry, and Lulu Rovira (Limardo), in the Economic Development Ministry, explored the media's complicity in perpetuating sexism, racism, and classism. In "World of Fantasy," Figueroa, describes television as a "brainwashing" tool for gender socialization and the enslaving of minds. She focuses on the broadcasters' promotion of racial and gender stereotypes. Specifically, Figueroa deconstructs how telenovelas, Spanish-language television soap operas directed at Puerto Rican and Latinx women, promote upper-class values, whiteness, and traditional gender roles. She emphasizes the marketing aspect, concluding that television "is used as a tool to sell us lies and try to make us believe those lies."[5] In "Makeup and Beauty," Limardo further analyzes the connection between capitalism and advertising in promoting standards of beauty based in racism, ageism, and classism. She writes, "We are made to feel ugly, inadequate, and inferior, when we don't live up to the false standards of 'beauty.'"[6] Limardo critiques the racism behind the endorsed ideals of whiteness, thinness, and youth, and its negative psychological, emotional, and physical effects on Third World women.

In addition to writing articles, women took part in the production and distribution of *Palante,* particularly in layout, design, translation, outreach, circulation, and sales. Among the women members who wrote or worked on the production of *Palante* were: Mecca Adai, Micky Agrait, Marta Arguello, Bernadette Baken, Iris Benítez, Lulu Carreras, Gloria Colón, Carmen Copeland, Aida Cruset, Jenny Figueroa, Gloria González, Mirta González, Beverly Kruset, Elsie López, Lulu Limardo, Iris López, Letty Lozano, Myrna Martínez, Nydia Mercado, Carmen Mercado, Raquel Merced, Connie Morales, Iris Morales, Denise Oliver, Luisa Ramírez, Isa Ríos, Olguie Robles, Gloria Rodríguez, Miriam Rodríguez, Heidy Ruiz, Becky Serrano, Lydia Silva, and Cleo Silvers.

Fig 7. *Palante* cover. *¡Liberación o Muerte!* June 5, 1970.

YOUNG LORDS PARTY FORMED

On June 5, 1970, *Palante* published startling news. The Young Lords' chapters in New York and Chicago had parted ways. Various reasons were cited. The New Yorkers complained the Chicago leaders failed to provide political guidance and did not produce the *Y.L.O.* newspaper on a regular basis. The Chicago leaders accused the New York group of trying to take over. Unable to resolve their differences, the organization split. The Chicagoans kept the name "Young Lords Organization," and the New Yorkers assumed the name the "Young Lords Party."[7]

The Central Committee of the Young Lords Party remained intact with Felipe Luciano as chairman, Pablo "Yoruba" Guzmán as minister of information, Juan González as minister of education and health, and Juan "Fi" Ortiz as minister of finance. David Pérez assumed the title "field marshal" in charge of developing new branches. To meet national responsibilities and challenges, the Young Lords Party added leadership levels that opened possibilities for women. By late June 1970, the Central Committee promoted Denise Oliver to minister of finance. Ortiz was moved to chief of staff.

Oliver was the first woman appointed to the Young Lords' Central Committee. An early YLO member, Oliver was one of thirteen persons arrested at the People's Church in 1969. She was a cofounder and influential member of the Women's Caucus. Serving as secretary of communications from April through mid-June 1970, she was promoted to information captain and then to the Central Committee. Other women were promoted to leadership positions: Lulu Carreras to lieutenant of finance; Gloria Cruz (later known as Gloria González) to lieutenant in the health ministry, and me to lieutenant in the education ministry.

CHANGES IN THE YOUNG LORDS PARTY'S CENTRAL COMMITTEE

Not long after the June split, the Young Lords Party reported a murder threat against the leadership. On July 31, 1970, the *Palante* newspaper announced:

> The Mafia has put out a $20,000 contract for the murder of chairman Felipe.[8]

The article speculated the contract was in retaliation for the Young Lords' campaign against heroin dealers in East Harlem. As a precaution, the Central Committee immediately assigned Luciano a twenty-four-hour security detail for his protection for an indefinite period.

A few weeks later, a hippie-looking white woman showed up at the East Harlem office and invited Luciano to a meeting that evening to discuss fundraising possibilities for the Young Lords Party. Luciano accepted the invitation, dismissed his security, and asked Pablo Guzmán to accompany him. Later that night, the Defense Ministry members received phone calls, alerting them that the men were missing but did not locate them. Luciano and Guzmán returned the next morning and later in that day met with the Central Committee members: Juan González, Denise Oliver, Juan "Fi" Ortiz, and David Pérez. Luciano reported that the woman who invited him to the meeting had drugged him and that he had sex with her. He gave no explanation why he dismissed his security. Knowing that the Young Lords Party was under constant FBI and police surveillance, the Central Committee members were stunned by Luciano's lack of security safeguards given the outstanding death threat. They demoted Luciano from the chairman position and responsibilities and called a general meeting to inform the Young Lords membership.

On September 5, 1970, the *New York Times* reported Luciano's removal from the Central Committee. They wrote that he was charged with "male chauvinism, unclear politics, political individualism, and lack of development" as reasons for the demotion.[9] Though the YLP's press release announced that Luciano would remain a member,[10] he resigned. A few Young Lords left with him. They argued that the demotion was too harsh a penalty, though all members were required to follow the same security protocols and rules of discipline. The *New York Times* also reported that Luciano's demotion "was seen by informants as moving the Young Lords Party into an open nationalist position in relation to the struggle for the independence of Puerto Rice."[11] This was an unexpected claim but perhaps a forecast of events later that year.

In the messy aftermath, the Central Committee retired the "chairman" title and replaced it with "minister of defense" as the Young Lords Party's highest rank. Juan González assumed this position and dropped the education and health minister title. The other Central Committee members—Guzmán, Oliver, Ortiz, and Pérez—kept their titles and roles. Gloria González (formerly Gloria Cruz) was promoted to the Central Committee as a second field marshal. González, cofounder of the Health Revolutionary Unity Movement (HRUM), had joined the YLO in January 1970. She and Juan González had celebrated their wedding that summer on July 26, 1970.[12] Luciano and Oliver had presided over the ceremony held on the first-year anniversary of the founding of the New York Young Lords.

From its inception, the Women's Caucus had advocated for promoting women to the Central Committee. Denise Oliver's appointment in June was a victory for the Women's Caucus and the Young Lords Party. In contrast, González had refused to take part in or support the Women's Caucus. Oliver and González represented different feminist perspectives, described in the following chapters. The struggles of the Women Caucus to increase representation in the YLP leadership showed that the mere presence of women did not translate into greater empowerment, as we had naïvely assumed it would. Not all women acted to end oppressive systems and norms. Some just sought gains for themselves. We learned that while increasing numbers was important, that alone might indicate greater progress than was true. Meaningful representation required action that brought about *collective* advances. The most successful demands of the Women's Caucus expanded benefits such as childcare, policies holding men accountable for sexual abuse, and campaigns for reproductive rights. They enriched the political education curriculum and the content of *Palante* and promoted nonsexist and nonracist language.

THE MEN'S CAUCUS: "CHANGE FROM THE TOP TO THE BOTTOM"

The Women's Caucus believed that if men knew the herstory of female oppression, they would join the fight to end the system of male supremacy. After all, men had significant relationships with women, including their mothers and other family members. In an experiment to change male chauvinist behavior, the Central Committee introduced a Men's Caucus to study the relationship between capitalism and women's oppression and raise consciousness about men's attitudes toward women. Defense Ministry cadre, David "Pelu" Jacobs, summarized, "It's tough for someone who has been dealing a certain way with women, whose father was dealing with women a certain way ... and now they have to change."[13] Richie Pérez, then Information Ministry captain, elaborated, "Male chauvinism is a problem every man has by virtue of being raised in this society. ... We recognize machismo is one of the biggest problems in making revolution."[14] He wrote:

> We not only have to change the political structure of this country; we've also got to change everything else. Revolution means change from the top to the bottom, and that includes the way we deal with each other as human beings.[15]

Pérez made a powerful connection between individual transformation and systemic change.

REVOLUTION WITHIN THE REVOLUTION: POSITION PAPER ON WOMEN

Shortly after the Young Lords' one-year anniversary, the Central Committee published the YLP Position Paper on Women as a full-page centerfold in *Palante*.[16] It presented the politics of the Women's Caucus and appeared in the issue dedicated to El Grito de Lares—the 1868 armed rebellion against Spanish colonial rule that launched Puerto Rico's national liberation struggle.[17] Expressing socialists, feminist, and nationalist ideas, the paper's analysis drew from diverse sources: caucus meetings and political education classes, exchanges with feminists of color, community organizing campaigns, feminist writings, and socialists texts.

The YLP Position Paper on Women opens with a description of "triple oppression," asserting that Third World women experience multiple and overlapping oppressions by gender, race/nationality, and class. Identifying capitalism as the major enemy, the paper declares the leading and integral role of Third World women in creating global social change. The position paper states:

> [T]he women's struggle is the revolution within the revolution. Puerto Rican women will be neither behind nor in front of their brothers but always alongside them in mutual respect and love.

Fig 8. *Palante* cover. YLP Position Paper on Women. 1970.

The Women's Caucus adopted the phrase, "the revolution within the revolution," from a speech delivered by Fidel Castro at the Congress of the Federation of Cuban Women in 1966. At the time, few Cuban women worked outside the home; 85 percent were homemakers, housebound and uneducated, living under a system reinforced by machismo and racism.[18] The Cuban government created programs to enable women to take part in the country's economic development. By the mid-1970s, the government issued the following pledge:

> The participation of women in society must be in absolute equality with men, and so long as any vestige of inequality remains, it is necessary to continue working to achieve this objective of the revolution.[19]

The Women's Caucus interpreted "the revolution within the revolution" to mean a present and ongoing struggle for gender justice, even under socialism. It rejected the nationalist argument that women's concerns should wait until *after* the revolution.

The YLP position paper examines a range of socialist feminist ideas. It discusses the institutions of marriage and family, reviewing their oppressive character and giving examples from across the world. Citing Engels's, *The Origin of the Family, Private Property, and the State,* the paper explains how the subordination of women began with the development of private property and rise of a privileged class of men. Capitalism reduced working-class women to household slaves and child-bearing machines to reproduce generations of laborers. The position paper argues that capitalism forces every person to sell their body, emphasizing that women of color are pushed into low-wage jobs where bosses and supervisors sexually harass, assault, and manhandle them.

The paper concludes:

> The Central Committee of the Young Lords Party has issued this position paper to explain and to educate about the role of sisters in the past and how we see sisters in the struggle now and in the future.

It was significant that Puerto Rican and African American socialist feminists persuaded the Young Lords Party, a revolutionary nationalist organization, to endorse a feminist perspective and analysis in September 1970.

THE WOMEN'S CAUCUS AND THE *NEW YORK TIMES*

The Women's Caucus attracted the interest of the *New York Times*. It was highly unusual for the corporate media to publish stories about the political community organizing work of young Puerto Rican, Latinx and African American women. On November 11, 1970, the newspaper published "Young Women Find a Place in High Command of Young Lords" in the "Food, Fashions, Family, and Furnishings" section, reserved for women's stories at the time.[20] The reporter interviewed four caucus members. Although it was not the article we would have written, it provided a rare public platform for young Puerto Rican, Latina, and African

American feminists. We were eighteen to twenty-three years old. We described our political activities, serving the community and organizing toward a socialist society. We emphasized our struggle for the rights of Puerto Ricans in the United States and the equality of women of color. "We are dealing with both male chauvinism and the passivity of the Puerto Rican woman," stated Olguie Robles, eighteen-year-old Education Ministry cadre from the Bronx branch. I added, "We do everything that the brothers do," emphasizing our equal responsibilities in organizing and leading campaigns. Martha Duarte, Defense Ministry cadre in the Lower East Side branch, made a distinction between revolution and reform. She explained, "We don't believe in electoral politics. It is the Band-Aid approach to a gaping wound." Central Committee member Denise Oliver explained, "Revolution is not just guns and fighting. Right now, we're in an educational phase." We concluded the interview by affirming that women in the Young Lords Party were committed to revolutionary change and social justice for all oppressed people.

7.
QUEER LIBERATION AND THE YOUNG LORDS PARTY

> We were all involved in different struggles,
> including myself and many other transgender people.
> But in these struggles, in the Civil Rights movement,
> in the war movement, in the women's movement,
> we were still outcasts. The only reason they tolerated
> the transgender community in some of these movements
> was because we were gung-ho; we were frontliners.
> We didn't take no shit from nobody.[1]
>
> —Sylvia Rivera, "Street Transvestite Action Revolutionaries"

The Third World Left in the United States was largely silent about queer liberation on June 28, 1969, when police raided the Stonewall Inn in Greenwich Village. Clashes between gay, lesbian, bisexual, and transgender activists and the police shook New York City streets for six days. The Stonewall Rebellion increased the visibility of the gay community in the United States and internationally. It was a turning point, and a new militancy emerged. Shortly after, activists who had taken part at Stonewall organized the Gay Liberation Front (GLF), on July 31, 1969.[2] Among the cofounders was Marsha P. Johnson, an African American self-identified drag queen. Sylvia Rivera, a Puerto Rican–Venezuelan transgender woman, joined them soon after.

The Young Lords Organization had formed a chapter in New York on July 26, 1969 and held its first rally in Tompkins Square Park in the East Village. Little more than a year later, the Young Lords opened a storefront office in the Lower East Side, a working-class neighborhood with a diverse population of African Americans, Latinx, Asians, European Jews, and Italians. The organization had strong ties to the area since many Young Lords were lifelong residents and activists in the community. Even before the storefront opened in September 1970, the YLO offered free breakfast, health screenings, and cultural activities in the neighborhood. The branch attracted new members, including several Puerto Rican lesbian and bisexual women who formed a Gay and Lesbian Caucus. Although documentation is scarce, this chapter describes the Young Lords' relationship with the LGBTQ movement and the activities of the YLP Gay and Lesbian Caucus, weaving fragments of recollections and history to prevent their total erasure.

THIRD WORLD QUEERS CHALLENGE RACISM AND HOMOPHOBIA

Several events amplified the prominence of the US queer liberation movement in 1970. Black, Latinx, and Asian gays and lesbians left the Gay Liberation Front shortly after it was formed and created Third World Gay Revolution (TWGR), citing racism as the main reason. An article in the newspaper *Come Out!* explained:

> Despite the many organizations emerging in the Gay Liberation movement, third world people haven't been able to relate to any of these. This is due to the inherent racism found in any white group with white leadership and white thinking.[3]

The TWGR appealed to the Third World Left for "immediate nondiscriminatory open admission/membership for radical homosexuals into all left-wing revolutionary groups." TWGR organizers wrote:

> Our straight sisters and brothers must recognize and support that we, third world gay women and men, are equal in every way within the revolutionary ranks. We each organize our people about different issues, but our struggles are the same against oppression, and we will defeat it together.[4]

The TWGR's politics paralleled those of the Black Panthers and the Young Lords. Members described their "triple oppression" by capitalism, racism, and sexism,[5] an analysis that aligned with socialist feminists of color. In the cited *Come Out!* article, two items linked to the Panthers and the Young Lords. One, an excerpt from the YLP's 13-Point Program, read: "We want the liberation of all Third World People." The other was a letter from Huey P. Newton, BPP chairman, titled "Letter to the Revolutionary Brothers and Sisters about the Women's Liberation and Gay Liberation Movements."[6] It was the text of a speech delivered by Newton on August 15, 1970 in New York City. It called for solidarity among the Black, women, and gay movements.

Newton's letter proposed building a coalition united against the racist, patriarchal capitalist state and acknowledged homosexuals as an oppressed group. Historian Ronald K. Porter credits James Baldwin and Jean Genet for encouraging Newton to reconsider his ideas about women's and gay liberation.[7] Newton states that his time in prison and talks with gay brothers "were largely responsible for a change in his thinking."[8] He was also influenced by the Stonewall Rebellion and the activism of gays, lesbians, and transgender people. Newton's letter proposed to "unite in a revolutionary fashion" with the women's and gay liberation organizations.[9] It opens with an appeal for respect for "all oppressed people," stating, "[H]omosexuals are not given freedom and liberty by anyone. … They might be the most oppressed people in the society,"[10] an impressive statement from a Black male nationalist leader in 1970. Newton calls on men to address their insecurities and fears about homosexuality. He reveals that he, too, had "hang-ups" about male homosexuality and that lesbians triggered fears of castration. He blames the "conditioning process" in US society that fosters this insecurity.[11] "Homosexuals are not enemies of the people," Newton concludes. He urges activists to drop the words "faggot" and "punk" from their vocabulary.[12] Historians Joshua Bloom and Waldo E. Martin remark on the letter's wide acclaim as the first major support of gay rights by a national Black organization.[13] Despite its male gaze, the letter brought attention to the queer movement and provoked discourse and debates in the New Left.

Newton's letter was published in the *Black Panther Party* newspaper issue that announced the Revolutionary People's Constitutional Convention. Planned for the 1970 Labor Day weekend in Philadelphia, the convention proposed to unify the US radical Left and draft a new version of the US Constitution.[14] About twelve to fifteen thousand activists from around the country attended,[15] including representatives of the Young Lords Party. Our delegation included Pablo "Yoruba" Guzmán, Denise Oliver, me, and other Young Lords cadre. On stage the first night, alongside Black Panther members, about twenty Young Lords from the New York and Philadelphia branches provided security, including one of our youngest members, Mark Ortiz.

Fig 9. Revolutionary People's Constitutional Convention. 1970.
Left to right: Iris Morales, Denise Oliver, and Pablo "Yoruba" Guzmán
(Courtesy: Michael Abramson)

White, Black, and people of color organizations, men and women, represented the gay liberation movement. In a show of unity, a gay contingent entered the plenary, chanting, "Gay power to Gay people! Black power to Black people!"[16]

Historian Jared E. Leighton describes the convention's aftermath in his dissertation "Freedom Indivisible: Gays and Lesbians in the African American Civil Rights Movement." Leighton writes that the increased interaction among the groups magnified homophobia, sexism, racism, and class differences:

> It seems white gay men expressed more unequivocal support of the BPP ..., while white lesbians had a more difficult relationship with the Panthers. LGBT people of color, like Third World Gay Liberation, also ... experienced hostility from the Panthers.[17]

A group of white lesbians from New York broke ties with the BPP, citing several grievances, including cancellation of their workshop, derogatory remarks, and acts of male intimidation.[18]

Third World Gay Revolution also registered grievances. After the convention, the TWGR released a revised 16-Point Platform and Program, adding three points to its superseded platform. One was likely a scathing critique of the Black Panther Party. It stated:

> We believe that so-called comrades who call themselves "revolutionaries" have failed to deal with their sexist attitudes. … Men still fight for the privileged position of man-on-the-top. Women quickly fall in line behind-their men.[19]

The other new points called for the abolition of capital punishment and the judicial system. TWGR's comprehensive program[20] demanded self-determination, women's liberation, equal employment, and decent and free housing. Several points denounced state-sanctioned violence and called for the abolition of the "fascist police force." The 16-Point Platform called for release of Third World gay and political prisoners from jails and mental institutions. It critiqued heteropatriarchy and denounced the "bourgeois nuclear family" as the unit of capitalism that generated the oppression of homosexuality. In sum, "radical queer activism called for a reordering of society, including conventional family structures and capitalist economic principles and concepts, such as private property."[21] The final point in the 16-Point Platform declared: "We want a new society—a revolutionary socialist society."

THE YOUNG LORDS PARTY AND THE LGBTQ MOVEMENT, 1970

During 1970, Pablo "Yoruba" Guzmán, YLP minister of information, met with activists from the Gay Liberation Front, the Third World Gay Revolution, and others, to become familiar with the goals and activities of the LGBTQ movement. The ongoing struggles with the Women's Caucus had created greater receptivity and openness to gender justice issues. When women formed the Gay and Lesbian Caucus (GLC) in the Lower East Side branch, they sought Guzmán as an adviser because of his relationship with the LGBTQ movement and his willingness to engage in discussions about sexual orientation and gender identity.

Gay, lesbian, and bisexual members joined the Young Lords Party for the same reasons as other Puerto Rican activists drawn by its militant platform and demands for the rights of Puerto Ricans. As was the case for Puerto Rican feminists, LGBTQ activists had few organizational options committed to this goal. As YLP cadre, LGBTQ members participated in and led community organizing campaigns, conducted door-to-door health testing, and represented the organization at public events. They took part in all required activities, including selling copies of *Palante* and attending general meetings, political education classes, and protests. Several LGBTQ members in the Defense Ministry provided security for Central Committee members and other leaders as assigned. Most LGBTQ members were not out, but neither were they closeted. They occupied an in-between space, a familiar one of coexistence. Micky Agrait, a tenant organizer in the Health and Field Ministry in the East Harlem branch, was the only out member in the New York organization.

Around the time the YLP opened the Lower East Side branch, Marsha P. Johnson and Sylvia Rivera founded Street Transvestite Action Revolutionaries (STAR). This organization was a house for LGBTQ youth, providing food and clothing, offering support to LGBTQ persons who were arrested, and sponsoring meetings and workshops for the gay and trans community. "STAR was for the street gay people, the street homeless people and anybody that needed help,"[22] Rivera explained.[23] Rivera was an ally of the Young Lords Party; she was not a cadre or member. Rivera's commitment to build STAR for homeless and other LGBTQ people was an all-consuming project. Street transvestites remained heavily marginalized within straight and gay communities alike, and Rivera understood that trans-identified people needed their own groups to address specific issues.[24]

In an interview years later, Rivera recalled marching with 10,000 people and the Young Lords to the United Nations on October 30, 1970. The marchers demanded an end to colonialism in Puerto Rico and an end to police violence in local communities. Rivera recalled that the

STAR organization joined the demonstration carrying the STAR banner, one of the first times it was displayed.[25] It marked a historic moment, highlighting solidarity among Third World gays, lesbians, and transgender people in an anti-imperialist alliance with Third World and other Left organizations.

THE YOUNG LORDS PARTY AND THE LGBTQ MOVEMENT, 1971

Early in 1971, the Young Lords Party published *Palante: The Young Lords*, a collaboration with photojournalist Michael Abramson and the first book detailing the organization's ideas and activities. The book consisting of historical accounts, essays by members, and beautiful black-and-white photographs became instantly popular. In the section titled "Revolution within the Revolution," Pablo "Yoruba" Guzmán writes about the gay liberation movement and sexual orientation and identity. Despite alliances with groups like the Third World Gay Revolution and Street Transvestite Action Revolutionaries, the Young Lords Party had made no public statement or published articles in the *Palante* newspaper about the oppression of queer people. Guzmán's essay expresses solidarity and support for the queer liberation movement and is significant as the only writing by a YLP leader on these themes. It synthesizes ideas from the LGBTQ movement, exchanges with members of the Young Lords' Gay and Lesbian Caucus, and Huey P. Newton's letter, discussed earlier.

Guzmán's opens the article briefly tracing the journey of the Young Lords Organization with gender justice issues. He acknowledges the group's early hostility to the women's liberation movement and credits the Women's Caucus with advancing the organization's understanding about the oppression and exploitation of "Third World women." The debates with the Women's Caucus were a precondition, the first step in moving the Young Lords Party to accept LGBTQ members. "The truth is that the idea of equality with gays was less acceptable than women's equality," Guzmán emphasizes. He adds, "It's a lot quicker for people to accept the fact that sisters should be in the front of the struggle than saying that we're gonna have gay people in the organization."[26] Guzmán critiques the irrational fear and hatred of gay people in society, and the role families in communities of color play, inculcating the belief that being gay is wrong, unnatural, or evil. He denounces ideas that cause gays to be rejected by family and friends, expelled from the community, and disdained by society.

Guzmán asserts, "Being gay is not a problem; the problem is that people do not understand what gay means." Society supports heterosexuality, assigning specific attributes to masculinity and femininity, such as men are strong and women weak. From birth, people are taught the roles, behaviors, and attributes considered appropriate to female or male identity. A person who departs from these is scorned as deviant. Seeking to provoke discussion about the meaning of gender, Guzmán introduces the following quote in bold black letters:

> We're saying that … it would be healthy for a man, if he wanted to cry, to go ahead and cry. It would also be healthy for a woman to pick up the gun.[27]

He explains:

> Gender is a false idea, because gender is merely traits that have been attributed through the years to a man or a woman.

Guzmán rejects the notion of inherent or inborn traits and concludes that the designations "man" and "woman" develop "half-people." He rejects the traditional male-female binary and concludes that becoming a "whole" human being requires a society without gender classifications. This conclusion was the seed of the idea that gender identity is a spectrum. Scholar activist Loretta Ross elaborates on the falsity of gender dualism:

> [T]he binary definitions of womanhood and manhood erect a false gender dualism that ignores the continuum of human experiences that include people who are lesbian, gay, bisexual, transgender, or gender nonconforming.[28]

At the time, we did not have the language of gender nonconforming or gender fluidity.

Guzmán's essay introduced a discussion about sexual orientation and gender identity that challenged "homophobic" ideas in the Young Lords Party. He emphasizes that shared struggles against oppression unify revolutionary people and advance revolutionary goals. Guzmán ends the article with an appeal to YLP members to build solidarity with the queer liberation movement. He declares the LGBTQ struggle a liberatory force for humanity.

Generally, the political discourse in the Young Lords Party did not include LGBTQ issues. However, after Guzmán's article, LGBTQ concerns surfaced in two internal documents, offering a hint about the struggle of queer members with the Central Committee. In July 1971 organization-wide retreat, the gay members in Puerto Rico criticized rising homophobia in the organization. By raising the problem in a written report, the members sought to engage the Central Committee in discussions about LGBTQ oppression. They also expected the leadership to open a dialogue among members. In response, the Central Committee wrote:

> The biggest problem of this period has been the oppression of homosexual cadres in the Party. No one should oppress anyone else for sexist reasons. ... We ask those people that have a good understanding to write up their feelings and to give it in to high levels of the Party so we can study ... and in the future take a complete position.

The Central Committee members acknowledged the oppression of homosexual cadres but offered no solutions, not even obvious ones like discussions among the membership, expanded political education study for the Young Lords, or collaborations with gay groups in Puerto Rico. Instead, they threw the issue back to the cadre "to write up their feelings." Then, they banned the "homosexual caucuses." The Puerto Rico caucus was only a few months old, but the Gay and Lesbian Caucus in New York had formed ten months earlier. The Central Committee members justified the shutdown of the caucuses:

> Homosexual caucuses, just like women's caucuses, are not the solution for resolving this contradiction. Inside the Party, all contradictions are resolved by waging ideological struggle.[29]

The response did not elaborate how "waging ideological struggle" would solve the problem. It was a missed opportunity. The shutdown of the "homosexual" caucuses in mid-1971 was a step backward, far removed from the solidarity with the queer liberation movement that Guzmán proposed.

Six months later, another LGBTQ reference appeared in the Central Committee's December 1971 communiqué. A Central Committee member reported that "a cadre at National [headquarters]" was preparing a paper on *bisexuality*[30] for the Young Lords Party Congress scheduled for July 1972. The mention indicated that queer members continued to raise LGBTQ issues to the Central Committee and were interested in bringing the discussions to the membership. However, these did not materialize. Part V details how the Central Committee's shift in political priorities in 1971 halted progress on these issues.

PART III. "WE DO NOT LIVE SINGLE-ISSUE LIVES"

There is no thing as a single-issue struggle
because we do not live single-issue lives.[1]

—Audre Lorde

During 1970, the Young Lords Party brought local, national, and international attention to the plight of Puerto Ricans in the United States and the colonial status of Puerto Rico. The organization gained popular support, provoked public discourse, and prompted policy and programmatic reforms. The Women's Caucus centered gender justice and moved feminist concerns onto the YLP's agenda. The next three chapters focus on the activism of women as leaders, strategists, spokespersons, organizers, and coordinators. Women took part in major YLP campaigns that year—protests at Lincoln Hospital for quality and affordable health care, struggles for prisoners' rights and criminal justice reform, and mobilizations to end the colonization of Puerto Rico.

Fig 10. Young Lords line up for a march. 1970.
(Courtesy of Michael Abramson.)

8.
POVERTY IS A HEALTH ISSUE:
PROTESTS AT LINCOLN HOSPITAL

> We want free publicly supported health care
> for treatment and prevention.[1]
>
> —10-Point Health Program, Young Lords Organization, 1970

From its beginnings in New York, the Young Lords Organization fought for quality health care for poor people. Programs such as free breakfasts and lead poisoning and tuberculosis screenings served low-income children and families. They gave prominence to the idea that poverty was a health issue. In April 1970, the Young Lords opened an office on Longwood Avenue and Kelly Street to serve the growing Puerto Rican population in the Bronx. Residents faced dehumanizing conditions—run-down housing, high unemployment, inadequate schools, police violence, and lack of social services.[2] People suffered high rates of infant mortality, tuberculosis, pneumonia, asthma, malnutrition, anemia, hepatitis, sickle cell anemia, and heroin addiction. The South Bronx was one of the poorest congressional districts in the United States. Public health care was urgent due to deteriorating community health services and the accelerating expansion of medical empires across New York City.[3] This chapter details the leadership role of women activists for health care as a human right in the Lincoln Hospital struggles in 1970.

Located at 141st Street and Bruckner Boulevard in the Bronx, Lincoln Hospital was the main public health institution available to the approximately four hundred thousand primarily poor and working-class Puerto Ricans and African Americans who lived in the area at the time.[4] Established in 1839, the nine-story, 346-bed facility had been a nursing home for Black people, many enslaved prior to the abolition of slavery in New York.[5] The dilapidated building featured lead-based paint peeling off walls, nonfunctioning elevators, and rodents and roaches running across the floors. Because of its substandard condition, the facility had been condemned thirty years earlier, but city officials kept it open for poor people of color.[6] Lincoln Hospital exemplified everything that was wrong with the US health-care system. Neighborhood people called it "the butcher shop."

Across New York City, public health services were in decline. Although low-income populations were growing, public hospitals and medical services had not expanded or improved. In 1969, the New York State legislature set up the Health and Hospitals Corporation (HHC) as a public benefit corporation. The HHC oversaw the budgets of eighteen municipal hospitals, including Lincoln. Under an affiliation agreement between the city and the Albert Einstein College of Medicine, Einstein's physicians delivered medical services, and hired and supervised the work of students, interns, and residents in exchange for a multi-million-dollar contract. Yet "Lincoln Hospital remained one of the country's worst urban hospitals."[7] A steady stream of poor patients arrived at the hospital, but the physician-administrators showed more interest in testing equipment, procedures, and drugs, and receiving city payments, than in healing people.

WORKERS' PROTESTS AT LINCOLN HOSPITAL

Lincoln Hospital was no stranger to worker and community protests. In 1969, a worker-management dispute erupted in the mental health clinic. More than one hundred workers, mostly African Americans and Puerto Ricans, evicted the director[8] and ran the clinic for almost thirty days with support from professional staff, members of the Black Panther Party and neighborhood service organizations, and local clergy.[9] At issue were demands for worker training, job upgrades, and worker participation in the administration,[10] as well as opposition to the hospital's increasing use of psychotropic drugs to treat patients.[11] The takeover ended with the arrest of twenty-two activists and sixty-seven workers fired, most of whom were later reinstated. According to the first-hand account of Dr. Fritzhugh Mullan in *White Coat, Clenched Fist: The Political Education of an American Physician,* the takeover's most important outcome was "the drawing together of people who were to be instrumental in subsequent events at Lincoln."[12]

Early in 1970, the HHC announced job freezes, service rollbacks, and deep budget cuts for Lincoln Hospital, to take effect at the start of the fiscal year on July 1, 1970.[13] Workers and activists quickly mobilized to fight the plan. At the forefront was the Health Revolutionary Unity Movement (HRUM), a network of hospital workers allied with the Young Lords and the Black Panthers. The HRUM's membership reflected the city's public hospital workforce, 80 percent Puerto Rican and African American, mostly women. Cleo Silvers, the HRUM's cochair and veteran of the 1969 mental health clinic takeover described earlier, organized the Think Lincoln Committee (TLC), uniting doctors and interns, other employees, and neighborhood residents.

Fig 11. Patient-Worker Complaint Table. Lincoln Hospital. 1970.
(Courtesy: Michael Abramson)

The TLC's approach was direct action. Among the committee's first actions was to set up a patient-worker complaint table in the hospital's emergency room entrance where most patients were likely to arrive and see the activists, addressing problems at Lincoln. It sent the message that the hospital was supposed to serve the people. The militants informed the recently hired Lincoln Hospital administrator, Dr. Antero Lacot, of their purpose. TLC volunteers staffed the complaint table eighteen hours a day and invited patients and workers to submit their grievances.[14] Complaints were handled directly and promptly with hospital staff.[15] TLC also circulated flyers and held rallies in the surrounding Bronx communities, spreading the word about the impending cuts. Through these interactions, the TLC created a list of demands. Carl Pastor, a leading organizer in the Young Lords' Health Ministry and HRUM member, commented that the hospital administrators were all too familiar with the grievances.[16]

The HRUM had its origins at the Gouverneur Health Center in the Lower East Side. In 1969, Gouverneur employed 350 workers, mostly area residents, when it announced plans to lay off ninety-six workers. Gloria González (then Gloria Cruz), Valerie Laguer, and other workers at the health center considered the union's response to the layoffs inadequate. Inspired by the Dodge Revolutionary Unity Movement (DRUM), an organization of African American auto workers in Detroit, the HRUM set out to build a revolutionary hospital workers' group as an alternative to the union.[17] Most HRUM members were African American and Puerto Rican women, although other people of color joined. At Gouverneur, the HRUM worked closely with I Wor Kuen, an organization formed in Chinatown in 1969.[18] IWK organized "serve the people" programs such as draft counseling and childcare and opened a free clinic dedicated to preventive health care and door-to-door tuberculosis screening. By exposing high TB rates, the group compelled New York City's health department to open a new X-ray unit in Chinatown.[19]

During this time, workers and health advocates at Metropolitan Hospital in East Harlem were also fighting budget cuts, and the Young Lords joined them in 1969. The group created a 10-Point Health Program, calling for community-worker control, free health care, door-to-door preventive health services, and employment of neighborhood residents.[20] Gloria González attended one of the meetings as the HRUM representative and began collaborating with the Young Lords on community health projects.

Patient services were worsening and so were conditions for overworked and underpaid staff.[21] Aiming to improve hospital and working conditions, the HRUM organized in New York's public hospitals and health clinics and developed active workers' collectives at Lincoln, Metropolitan, Morisania, Fordham, and Greenpoint hospitals, as well as at the Gouverneur and NENA Health Centers, among others. The HRUM workers adopted the 10-Point Health Program cited earlier and published the pamphlet titled "Ideology, History, Patients' and Workers' Rights." It described the scope of the struggle:

> We are faced with fighting racism, the corrupt health system, the hospital administration, and the union leadership. At the same time, we must struggle with male chauvinism and female passivity in our own ranks.[22]

To communicate and organize with fellow workers and community members, the HRUM also produced a newspaper, *For the People's Health.* The first issue in February 1970 printed ten thousand copies.

Kathy Larkin, an HRUM organizer and spokesperson, explained the organizing approach and outreach to workers. "We lay out what the problems are and challenge them to see the issues."[23] Due to the high concentration of women workers, organizers emphasized the intersectionality of women's exploitation by class, race, and gender. The HRUM pamphlet described the situation for "Third World women."

> Our wages are lower than those of white women workers. Working in hospitals as clerks, aides etc. we take insults from racist supervisors (who are usually men) and male workers who, because of their machismo, see us as objects to be pinched, propositioned, and treated as mentally inferior.[24]

Third World women were relegated to lower-status, lower-paid roles, the "dead-end jobs," and faced harsh realities of gender bias and harassment.

Demands of Black and Puerto Rican women hospital workers included a decent living wage and "working conditions fit for human beings."[25] Because they spent up to 50 percent of their wages for childcare expenses, women workers demanded that the hospital finance community-worker-controlled free day-care centers in or near the hospital to meet their needs.[26]

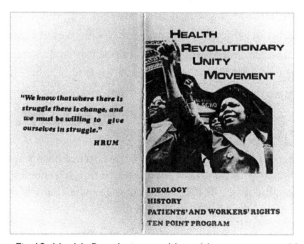

Fig 12. Health Revolutionary Unity Movement pamphlet. 1971.

As workers, mothers, women, and patients, they organized and collectively challenged health institutions.

The HRUM members prioritized "worker-patient-community unity and control."[27] They explained:

> We believe that the duty of every health worker is to fight for decent medical care and the human rights of every patient receiving that care. Patients and workers should be able to aid and communicate with each other without fear of reprisal.[28]

> We say, all workers must become patient advocates, that is, defend the rights of the patients against bad patient care and disrespect on the part of doctors and hospital administrators.[29]

The belief in worker-patient-community unity emphasized that workers in public hospitals were also its patients and community members. The HRUM's ongoing day-to-day organizing at Lincoln Hospital and the workers' militancy created the conditions and provided the support for the hospital takeovers and protests that took place in 1970.

THE LINCOLN HOSPITAL TAKEOVER

By July 14, 1970, Lincoln Hospital administrators had not responded to the workers' demands concerning budget cutbacks. The Young Lords' Central Committee together with the HRUM and Think Lincoln Committee leaders devised a plan to take over the hospital to dramatize the situation. They informed the Young Lords cadre of the planned action at a special members' meeting, taking security precautions so information was not leaked to the police or press. Members stayed together at the location until 4:00 a.m. when about fifty Young Lords loaded into the back of a truck headed to Lincoln Hospital. The driver, Willie Santiago, was a District 65 union member and longtime supporter of the Young Lords. When he arrived at the hospital, members rushed out of the truck. Those responsible for security went first. Others followed to hang banners from windows declaring, "Welcome to the People's Hospital, Bienvenidos al Hospital del Pueblo." A few members hoisted a Puerto Rican flag on the roof. All others went to designated spaces to conduct health screenings, hold political education classes, and set up day care for children. Members of the HRUM, Black Panther Party, TLC, and hospital staff joined the Young Lords. Approximately two dozen physicians from the Lincoln Pediatric Collective, who had arrived two weeks earlier for internships and residencies, found themselves in the middle of this extraordinary event. They, too, joined,[30] and patient services continued uninterrupted.

In the hospital auditorium, reporters, activists, workers, patients, and doctors gathered for a press conference. Two huge banners at the back of the stage declared: "Lincoln Hospital Must Serve the People, El hospital tiene que servirle al pueblo." A table at the center of the stage was crowded with reporters' microphones. The HRUM cochairs, Cleo Silvers and Gloria González, and the YLP minister of information, Pablo "Yoruba" Guzmán, outlined seven demands. The first, "no cutbacks in services or jobs," was followed by the demand for a new Lincoln Hospital. Other points called for a minimum wage, a childcare center for patients and workers, door-to-door preventative health care programs, and a twenty-four-hour complaint table staffed by patients and workers. The final demand called for "total self-determination" and an oversight board of community residents and workers.[31]

Throughout the day, representatives of TLC, the HRUM, and the Young Lords met with the hospital's negotiators, including Dr. Antero Lacot, the hospital administrator; Sid Davidoff, Mayor John Lindsay's representative; and HHC personnel.[32] At about 5 p.m., Dr. Lacot called an emergency medical staff meeting with approximately one hundred persons.[33] Lacot reported the negotiations had ended and that he had authorized the police to retake the hospital. At that moment, nearly half the physicians left the room and went to join the activists.[34]

As police surrounded the building, someone suggested that the Young Lords exit wearing the white smocks worn by hospital personnel. The Young Lords left the building accompanied by workers and doctors. Five blocks from the hospital, the police recognized Pablo "Yoruba" Guzmán accompanied by Luis Pérez, also a Young Lord. The police chased them, shot at them, caught them, and charged them with possession of karate sticks. The judge threw out the case, describing it as totally absurd.[35]

The Young Lords Party declared a political victory. City and health officials agreed to two demands—no cutbacks in services and the establishment of preventative health screenings.[36] The takeover demonstrated the power of worker-patient-community organizing. Although it lasted only twelve hours, it brought national and international attention to the horrendous public health services and working conditions for Puerto Rican and African Americans in New York's public hospitals, and the city's indifference.

DEMANDS FOR LEGAL AND SAFE ABORTIONS

Less than a week after the takeover, another protest exploded at Lincoln Hospital. At the center was the issue of abortion. During the 1960s, abortion was illegal in all fifty states. According to a 1967 report, approximately eight hundred thousand abortions (mostly illegal) were performed annually.[37] The criminalization of abortion disproportionately affected low-income women of color. Just as is true today, wealthy women could obtain a safe abortion by paying a private doctor an exorbitant fee or by traveling to a country where it was legal. Restrictive laws forced poor and working women to resort to unsafe, clandestine, and often fatal procedures. Thousands died through botched or self-induced "clothes hanger" abortions.

In July 1970, New York State legalized abortion and suddenly had the most liberal abortion law in the country. New York allowed abortions to be performed within twenty-four weeks of pregnancy and at any time if the woman's life was at risk.[38] On July 20, Carmen Rodríguez, a thirty-one-year-old mother of two and a South Bronx resident, entered Lincoln Hospital for an abortion under the new law. Rodríguez was already a Lincoln Hospital patient being treated for rheumatic heart disease.[39] Although doctors recorded her condition in her medical record, the doctor performing the abortion did not bother to read it. Saline got into her bloodstream, causing fluid accumulation in her lungs, and Rodríguez went into a coma from which she never recovered. She died from the botched abortion, the first death under the new law.[40]

Protestors mobilized. "Murder!" they shouted. The Young Lords, the HRUM, the Black Panther Party, and other advocates demanded justice. Seeking to quiet the outrage, Dr. Lacot consented to a public meeting. He reported that Rodríguez's death, though unfortunate, was "medically acceptable."[41] His statement further enflamed the community, and the protesters demanded the firing of Dr. Joseph J. Smith, head of the Obstetrics and Gynecology Department.[42] Smith left grudgingly, accusing the Young Lords of creating a hostile work environment. Twenty-seven doctors and residents in the OB-GYN unit, in support of Smith, walked out, shutting down the department.[43] Ten days later, they returned on condition that the activists be barred. The administrators accommodated them and obtained a restraining order, stipulating that any member of the Young Lords Party, the Health Revolutionary Unity Movement, or the Think Lincoln Committee would be arrested if "interfering with patient care and medical services."[44]

The right to abortion was fiercely debated even in the social justice movement. Generally, nationalist organizations opposed abortion. At its inception, the Black Panther Party considered abortion genocide.[45] Panther women successfully shifted the organization's rhetoric away from abortion as genocide to a discourse about the importance of health care and safe, legal abortions.[46] Puerto Rican nationalist and pro-independence organizations viewed abortion as foreign and as a form of colonial oppression.[47] The strict nationalist viewpoint called on Puerto Rican women to have children to save the nation from genocide.

The Young Lords Party distinguished itself by supporting a woman's right to make autonomous choices about her reproduction. The Women's Caucus believed that the decision to carry a pregnancy to term belonged to the woman and no one else—not the government, church, parents, husband, or boyfriend.[48] We believed in a woman's right to control her body without coercion or interference. Furthermore, caucus members viewed abortion as necessary in a society that expected women to bear the financial, social, emotional, and spiritual responsibilities of raising children but kept women in low-wage jobs or unemployed and provided no childcare or housework support.

Although New York's abortion law expanded women's rights, lawmakers failed to consider the life-threatening risks women of color faced at public institutions. Without access to affordable quality health care, the right to abortion was meaningless, as the case of Carmen Rodríguez showed. The Women's Caucus linked the right to abortion to demands for safe and quality health care for poor and working-class women of color. We spearheaded demands for reproductive rights, pulling from the ideologies of both feminists of color and nationalists.[49] Feminist politics demanded a woman's right to control her reproduction. Nationalist politics emphasized self-determination. Together these ideas forged a liberatory perspective centered on the needs of women of color and poor communities.

The Women's Caucus envisioned abortions under community control of a board composed of caring neighborhood residents, hospital workers, and medical professionals to oversee policies and procedures. In *Palante,* Gloria Colón from the YLP's Education Ministry outlined the criteria for community-controlled abortions:

> We believe that abortions should be legal if they are community-controlled, if they are safe, if our people are educated about the risks, and if doctors do not sterilize our sisters while performing abortions.[50]

Colón's warning about sterilization was justified. Chapter 5 documents how women of color in the United States and Puerto Rico were routinely targeted for involuntary and coerced sterilization procedures.

In the article "Abortions under Community Control," historian Jennifer Nelson interviews Olguie Robles, a former Young Lord and member of the Women's Caucus. Robles confirms the Young Lords' political views about abortion. Members believed that poor women needed options if they could not afford to adequately take care of a child. Robles also points out that most women would not choose abortion if they had the resources to raise children.[51] The idea of poverty as a limitation on reproductive choice was reflected in the YLP Position Paper on Women. It concludes, "Change the system so that women can freely be allowed to have as many children as they want."[52] The Women's Caucus in the Young Lords believed that a socialist society would provide the material basis to meet the childcare, health, and financial needs of women and children.

THE LINCOLN DETOX PROGRAM

A few months after Carmen Rodríguez's death, another community protest erupted at Lincoln when activists approached the hospital appealing for drug addiction treatment services. A year earlier, in a message to Congress, President Nixon, had declared a "War on Drugs," labeling drug abuse as public enemy number one. Nixon reported, "New York City alone has records of some 40,000 heroin addicts, and the number rises between 7,000 and 9,000 a year."[53] But instead of providing treatment services, state and federal governments rolled out punitive policies and measures, such as mandatory sentencing and no-knock warrants that disproportionately and adversely affected African Americans and Puerto Ricans.

Grassroots activists in New York organized to end the drug invasion and rising heroin deaths. Youths under sixteen years old died of overdoses at the rate of one a week.[54] Young people of color suffered the impact of heroin addiction, but no hospital programs existed for them. Frustrated by the city's inaction, Black women formed Mothers Against Drugs (MAD) to fight the heroin epidemic. At the time, I was a teacher at the Academy for Black and Latin Education (ABLE), an independent storefront school inspired by the philosophy of Black Power and self-determination.[55] Many of our students were strung out on heroin. The director, Dave Walker, approached the local hospital, seeking treatment services but was turned away. In December 1969, a twelve-year-old boy named Walter Van Der Meer, died from an overdose in the bathroom of a Harlem tenement on West 117th Street. He was the youngest child on record to die from a heroin overdose in the city. Outrage spread throughout the community. Angered by the lack of response from the city, the police, and health institutions, ABLE and MAD joined forces in early January 1970 and occupied the office of Community Psychiatry at St. Luke's Hospital, demanding treatment services. The sit-in lasted four days and ended with a joint statement by hospital administrators and community activists, announcing the opening of a twenty-eight-bed detoxification center for adolescents, the first such hospital treatment available for youth in the city.[56]

In the South Bronx, the heroin epidemic affected one in four people.[57] Neighborhood residents formed the South Bronx Drug Coalition (SBDC) together with the Young Lords, the Black Panthers, the HRUM, and ex-addicts. On November 10, 1970, they occupied the sixth floor of Lincoln Hospital's Nurses' Residence, the third major protest at the hospital that year. Negotiations resulted in the Lincoln Hospital Detox Program, which treated thousands of people over an eight-year period. The Detox Program become internationally known for its innovative treatment, combining acupuncture and political education.

PEDIATRICS COLLECTIVE DEMANDS COMMUNITY-WORKER CONTROL

While the SBDC takeover was in progress, another crisis brewed in Lincoln's Pediatrics Department, exposing sharp differences between the department head, Dr. Arnold Einhorn, and about thirty resident doctors and interns, members of the Pediatrics Collective.[58] The group of physicians—white and predominantly Jewish—were committed to creating community-based programs. Early in November, administrators from the Albert Einstein College of Medicine informed the doctors' collective of plans to hire Dr. Helen Rodríguez Trías, a pediatrician and women's rights advocate from Puerto Rico, as the department's assistant director. They expected a short transition period after which Dr. Rodríguez Trías would become the department head. However, Dr. Einhorn refused, and the Pediatrics Collective demanded his resignation, citing his "inability to administer the department and his resistance to community-worker control."[59] Several Jewish organizations denounced Einhorn's removal, claiming discrimination because he was Jewish. However, a city civil rights investigation concluded that the action was due to "fundamental and irreconcilable disagreement over philosophy and goals," not ethnic discrimination.[60]

The Lincoln Hospital protests in 1970 reflected a broader societal discourse about medical care in the United States. The HRUM, Young Lords, Black Panthers, and doctors collaborated on a Patients' Bill of Rights. It laid out basic requirements for the doctor-patient relationship, such as treating patients with respect; explaining the diagnosis, treatment, and medication; and providing access to medical records. The original version advocated for day-care centers in all hospital facilities and for preventative health programs.[61] Cleo Silvers noted that a Patients' Bill of Rights hangs on every hospital wall today, even if watered down from the original version.

At the heart of the Lincoln Hospital struggles was the belief that health care was a human right. African American and Puerto Rican women played a vital role, demanding that people most affected by hospital policies and practices—the patients, workers, and community residents—should have a say in running the institution and setting its priorities. Lincoln Hospital represented "one of the first thin threads of a sustained struggle to achieve worker-community control within a health institution."[62] The protests achieved some internal reforms in operations, but the inequalities and power imbalances were overwhelming. Long-standing structural problems embedded in the expanding "medical industrial complex"[63] called for a total and complete overhaul, which despite progress in some areas remains even more urgent today.

9.

UPRISINGS AGAINST THE NEW YORK CITY CRIMINAL JUSTICE SYSTEM

And, if I know anything at all,
It's that a wall is just a wall
And nothing more at all.
It can be broken down.[1]

—Assata Shakur, "Affirmation," 1987

The call by politicians for "law and order" in the 1960s triggered a get-tough-on-crime politics that exploded into a zeal for incarceration[2] and moved the United States into position to become the world's leading jailer.[3] In 1970, New York City jails overflowed with poor and working-class African Americans and Puerto Ricans, who made up 85 percent of the city's jail population.[4] Most were charged but not convicted of a crime. They were in jail mainly because they could not afford to pay exorbitant bails.[5] The oppression and violence of the criminal justice system was a central concern for low-income communities. Overcrowding in the jails was a huge problem. The Manhattan Detention Center, known as "the Tombs," for example, a facility designed for a maximum of 932 men, was 213 percent over capacity.[6] Even a report from the Board of Corrections acknowledged that the jails kept fellow human beings caged like animals,[7] evidencing the city's disdain for African Americans and Puerto Ricans. Walls separating social movements from prisoners "grew increasingly permeable."[8]

Most New Yorkers thought little about what went on in the city's jails.[9] Five facilities—the Manhattan Detention Center, the Queens Detention Center branches in Long Island City and Kew Gardens, the Brooklyn House of Detention, and Rikers Island—lodged male prisoners. The Women's House of Detention held women charged with a crime. This chapter discusses remarkable New York City jail and community protests in 1970, strategies in the emergent prisoners' rights movement, and the activism of feminists of color.

THE WOMEN'S HOUSE OF D

From 1932 to 1974, the Women's House of Detention, known as "the House of D," was a fixture of state violence and repression. Black feminist Audre Lorde described it as "a defiant pocket of female resistance, ever-present as a reminder of the possibility, as well as the punishment."[10] The eleven-story building was then located in the West Village at the intersection of Greenwich Avenue, West Tenth Street, and Sixth Avenue. It housed poor and working-class women, most women of color in jail for crimes of survival, poverty, and desperation. They were young and old, working poor, mothers, lesbians, sex workers, and activists.

Throughout its history, the House of D imprisoned many high-profile and well-known political activists. Among them, in 1950, Rosa Collazo and Carmen Torresola were held for almost two months on $50,000 bail each.[11] They were accused of collaborating with their spouses, Oscar Collazo and Griselio Torresola, the Puerto Rican Nationalists who attempted to assassinate President Truman. According to historian Olga Jiménez de Wagenheim, the women were released in December 1950 because the prosecution failed to make a case.[12] In 1954, Collazo and Torresola were arrested again after four Nationalist Party members shot into the US House of Representatives. The two women were held at the Women's House of D and subsequently convicted of violations of the Smith Act, a statute criminalizing a range of activities considered subversive or advocating the overthrow of the US government.[13] Collazo was sentenced to six and Torresola to four years. They were shipped to Alderson federal prison in West Virginia, along with Lolita Lebrón who had participated in the attack on Congress.[14]

In 1951, Claudia Jones, a Black socialist feminist; Elizabeth Gurley Flynn, a labor organizer and founding member of the American Civil Liberties Union; and others were held at the House of D, awaiting transfer to a federal prison. Jones and Flynn were leaders of the US Communist Party's Women's Commission. They were charged with "un-American activities" under the Smith Act. Less than twenty years later, Black Panther leaders Afeni Shakur and Joan Bird were incarcerated at the House of D, held on bail of $100,000 each. Arrested on April 2, 1969 in the case known as "the Panther 21," they faced 156 counts of "conspiracy" to blow up subway and police stations, department stores, railroads, and the New York Botanical Gardens. Eventually, they were acquitted of all charges. During their detention, thousands of protestors demanded their release, holding demonstrations in front of the jail. The protests brought visibility to the political prisoners and linked activists on the outside with those behind jailhouse walls.

Shakur and Bird were already incarcerated in the House of D on June 28, 1969, when "a mix of queens, gay men, and lesbians, most of them people of color, and many of them 'street kids,'" fought back the police raid at the Stonewall Inn.[15] A group of detainees expressed solidarity by setting fire and throwing their few possessions out the windows. They chanted, "Gay power! Gay power!," according to an oral history with Arcus Flynn, an early member of Daughters of Bilitis, one of the first lesbian organizations in the United States.[16] Activists from the Gay Liberation Front helped organize twenty-four-hour-a-day protests outside the jail between Christmas and New Year's, 1969, calling for "peace, freedom, and the rights of all peoples."[17]

On International Women's Day, March 7, 1970, the Women's Caucus of the organization Youth against War and Fascism (YAWF) rallied at Union Square Park on Fourteenth Street. YAWF member Deirdre Griswold explained that the demonstration was reclaiming the day's feminist socialist origins[18] by raising "the struggle of the most oppressed women."[19] Among the rally speakers was Flo Kennedy, a well-known African American feminist activist, and Iris Benítez, information lieutenant in the Young Lords Organization. Benítez spoke about the police murder of Antonia Martínez a few days earlier. Martínez, a university student, was killed in Puerto Rico during protests against the US Reserve Officers' Training Corps (ROTC). Benítez declared, "The role of police and prisons are the same in the colony of Puerto Rico as in the United States—to oppress poor and working people." When the rally ended, members of the Young Lords' Women's Caucus and Benítez joined demonstrators heading downtown. Griswold elaborated, "Marching from the rally to the House of Detention drew attention to the plight of poor and working-class women, in particular, and to women political prisoners."[20] Protesters carried huge banners, calling for free and legal abortions, equal pay for equal work, an end to job discrimination, and freedom for women political prisoners.

At the front of the Women's House of D, more than one thousand protesters chanted, "Free our sisters! Free ourselves!"[21] From behind the barred windows, women with raised fists shouted words of solidarity to the protesters below. For months afterward, demonstrators gathered outside the jail. The Women's House of D became an important site and symbol of political protest. In June, for the first anniversary of the Stonewall Rebellion, gay, lesbian, trans, and other people marched past the jail, chanting, "Free our sisters! Free ourselves!"[22] In July, the Gay Liberation Front marched against police harassment and ended the protest at the House of D.[23] African American and Puerto Rican detainees, feminists, gays, lesbians, trans people, revolutionary nationalists, and prisoners united in protest against the criminal justice system.

1970 TAKEOVER OF CITY JAILS

On the morning of August 10, 1970, the Tombs erupted in protest.[24] Inhumane living conditions and severe overcrowding at the men's prisons produced a human rights crisis. Although Mayor John Lindsay had in his possession a scathing report about jail conditions, he had done little to remedy the situation.[25] Prisoners detailed a long list of grievances: vicious daily beatings by guards, moldy and rotten food, cells overrun with vermin, substandard medical care, inadequate legal representation, delayed trials, excessive bail, and restricted access to legal books.[26] They complained that guards made sexual slurs and indecent propositions to their mothers, wives, sisters, and girlfriends who arrived at the jail to visit. To add insult to injury, the jail lacked adequate bathing facilities, and showers were rare.[27]

The immediate trigger of the August protest was the beating of a Black detainee by three white guards.[28] It provoked 225 men to take five guards as hostages.[29] Most detainees rejected the explanation that the beating was the result of individual "bad apples." They insisted racial violence was integral to the prison system.[30] In this conclusion, they found common ground with the politics of the Black Panthers and the Young Lords. Within the Tombs, the detainees organized the Inmates Liberation Front (ILF) and played a leading role in the uprising. Victor Martínez, its cofounder, subsequently joined the Young Lords Party and affiliated the ILF as a "people's organization."

Fig 13. Young Lord at rally in support of prison rebellions. 1970.
(Courtesy: Michael Abramson)

Men imprisoned at other city jails soon followed in protest, as historian Heather Ann Thompson describes:

> More than 900 men at the Queens House of Detention in Kew Gardens, along with hundreds more at the dreaded Brooklyn House of Detention for Men and a group of young people on Rikers Island had also launched their own protests.[31]

On October 1, 1970, the Queens House of Detention in Long Island City erupted. Inmates cited grievances like those of prisoners in the Tombs. Additional demands included more Spanish-speaking staff, access to the *Palante* and *Black Panther* newspapers, and the release of Afeni Shakur, still being held in the Women's House of D. Supporters of the uprising gathered outside the jail in solidarity.

Nine Black Panther Party members were awaiting trial at the Queens House in Long Island City in connection with the Panther 21 case.[32] They played a leading role. Insisting that the criminal justice system imposed excessively high bail on many prisoners, the detainees demanded that a judge come to the jail to hear bail reduction cases.[33] In an extraordinary action, three state supreme court justices arrived for this purpose. Acknowledging exorbitant bails, they released thirteen detainees that day.[34] Among those released was Gilbert Jiménez who subsequently joined the YLP and organized with the Inmates Liberation Front.[35]

After the bail hearing victory, the police commissioner and Mayor Lindsay ordered the police to retake the jails by force if necessary. By October 6, they had violently squashed the uprisings. With the prisoners back in confinement, the guards retaliated brutally against them for taking part in the protests.[36] The horrific jail conditions were not addressed.

YOUNG LORDS IN THE TOMBS AND COMMUNITY PROTESTS

Shortly after the jail uprisings, undercover narcotics agents arrested two Young Lords, Julio Roldán and Bobby Lemus, on October 14, accusing the two men of setting a fire in the East Harlem building where they lived. The police agents charged them with first-degree arson. Their actions were part of the pattern of police harassment against the Young Lords Party, described in chapter 14. While in custody, the two Young Lords were subjected to police abuse, denied access to their attorney, and processed with condescension and disdain. The judge imposed $1,500 bail on each and dispatched them to the Tombs. Before the Young Lords Party could raise and post bail, the guards reported that Roldán was found hanged in his cell. They labeled it a "suicide." Their claim was among several suspicious jail "suicides" the police announced that year, and the community did not believe it. "Murder!" declared the Young Lords. As expected, the New York Board of Corrections alleged that Roldán had died by his own hand,[37] although the police were responsible for Roldán while in their custody, and Roldán's family pathologist found evidence of a beating,[38]

Enraged by Roldán's death, more than two thousand people marched through the streets of East Harlem in a funeral procession and protest. Representatives from Third World Left organizations served as pallbearers, including Black Panthers, the Puerto Rican Student Union, the Movimiento Pro Independencia, I Wor Kuen,[39] Justicia Latina, and Los Siete de la Raza.[40] They carried Roldán's casket to the People's Church on 111th Street and Lexington Avenue. Young Lords armed with carbines and automatic weapons entered the church with two hundred supporters[41] and opened the church to the public. People arrived to pay their respects to Julio Roldán. The protestors made two demands to the city: to fund a defense center at the People's Church and to allow local clergy to investigate the prisons. The new pastor at the People's Church provided space for the Inmates Liberation Front, and members offered free legal programs to the community. However, the city refused to fund a defense center and lacked the political will to reform the prison system.

Fig 14. Justicia Latina activists at Julio Roldán's funeral. 1970.
(Courtesy: Michael Abramson)

Fully expecting the police to storm the church, the Central Committee appointed a special squad made up of Young Lords to train and remain in the building to defend against the assault. Several men assigned to the squad, quit. They called it a suicide mission and resigned from the Young Lords Party. The three women in the squad stayed to the end. The truth is, we were inadequately equipped, trained, and prepared. As police surrounded the church, Mayor Lindsay's negotiators agreed to amnesty for the protesters on condition that the police would find no weapons when they entered.[42] With the help of neighborhood residents, the Defense Ministry removed the guns. The second People's Church takeover ended in early December 1970. A bloodbath was averted.

THE WOMEN'S BAIL FUND

Mecca Adai, a leading Information Ministry cadre in the Young Lords Party, wrote an urgent appeal in the *Palante* newspaper, bringing attention to the deplorable conditions that women confronted in the House of D. Adai explains:

> For the past few months, newspapers and magazines all over the country have been writing articles about the prisons. … [W]e can see that in every article the author deals only with what's been happening inside the concentration camps for men. No attention has been paid to our sisters who are being held inside of the Women's House of Detention. …
>
> [W]e write articles in *Palante* to educate our people about our sisters and to explain that we must fight for the liberation of all our people—not just for half of our population.[43]

Like the men held in New York City jails, most women detainees were African American and Puerto Rican, poor and working class. They were in detention because they could not afford the $100 to $1,000 bail, which amounted to no bail at all.[44]

Adai chronicles the gendered and racist punishment women encountered from the moment of arrest. Women lacked proper legal representation, and the state routinely sent their children into the foster care system. Inside the jail, the women confronted sexual and racial violence, and other exploitation and degradation. Officials frequently deprived detainees of basic toiletries, such as toothpaste and soap. To obtain the items, women often had to sell their bodies. Assigned to work in the jail's kitchen and laundry, their labor was exploited for two to ten cents an hour. The detainees also accused administrators of racially dividing the cells and promoting racial violence.[45] Adai denounced the lack of educational programs and support services for the women.

During 1970, the House of D imprisoned Black Panther Party leaders Afeni Shakur and Joan Bird, for ten and fifteen months, respectively. Angela Davis was held for nine weeks from October to December 1970, awaiting transfer to California in connection with kidnapping and murder charges there. Their cases generated international publicity and helped bring media attention to the circumstances of political prisoners, as well as poor and working-class women prisoners.

Shakur described her experience at the Women's House of D in an article published in *Palante*.[46] She details the systemic cruelty and scorn that poor women of color faced in the judicial system. Class-based, racist, and sexist assumptions drove the process at each step from arrest to booking, appearance before a judge, setting of bail, and legal aid attorney assignment.[47] Shakur urged activists to organize "brigades of women" from the outside to build relationships directly with detainees and advocate for their rights. She proposed an "inside/outside" strategy to broaden the prisoners' rights movement and compel the criminal justice system to reform jail conditions.[48] Angela Davis also wrote about her experience at the House of D, emphasizing that "women's prisons have held on to oppressive patriarchal practices" and forms of state-sanctioned violence against women that receive little attention.[49] Specifically, she denounced the mandatory strip search—the internal examination of a woman's body cavities—explaining that a woman's refusal to submit landed her in solitary confinement.[50]

On December 20, 1970, another protest took place in front of the Women's House of D. Hundreds of African American, Puerto Rican, Asian, and white women rallied. Joan Bird, recently released from the jail, led the demonstrators in songs and chants: "Hey Hey, Ho, Ho, House of D has gotta go," and "The rich set the bail, the poor go to jail!" Members from the Young Lords' Women's Caucus led chants in Spanish.[51]

From behind the prison windows, women waved and shouted down to the crowd. Angela Davis stood and chanted with them.

Rally speakers included women from the BPP, the YAWF, the Young Lords, I Wor Kuen, and the Puerto Rican Student Union.[52] They detailed the atrocious jail conditions and advocated for the rights of the women behind bars. Several speakers announced the formation of a bail fund to aid the release of "non-movement women," specifically those with bail amounts less than $500.[53] "Third World and White women" from the Black Panther Party, the Young Lords Party, the Anti-Imperialist Women's Collective, and Youth against War and Fascism[54] had joined forces to raise awareness about jail conditions and provide support to the detainees. The crowd cheered when a representative announced, "This morning the bail fund secured the release of two detainees."[55] For six months, the organizers had conducted fundraising, published information about injustices at the House of D, contacted women inside the prison, and created legal information aids in English and Spanish. The women in the Young Lords took part, rallying, speaking, helping to raise funds, and bringing to the public's attention the injustices faced by Black, Puerto Rican, and other women of color in prison. Women activists advanced the struggle for justice and unity from inside and outside prison walls. As the author Tony Platt states, "One important legacy was the successful effort to make the prison cell into an outpost of a broader agenda for social and economic equality."[56]

According to historian and author of *Our Trials* Emily L. Thuma, as of 2019, the rate of women's imprisonment was eight times greater than in the 1970s. Black, Latinx, and Indigenous communities continue to be disproportionately represented and affected by mass incarceration.[57] Today, women are "the fastest growing segment of the incarcerated population"; more than two-thirds are women of color.[58] Although the United States incarcerates more women than any other nation, women in prison remain invisible,[59] echoing Adai's report more than fifty years ago. The New York jail uprisings and community protests in 1970 involved inside/outside organizing strategies to draw attention to the deep-rooted racial and economic inequality fueling the prison industrial complex that we are still dealing with today.

10.
FREE PUERTO RICO NOW!
ORGANIZING WITH STUDENTS

> Unless we act now, we may be the last
> Puerto Ricans on this planet.[1]
>
> —Puerto Rican Student Union, 1970

E qual access to education was at the forefront of the national civil rights movement. The US Supreme Court's ruling in Brown v. Board of Education in 1954 had declared unconstitutional the segregation of schools based on race, and the Civil Rights Act in 1964 prohibited discrimination in educational programs. Yet access to higher public education for Black and other people of color was still limited. In New York, educators, parents, community activists, students, and progressive politicians engaged in vigorous struggles and protests to open doors. During the 1960s, nearly one million African Americans and Puerto Ricans had moved to the city,[2] but the student population at the public universities did not reflect the changing demographics. In 1961, the City University of New York (CUNY), the nation's first free public institution of higher learning, was 94 to 97 percent white and middle class.[3] The City College of New York (CCNY), located in Harlem, was "especially dissonant, having an almost entirely white student population."[4]

By the mid-1960s, the education rights movement was gaining ground. Public university officials discussed recruiting "economically and educationally disadvantaged"[5] youth. The CCNY Faculty Council agree to admit "some of the disadvantaged New York City high school graduates who would not be eligible for admission to the College but who might nevertheless be judged as having the potential for successful college work."[6] In the fall of 1965, CCNY piloted a "pre-baccalaureate" program intended as a five-year program with the first year dedicated to remediation courses. It enrolled 113 African American and Puerto Rican students from low-income neighborhoods, including me.

Among my classmates were Henry Arce, Eduardo "Pancho" Cruz, Francine Covington, Khadija DeLoache, Mary McRae, Cenen Moreno, Louis Reyes Rivera, and Sekou Sundiata; they all went on to make important contributions to Black and Latinx communities and to the fields of arts and politics. Our first professors included Allen Ballard, Toni Cade Bambara, Barbara Christian, Addison Gayle, and Anthony Penale, passionate and dedicated educators.

The "pre-bac" program enrolled low-income students of color, providing an opportunity for a college education. But at the end of the first year, the program was threatened with budget cuts. Administrators and faculty mobilized quickly, contracting buses to take students to Albany to protest the cuts and petition the state legislature for refunding. Students eager to secure the program's survival rapidly filled the buses. Five students were asked to speak to the state legislators on behalf of the program, and I was among them. Due to a convergence of factors, the New York state legislature expanded the pre-baccalaureate program to other CUNY senior colleges, creating SEEK (Search for Education, Elevation, and Knowledge). Our trip to Albany was victorious!

SEEK opened doors to the first generation of Puerto Rican students in New York to enter college in historically significant numbers. The majority from working-class homes were the first in their families to attend college. Recognizing the importance of uniting to navigate the university system, Puerto Rican students formed advocacy groups on university campuses. At City College, Henry Arce, Eduardo "Pancho" Cruz, myself, and several others formed Puerto Ricans Involved in Student Action (PRISA) in the spring of 1968. At Lehman College, Hildamar Ortiz and Myrna Martínez cofounded the student organization named UNICA in 1969.[7] Puerto Ricans joined with African American students to advocate for increased admission of students of color, inclusion of Puerto Rican and African American studies in the curriculum, and the hiring of African American and Puerto Rican professors.

On April 22, 1969, a City College alliance of African American and Puerto Rican students walked out of classes, renamed the college "Harlem University," and occupied the campus for two weeks. The demands included creating "a school of Black and Puerto Rican studies" and admitting an entering freshman class "reflective of the city's high school population." That spring, students mobilized throughout the CUNY system, organizing sit-ins and rallies at Brooklyn College, Queens College, Queensborough Community College, Bronx Community College, and the Borough of Manhattan Community College.[8] The African American and Latinx communities expressed overwhelming support in favor of the student demands. By July 1969, negotiations with the CUNY administration culminated in an open admission policy.[9] The Board of Higher Education guaranteed every New York City high school graduate a seat in one of the CUNY colleges. The historic and groundbreaking victory also mandated Black and Puerto Rican studies programs at the twenty-five campuses in the largest urban university system in the United States.

THE PUERTO RICAN STUDENT UNION (PRSU)

By the fall of 1969, Puerto Rican student groups were collaborating across campuses on school-related issues but also to publicize events in Puerto Rico. In November, Puerto Rican student and community groups met at St. Mark's Church in the Lower East Side to support Edwin Feliciano Grafals,[10] a member of the Movimiento Pro Independencia (MPI), sentenced to a one-year sentence for resisting induction into the US army. University of Puerto Rico (UPR) students protested his sentence at the ROTC building, and seven were arrested.[11] The protestors denounced Puerto Rico's colonial status and the induction of men in Puerto Rico into the US army, while college men in the United States got draft deferments. Puerto Rican activists in New York rallied to support the arrested UPR students.

Mirta González, Information Ministry cadre, reported in the *Y.L.O.* newsletter: "A number of Puerto Rican organizations formed a committee to publicize and defend the struggle and repression against the freedom fighters on the island."[12] Under the name "Puerto Rican United Front," the ad hoc group raised funds for the UPR students, sent dozens of protest telegrams to the colonial government and the UPR administration, issued a joint press release, and conducted an information campaign in the United States. The committee's representatives included several student organizations: L.U.C.H.A[13] (New York University), PRISA (City College), UNICA [14] (Lehman College), and

United Puerto Rican Students (Rutgers University–Newark), as well as the MPI and the Young Lords Organization.

Fig 15. ¡Despierta Boricua! Graphic, *Palante*. 1970.

Cross-campus activities helped foster a radical Puerto Rican student network. In December 1969, more than one hundred students from fifteen universities in the New York metropolitan area convened a two-day conference to form the Puerto Rican Student Union (PRSU) (La Unión Estudiantil Boricua).[15] Their discussions resulted in agreement on PRSU's mission: to advocate for the interests of Puerto Rican college students, organize for the rights of Puerto Ricans in the United States, and support Puerto Rico's independence movement. During the conference, students heard about the Young Lords' takeover at the People's Church. A solidarity contingent formed quickly and went to the church to join the Young Lords. At the end of the church takeover, ten PRSU members were among those arrested.[16]

In March 1970, the PRSU opened a storefront office on East 138th Street in the Bronx. Committed to student-community unity, PRSU members worked with neighborhood residents to clean up an abandoned lot across the street and transformed it into a beautiful public outdoor gathering space. They named it La Plaza Borinqueña, and it became a popular place for political, and cultural events. PRSU members were also active in organizing for tenants' rights, health care, and an end to police brutality,[17] as well as presenting educational programs about Puerto Rico's colonial status and the independence movement.

CAMPAIGN TO SUPPORT THE INDEPENDENCE OF PUERTO RICO

From the outset, the Puerto Rican Student Union and the Young Lords had a close working relationship. Many Young Lords had been active in the early Puerto Rican student struggles, and the PRSU was an earlier supporter of the Young Lords Organization, as mentioned. The YLP and PRSU shared political views and commitments to advance Puerto Rico's struggle for national liberation. Seeking to expand the base of support for Puerto Rico's independence, the PRSU and the Young Lords Party planned major activities in the fall of 1970. They included the first Puerto Rican student conference in the United States and a mass demonstration to the United Nations.

Fig 16. Puerto Rican Student Conference. September 1970.
Hildamar Ortiz and Iris Morales make opening remarks.
(Courtesy: Michael Abramson)

Hildamar Ortiz and I served as the main coordinators of the Puerto Rican student conference, representing the PRSU and the YLP, respectively. More than one thousand students participated in the two-day conference held at Columbia University on September 23 and 24.[18] The objective was to encourage high school and college students to form "Free Puerto Rico" or "Liberate Puerto Rico Now" committees in their schools and campuses. The conference keynote speaker, Flavia Rivera from La Federación Universitaria Pro Independencia de Puerto Rico (FUPI), reported on student struggles in the archipelago. Denise Oliver from the YLP Central Committee spoke about the historic revolutionary role of students. Puerto Rican and African American women activists led and cofacilitated workshops on topics such as Puerto Rican history and culture; the role of women in the revolution; political prisoners; Third World unity; education and the media; and socialism. On the last day of the conference, I reported that several "Liberate Puerto Rico Now!" had already been formed at schools and reminded students about the upcoming march to the United Nations scheduled for October 30.[19] When the conference ended, participants marched to La Plaza Borinqueña in the Bronx to celebrate and rally for the independence of Puerto Rico.

On Friday, October 30, 1970, marchers gathered in Harlem at 125th Street and Lexington Avenue headed to the United Nations on Forty-Seventh Street. Ten thousand people marched to bring international attention to Puerto Rico's colonial status. They included members from a broad spectrum of allied and social justice organizations— the Black Panther Party, El Comité, Frente Estudiantil Revolucionario Dominicano, FUPI, the Gay Liberation Front, the Health Revolutionary Unity Movement, I Wor Kuen, Justicia Latina, the MPI, Resistencia Puertorriqueña, STAR, Third World Gay Liberation, Third World Women's Alliance, Youth against War and Fascism, and others.

The mass mobilization united with three main demands: an end to colonialism in Puerto Rico, an end to police brutality in local communities, and the release of Puerto Rican Nationalist political prisoners: Oscar Collazo, Lolita Lebrón, Rafael Cancel Miranda, Andrés Figueroa Cordero, Irvin Flores Rodríguez, and Carlos Feliciano. As discussed earlier, the Nationalists were in prison for actions opposing US colonialism in Puerto Rico. Collazo participated in the attempted assassination of President Truman in 1950 and was sentenced to life imprisonment. Lebrón, Cancel Miranda, Figueroa Cordero, and Flores Rodríguez took part in the 1954 shooting in the House of Representatives. Convicted of "seditious conspiracy," they were each sentenced up to seventy-five years in prison.[20] Feliciano, accused of several bombings in New York City, was subsequently acquitted in 1975.

October 30, 1970 marked the twentieth anniversary of the Jayuya Uprising against the US government in Puerto Rico, known as the 1950 Rebellion, referenced in chapter 2. The Nationalist Party organized revolts in eleven towns, including Jayuya, Peñuelas, Utuado, Ponce, San Juan, Mayagüez, Arecibo, and Naranjito.[21] Their goal was to denounce US colonialism and bring international attention to Puerto Rico's continuing colonial status. The rebellion began in Peñuelas where three Nationalists were killed immediately. In Jayuya, Nationalists took up arms, attacked police headquarters, and held the town. Blanca Canales, a leader of the rebellion, raised the Puerto Rican flag in the town plaza in defiance of the Gag Law and declared Puerto Rico a free republic. The US and Puerto Rican governments responded swiftly. President Truman declared martial law and ordered the army and air force to attack. US bomber planes, land-based artillery, mortar fire, and grenades crushed the revolt. Mass arrests followed.[22] In a public broadcast, Puerto Rico's Governor Luis Muñoz Marin declared his support for the US government and called the uprising "a conspiracy against democracy helped by the Communists."[23] More than twenty-three Nationalists were killed and many more wounded.[24] For her actions in the rebellion, the District Court of Arecibo, Puerto Rico and the US Federal Court in San Juan sentenced Canales to a combined term of life imprisonment plus sixty years to be served at the Alderson Federal Prison in West Virginia.[25]

While at the Alderson prison, Canales met Claudia Jones, the Trinidad-born, US Communist Party member, and feminist who was there awaiting deportation from the United States. Since 1948, Jones had been fighting deportation. Prior to arriving at Alderson, she had been detained at various sites, including Ellis Island and the Women's House of Detention in New York City. According to Jones's FBI file, her crime was "practicing the ideas of communism" for which she was declared an enemy of the state.[26] Deported in 1955, Jones lived the rest of her life in London.[27]

Jones and Canales became friends during the time they were detained at Alderson Federal Prison. United by deeply held anti-imperialist beliefs and commitments, Jones wrote a poem dedicated to Canales, titled, "For Consuela—Anti-Fascista."[28] It opens with the following verse:

> It seems I knew you long before our common ties—
> of conscious choice
> Threw under single skies, those like us
> Who, fused by our mold
> Became their targets, as of old.

The final verses declare:

> We swear that we will never rest
> Until they hear not plea
> But sainted sacrifice to set
> A small proud nation free
>
> O anti-fascist sister—you whose eye turn to stars still
> I've learned your wondrous secret—source of spirit and
> of will
> I've learned that what sustains your heart—
> mind and peace of soul
> Is knowledge that their justice—can never reach its goal.

According to Jones's biographer, Carole Boyce Davies, the poem "recognizes the power of women in leadership positions in the political struggle for radical social change" and describes the identification between them as Caribbean sisters linked by their commitment to "a politics of decolonization."[29]

In 1956, Blanca Canales was transferred to a prison in Puerto Rico, where she remained until 1967, when Governor Roberto Sánchez Vilella pardoned her. Canales remained a vocal *independentista* until her death in 1996.[30]

Fig 17. United Nations demonstration. October 30, 1970.
(Courtesy: Michael Abramson)

PART IV.
NATIONALISMS AND FEMINISMS

Río Grande de Loíza! … Great river.
Great flood of tears. The greatest of all
our island's tears save those greater
that come from the eyes of my soul
for my enslaved people.[1]

—Julia de Burgos, "Río Grande de Loíza," 1938

"Tengo Puerto Rico En Mi Corazón."

"I Have Puerto Rico in My Heart."

—The Young Lords Organization, 1968

11.
"REBELLION RUSHIN' DOWN
THE WRONG ROAD"[1]

> [W]e have to think of two analyses because
> we have to think of two struggles which are
> interrelated and at the same time not related…
> In other words, we have to make one analysis
> for the Puerto Rican nation that includes Puerto Rico…
> then another one for the Puerto Ricans who are
> struggling in the United States.[2]
>
> —Pablo "Yoruba" Guzmán, Minister of Information,
> Young Lords Party, 1971

T he Young Lords Party ended 1970 with an impressive list of social justice victories. The organization's political ideas and actions had earned broad public support, created new chapters, and developed affiliated groups across the northeastern United States, especially in New York, Pennsylvania, Connecticut, Massachusetts, and New Jersey. Through grassroots organizing, collective leadership, bold protests, collaborations, and strategic use of mass media, the Young Lords had activated public discourse, achieved policy changes, and brought about reforms in low-income Puerto Rican communities.

Reflecting on the intense activities that year, Pablo "Yoruba" Guzmán wrote "Why a Young Lords Party?" in the December issue of *Palante.* He concludes:

> There would be no Young Lords Party if there were no capitalism and no racism. Since both exist, a force has arisen to stamp both evils out. We also are on the move against a force just as deadly: machismo.[3]

Guzmán's statement made it clear that the Young Lords Party developed in response to oppression. Declaring machismo "a force just as deadly" as capitalism and racism was a significant step forward for the organization's commitment to gender justice. By describing capitalism, racism, and machismo as related systems of domination, Guzmán allied the

Young Lords Party with the analysis of US socialist feminists of color, rejecting the nationalist position that the struggle for the emancipation of women was secondary. It was the first time a male Central Committee leader publicly supported this position, and it encouraged the liberatory hopes of Puerto Rican and African American women in the organization.

Around this time, the Central Committee—Juan González, Pablo "Yoruba" Guzmán, David Pérez, Juan 'Fi' Ortiz, Denise Oliver, and Gloria González—went into a leadership retreat to review the Young Lords' activities since September 1970 and set goals for the coming year. As the first major convening since Felipe Luciano's demotion and resignation and Gloria González's promotion, the retreat took on amplified importance regarding the YLP's future. After meeting for eight days, the group produced a twenty-two-page document titled "Report of Central Committee Evaluation and Retreat." Field marshal David Pérez summarized key changes planned for 1971.[4] First was the opening of YLP branches in Puerto Rico. Second was the shift to developing "people's organizations" in the United States.

This chapter discusses the shift in political priorities in 1971 and the consequences for gender and racial justice organizing and the future of the Young Lords Party.

THE "DIVIDED NATION" DEBATE

The Central Committee's December 1970 retreat centered questions related to Puerto Rico. What was the role of Puerto Ricans in the United States to the independence struggle of Puerto Rico? And what should be the relationship of the Young Lords Party to Puerto Rico? Field marshal Gloria González took the lead and introduced the concept of "divided nation." González theorized that Puerto Ricans constituted one nation, separated geographically, with one-third in exile in the United States severed from the two-thirds in Puerto Rico.[5] She concluded that the Puerto Rican nation needed to be united and proposed opening YLP branches in Puerto Rico for this purpose. The idea of Puerto Ricans as one people had tremendous nationalist appeal. González emphasized that the Central Committee had already begun to consider the possibility of opening Puerto Rico branches in the summer of 1970. She claimed that Juan González and Juan "Fi" Ortiz had traveled to the archipelago in August "to begin preparations *to unite the nation.*"[6] Her explanation of the Puerto Rico trip conflicted with the account given by Juan González and Ortiz in *Palante.* They wrote,

> The purpose of this trip was to make a formal and official contact with other political parties, push the student conference [September 23], and get a better sense of the realities of the political situation in Puerto Rico.[7]

Hence, as far as the Young Lords cadre and public knew, the trips to the archipelago in the summer of 1970 were exploratory to get a better understanding of the political movement and situation in Puerto Rico. Thus, it was surprising when Gloria González reported that the Central Committee had decided in September to proceed secretly (*clandestinamente*) to prepare the Young Lords Party for the move to Puerto Rico.[8]

Juan González, Gloria González, and Pérez were proponents of expanding the Young Lords Party to Puerto Rico. Guzmán, Oliver, and Ortiz were opposed, insisting that the YLP's role was to organize inside the United States. "The Young Lords Party has zero experience in Puerto Rico," they exclaimed. "The people in Puerto Rico will lead the struggle for national liberation," they emphasized. Unlike the pro-expansion proponents who were born in Puerto Rico, Guzmán, Ortiz, and Oliver were born and raised in the United States. They were Afro-Boricuas and African American and identified closely with the African American experience and social justice movements. Furthermore, during their trips to the archipelago, they encountered anti-Black racism, class elitism, and gender discrimination even in the pro-independence movement. "How will the Young Lords Party tackle these issues?" they asked.

Gloria González put forth her ideas. She replied that the Young Lords Party would organize the most exploited people, "the working class, the poor, the lumpen, the jibaro, and the Afro-Puertorriqueño."[9] Her main argument was that Puerto Rico's working class was without revolutionary leadership. She argued that the pro-independence organizations—Movimiento Pro Independencia (MPI) and the Puerto Rican Independence Party—represented the middle and upper classes, not the exploited sectors. She claimed the Young Lords would fill the leadership vacuum and "reunify the nation"[10] though she did not explain what "reunification" meant. Nor did she explain how the Young Lords would re-unify Puerto Ricans living in two nations—one the colonizer and the other the colonized.

A strong undercurrent in the debate was a questioning of who was really Puerto Rican and loyal to Puerto Rico's liberation. At the time, heated and passionate arguments in the Puerto Rican Left movement debated who was a "true" Puerto Rican or Boricua, and a "linguistic chauvinism privileged Spanish over English"[11] as a marker of authenticity. It is significant that Gloria González's four-page explanation of "divided nation" was in Spanish, which many Young Lords could not read. As the only Central Committee member writing in Spanish, González positioned herself as the most authentic Puerto Rican in the leadership. She injected a narrow nationalist element into the debate, claiming that a "real" Puerto Rican would support the YLP move to the archipelago.

Although David Pérez reported full agreement with the move to Puerto Rico and the "new political lines" in the December 1970 retreat, this was not true. When the Central Committee voted on whether to open branches in Puerto Rico, the outcome was a tie—three for and three opposed. Juan González, as minister of defense and the highest-ranking member, entered the deciding vote to expand the Young Lords Party to Puerto Rico. Guzmán, Oliver, and Ortiz were opposed to the move but accepted the decision pursuant to the interpretation that the principles of democratic centralism permitted the highest-ranking person to break a tie. Nonetheless, the decision left a bitter taste and opened a pandora's box. Why proceed with such a critical result without full Central Committee agreement or consensus? Given the split in the leadership, why not bring the question to the general membership for thorough discussion or table it for further evaluation? What was the urgency? The Young Lords Party was barely a year and a half old. Whose interests did the rushed decision serve? These questions remained unanswered.

STRUGGLE WITH MALE CHAUVINISM AND SEXISM CONTINUES

The debate about the expansion to Puerto Rico dominated the December retreat, but the Central Committee also reported long discussions about male chauvinism and the status of women in the organization. This was no surprise since struggles with the Women's Caucus were ongoing.

Also, for the first time, two women—Denise Oliver and Gloria Gonzá-lez—sat on the Central Committee. The group acknowledged that male chauvinism was a problem in every branch and at all levels.[12] They cited low numbers of women officers and admitted failing to promote several women who showed leadership ability but gave no reason. They merely stated, "extra efforts must be made to educate sisters out of passivity and prepare them to become officers."[13] But, they did not specify what the "extra efforts" were, and none materialized. The Central Committee agreed that the *Palante* newspaper was still too male oriented in view-point and content. One member added, "A normal working woman would find little to interest her," conceding the need to be more attentive to and inclusive of women's concerns and interests. The Central Com-mittee also reprimanded the Young Lords for not studying sufficiently the YLP Position Paper on Women published that September and in-structed all members to memorize whole sections and be able to speak about it.[14] Seeking to expand the discourse, Oliver introduced the con-cept of "sexism,"[15] explained in the retreat report as the ideology of a di-vision between men and women[16] that believes men are inherently supe-rior and discriminates based on gender. The Central Committee prom-ised a fuller discussion about sexism in the future.

During 1970, the Central Committee responded to the ten demands presented by the Women's Caucus, but one was pending—the right of women to caucus. Unexpectedly, the Central Committee members wrote: "The female caucus is not the right solution. … Separate caucuses are not the answer."[17] With these simple statements, the Central Com-mittee disbanded the Women's and Men's Caucuses, though they were sites of learning and promoted political discourse. The Women's Caucus led the development of feminist thinking and practices in the Young Lords Party. Caucus members led struggles for women's rights, provided opportunities for women to strategize together, and helped recruit new members. Most cadres credited the caucuses with advancing their un-derstanding of gender oppression and aiding their personal political growth and transformation. But the Central Committee had not engaged the membership in making the decision to disband the caucuses. As dis-cussed in chapter 7, the homosexual caucuses later met the same fate. In retrospect, the Puerto Rico project proponents sought to eliminate all potential groupings that might challenge their new political direction.

Ironically, the Central Committee's retreat report included a section titled "Democratic Centralism," declaring the general membership meeting and discussion as "the core of democracy in the Party."[18] It emphasized the importance of engaging the rank and file in dialogue and debate to reach the majority decisions to be implemented. However, the Central Committee did not practice "democratic centralism" in the conclusions it reported in the retreat document. Instead, the Central Committee ended 1970 with *clandestine* actions and unilateral decisions severely impacting the Young Lords Party's political work, integrity, and future.

The December retreat report was full of theories, promises, mixed messages, and inconsistencies, but few concrete plans. It was a turning point, introducing ideas and approaches that moved the Young Lords Party down an ominous road. First was the Central Committee's unilateral decision-making, bypassing cadre participation and eroding democratic centralism. Second was the decision to open branches in Puerto Rico. Third was the shutdown of the Women's Caucus. The retreat report forecast shattering changes.

CENTRAL COMMITTEE DECISION TO EXPAND TO PUERTO RICO

After the December retreat, the Central Committee called a general membership meeting early in January 1971 and distributed to each Young Lord the twenty-two-page "Report of the Central Committee Evaluation and Retreat." We had waited for it anxiously. On that cold and overcast day, I wondered if a storm was coming. Its main announcement was the decision to open YLP branches in Puerto Rico presented as a fait accompli. The retreat document did not present the arguments for and against the move or the divergent views among the leadership. Instead, the Central Committee members asked the cadre, "What do you think about the plan to open branches in Puerto Rico?" A flood of thoughts raced through my mind like a flipbook, illustrating US colonialism in Puerto Rico and the struggles of the Nationalist Party and other activists to end it. I imagined many Young Lords had similar thoughts and feelings. We all had strong emotional connections to Puerto Rico.

Some Young Lords quickly jumped on the idea of opening branches in Puerto Rico, romanticizing a direct fight against US colonialism. A few even said the Young Lords should shut down the US organization and move to Puerto Rico. Many disagreed with these viewpoints, saying the mission of the Young Lords was to organize for the rights of Puerto Ricans in the United States. Most, like myself, expected a discussion, not a hurried poll. We had questions. Why was the Central Committee taking this direction? How would it affect organizing in the United States? What changes were anticipated with branches in two countries? Would the Young Lords in Puerto Rico follow the 13-Point Program or have its own? Where would funds for the expansion come from? How would the Young Lords collaborate with existing organizations in Puerto Rico? How would the Central Committee organize against racism in Puerto Rico? How would the YLP advance women's rights? Who would be assigned to go?

Unquestionably, all Young Lords were committed to the decolonization of Puerto Rico. The hesitancy about the Central Committee's announcement sprang from lack of discussion and clear analysis. Despite the gung-ho attitude, no plan was presented for how the move would unfold. The decision felt rushed, inadequately thought out, and unorganized. With the limited information, we could not assess what the move meant for the Young Lords Party or the extent of what was at stake.

Not long after the cadre received the retreat report, the Central Committee summoned over fifty cadres to a special meeting. It became clear that the focus was on Carlos Aponte, a member since January 1970 and captain in the Education Ministry, highly respected for his knowledge of Puerto Rican history. Aponte was a Vietnam War veteran and had organized with the Black Panther Party in California. Aponte had asked the Central Committee members about the reasons for the move to Puerto Rico. However, the special meeting was not to answer his questions. Instead, he was interrogated about his background and activities. Gloria and Juan González took the lead. They accused Aponte of being a police agent. The evidence consisted of insinuations, name calling, and guilt by association. They pointed to Aponte's four-year service in the US air force. They cited his attendance at early meetings of the Black Panther Party and the Puerto Rican Student Union and his travel to Cuba with the Venceremos Brigade.[19] At the end of the interrogation, the Central Committee expelled Aponte from the Young Lords Party and published his photograph and biography in the *Palante* newspaper with those of other alleged agents.[20] According to the Central Committee, Aponte was "one of the highest-level agents" in the organization.[21] Years later, Juan González wrote about the incident, regretting the leading role he played in "the sham trial."[22]

The vicious grilling of Aponte was shocking. It caused anxiety among the cadre about being labeled "an agent" for asking questions or voicing an opposing opinion. Most of us recognized the move to Puerto Rico was a major change, but we were not yet clear about its ideological, organizational, and political consequences. We did not foresee that the move was the first step in a tsunami that would dramatically alter the Young Lords Party.

Around this time, the book, *Palante: The Young Lords Party,* was published. In an essay by Pablo "Yoruba" Guzmán,[23] he discusses the relationship between the Puerto Rican struggles in the United States and Puerto Rico. He proposes two investigations to evaluate the political conditions in each country and plan accordingly. Believing that Guzmán's article reflected the Central Committee's point of view, reassured many of us. However, we later learned that the proponents of the Puerto Rico expansion did not support Guzmán's proposal.

RESTRUCTURING THE YOUNG LORDS PARTY

From January through July 1971, the Central Committee focused on opening YLP branches in Puerto Rico. *Palante* expanded its coverage regarding Puerto Rico's history and politics to increase public awareness about US colonialism and the colonial government. The first *Palante* issue in 1971 featured Luis A. Ferré, Puerto Rico's governor and founder of the pro-statehood New Progressive Party, as "pig of the year."[24] "You are doing nothing but selling our people down the drain," the article concluded. It highlighted Ferré's millionaire status, banking and business interests, and Puerto Rico's 35 percent unemployment under his tenure.

Fig 18. *Palante* newspaper. "Why Rebellion?" 1971.

Palante's reporting included a thirteen-part series titled "History of Borikén" tracing the archipelago's evolution from its Indigenous roots to the Spanish colonization and enslavement of Indigenous and African people. The series recapped the Spanish Cuban American War, when eighteen thousand US troops invaded the southern town of Guánica, Puerto Rico.[25] On July 25, 1898, Spain ceded Puerto Rico to the United States. The US government immediately implemented policies aimed at "Americanizing the island" and manufacturing consent for its rule.[26] They imposed English as Puerto Rico's official language.

From 1900 to 1946, US governors, politicians, and military men ruled Puerto Rico. They paraded their contempt for the people and opened opportunities for US corporate exploitation of the land and natural resources. In 1917, Congress passed the Jones Act, making Puerto Ricans citizens of the United States and drafting men into the military. Yet the US government prohibited Puerto Ricans from voting for president or electing congressional representatives. The extraction policies of US corporations triggered an economic crisis. Exploitation and poverty escalated. Puerto Rican workers organized for decent wages and conditions, and strikes intensified.

In 1930, the Puerto Rican Nationalist Party elected Pedro Albizu Campos, an Afro-Boricua and Harvard Law School graduate, as president, and the party stepped up demands to end US colonialism. In 1948, the colonial government passed Law 53, known as the Gag Law or *Ley de la Mordaza,* to suppress the pro-independence movement. It criminalized owning or displaying a Puerto Rican flag, singing a patriotic song, speaking or writing about independence, or assembling in support of sovereignty and independence. Anyone disobeying the law could be sentenced to ten years imprisonment, fined $10,000, or both. Hundreds of patriots were imprisoned under this law.

The move to Puerto Rico was all-consuming for the Young Lords Party, an organization with limited financial resources and reliant on volunteers. Juan González, minister of defense, urged members to prepare. Signaling new priorities, he wrote, "The slogan we should remember is 'Consolidate the base' (US branches) to 'prepare the front' (Puerto Rico)."[27] With this catchphrase, the Central Committee launched Ofensiva Rompe Cadenas or the "Break the Chains Offensive," shifting the resources of the Young Lords Party to the Puerto Rico project. With whirlwind speed, the Central Committee shuffled people to new assignments and closed "serve the people" programs. Without regard to the impact on local neighborhoods and residents, they restructured the New York organization. They transferred cadres out of the YLP storefront offices to a section called the Committee to Defend the Community, which had no physical location. Gloria González insisted that the pull away from US communities was necessary. "In order for us to move forward in one area—preparing for the move to Puerto Rico—we had to sacrifice in the area of community work," she wrote.[28] The hub of the Young Lords Party, the East Harlem office, closed. It was "a rebellion rushin' down the wrong road."

On March 21, 1971, the Young Lords arrived in Puerto Rico. Gloria González, Juan González, Richie Pérez (then deputy minister of information), and other Young Lords marched with eighty nationalists in the city of Ponce. The date marked the Ponce Massacre of 1937, when police shot into a peaceful demonstration, killing eighteen persons, and seriously wounding two hundred others.[29] Led by Gloria González, the Young Lords Party opened two branches in Puerto Rico—one in Aguadilla in the northwest and another in Santurce in the northeast.

Back in US communities, people asked, "Where are the Young Lords?" The move to Puerto Rico caused a decline in new recruits and hastened the departure of veteran members such as Denise Oliver, minister of finance, who resigned in February 1971. A short item in *Palante* noted Oliver's resignation but did not mention her opposition to the YLP expansion to Puerto Rico. As the sole revolutionary socialist feminist on the Central Committee, Oliver's departure had major ramifications for the Young Lords' feminist organizing and agenda.

As the Young Lords' activities waned in the United States, organizations like the Movimiento Pro Independencia (MPI) filled the void. Although MPI's focus had been to build support for Puerto Rico's independence movement,[30] the Young Lords' success had spurred the older MPI members to reconceptualize their mission.[31] They made "a strategic decision" to organize for the rights of Puerto Ricans in the United States.[32]

12.
THE WOMEN'S UNION AND
THE 12-POINT PROGRAM

> Whenever any people are victims of abuse,
> it's only natural that they fight against it.
> The Third World Woman, as the most
> oppressed person in the world today,
> is no exception.[1]
>
> —The Women's Union, *La Luchadora*, 1971

As the Young Lords Party opened new branches in Puerto Rico in 1971, the Young Lords in the United States focused on developing "people's organizations." The Central Committee described them as democratic entities made up of activists working in diverse sectors to advance political, economic, and social justice. By building with distinct constituencies, the YLP proposed to expand the mass movement. Field marshal David Pérez explained, "The people's organizations are the mass movement the Party leads." He declared, "If we serve, guide, and protect them, they will definitely follow us."[2] The Health Revolutionary Unity Movement and the Puerto Rican Student Union, discussed in chapters 8 and 10, respectively, affiliated with the Young Lords Party as peoples' organizations. They connected the YLP with thousands of health care workers and working-class students. As independent groups, the HRUM and the PRSU selected their steering committees and set their political priorities. The YLP Central Committee assigned Young Lords to take part in the everyday work of each people's organization.[3] The Inmates Liberation Front, emerging from the 1970 New York City jail uprisings discussed in chapter 9, was also a people's organization. Pérez described it as "the organizing group of the lumpen,"[4] adding that "the two most important parts of Puerto Rican society are the lumpen and the workers."[5] However, the ILF's relationship with the YLP was short-lived.

In addition to the existing people's organizations, the Central Committee members proposed to create new ones. They prioritized a "workers' group" and appointed Gloria González to organize the Workers' Federation and me to the Women's Union. Given my disappointment with the shutdown of the Women's Caucus, I welcomed the project, envisioning an organization led by women of color focused on advancing women's rights and social justice. This chapter reviews the activities of the Women's Union and its relationship with the Young Lords Party.

FIGHTING GENDER, RACIAL, AND CLASS OPPRESSIONS

Dire economic, social, and political conditions confronting Black women and Latinas in the United States at the time heightened the need to fight gender, racial, and class oppressions simultaneously. Both the government and corporate media vilified poor and working-class women of color. In 1965, Assistant Secretary of Labor Daniel Patrick Moynihan released a report, "The Negro Family: The Case for National Action,"[6] that rapidly gathered momentum across the mainstream political spectrum.[7] "Moynihan maintained that cyclical poverty among Black urban families was related to deficiencies in their family structure and their dependence on welfare," writes historian Chong Chon-Smith.[8] Moynihan's report revived a racial conversation, providing ideas and language for conservative assaults on working-class and poor Black communities.[9] In Moynihan's opinion, the relative absence of nuclear families and the rise of single mothers prevented progress toward economic and political equality. He argued that "unstable" Black family structures produced what he labeled a "tangle of pathology"—high rates of delinquency, joblessness, school failure, crime, and fatherlessness.[10] Moynihan blamed the Black "matriarchy" as the primary barrier to racial equality. He and other officials promoted stereotypes of African American women and Latinas as lazy freeloaders. Racist corporate media accused them of defective parenting and rearing unemployable workers.

Black feminists denounced Moynihan's report for its racism, sexism, and defense of capitalism. They called for increased economic opportunities for African American men and women alike. Activist Pauli Murray blasted Moynihan's explanation of African American "matriarchy." She criticized it as "a grave disservice to the thousands of Negro women in the United States who have struggled to prepare themselves for employment in a limited job market."[11] The National Organization for Women also condemned the Moynihan report, asserting:

> People are poor for one reason—the economic system in the United States is not structured to eliminate poverty, and it is not intended to be. It depends upon a cheap reserve of labor—extracted primarily from women and minorities and especially minority women.[12]

Fifty years later, anthropologist and activist author Susan Greenbaum, in a piece titled "Where's the Obituary for the Moynihan Report?," concludes:

> The Moynihan Report was misguided in conception and defective in its research. It survives today only because it feeds the narrative that poor people cause their own problems, and the economy is not to blame.[13]

The ideas in the Moynihan report persist to justify racial, gender, and class inequality.

THE WOMEN'S UNION: A PEOPLE'S ORGANIZATION

Early in 1971, the Young Lords Party circulated flyers to announce the formation of the Women's Union. I was assigned to create this new people's organization. The Central Committee appointed Gloria González, the only female in the top leadership after Denise Oliver's resignation, as their liaison to the project. Because González had refused to join and take part in the Women's Caucus and voted to disband it, I was troubled by her track record and what it would mean for the Women's Union.

In keeping with the Central Committee's description of people's organizations, the WU was formed to advance the interests of women of color and develop as a mass-based group with its own steering committee, political priorities, and membership. By April 1971, the first steering committee was organized with Elsie López, an East Harlem resident and lifelong *independentista* from Puerto Rico; Yvonne, a Puerto Rican student activist from the Bronx; me as the Young Lords' organizer; and Gloria González in absentia, since she was in Puerto Rico, overseeing the new branches. The WU's early activities were informational women-centered meetings and political education workshops. Puerto Rican, Latinx, and African American women—students, mothers, homemakers, workers, activists, socialists, and nationalists—attended. The WU participants expressed similar political aspirations as Black women's organizations described by historian Kimberly Springer in *Living for the Revolution.*

> [They] sought to attain visibility and allies for a movement that encompassed race, gender, and class questions of social justice through their activities and myriad other traditional ways of organizing of the time period.[14]

The WU members were eager to build a militant, activist organization to address the social and political concerns of Puerto Rican and other women of color.

As the Women's Union formed and organized initial activities, sharp differences of opinion surfaced with the Central Committee. The first concerned the WU's autonomy and political priorities. As a people's organization, the Women's Union expected to direct its affairs, but Gloria González, as the Central Committee's liaison, sought to exert total control, ignoring the ideas and wishes of the WU steering committee and members. Before the WU could get off the ground, the Central Committee set the WU's political priorities, violating the principle that people's organizations were independent entities. González did not take part in the day-to-day organizing, but she ordered the Women's Union to establish a public day-care center in East Harlem. Because childcare was a foremost concern, the WU members followed her directive and began the process. However, the Central Committee provided no support, financial or other resources to the project, and it stalled. In González's absence, the members of the Women's Union proceeded to develop other projects and activities. The conflict over who sets the political priorities led to a second question: What was the mission of the Women's Union? Different points of view emerged and clashed later that year as discussed in the following chapters.

While González was in Puerto Rico, the Women's Union took part in gender-related and social justice organizing activities, building on the activism of the Women's Caucus and US feminists of color. Members drafted a 12-Point Program and rules of discipline, facilitated political education workshops, participated in social justice protests, and produced a bilingual newspaper. Puerto Rican women expressed enthusiasm for an organization dedicated to the rights of women of color. The Women's Union grew rapidly.

THE 12-POINT PROGRAM: A SOCIALIST FEMINIST AGENDA

As a mass organization, the WU's 12-Point Program included socialist, feminist, and revolutionary nationalist members and ideas. The core demand was "equality for women—down with machismo and sexism." The program reflected members' lived experiences. It focused on issues affecting working poor and disenfranchised women in communities of color, including welfare mothers, street sex workers, drug-addicted women, and women in prison.[15] Recognizing male supremacy, gender oppression, and capitalism as intertwined forms of domination, it emphasized the "triple oppression" of women of color by class, race, and gender.

High on the list of concerns, the 12-Point Program called for full employment with equal pay, emphasizing that women of color were paid substantially less than both men and white women. Childcare was a related issue, and the WU demanded "day-care facilities provided by the work institution." As discussed earlier, without day care, mothers with young children could not hold jobs outside the home. Few affordable options existed, mainly restricted to informal networks of family, friends, neighbors, and strangers. Because childcare was so critical, many of the Young Lords' campaigns included it as a demand. For example, the People's Church occupation requested space for "a free day-care center for the mothers of the community" and for breakfast programs. The Lincoln Hospital takeover demanded "the establishment of a childcare center for both patients and working parents at the hospital." The demands of the YLO women member for childcare resulted in a policy that enlisted both men and women to care for children so that mothers could take part in political activities.

The Women's Union joined protests with mothers at welfare centers to demand state resources desperately required for childcare, employment, health care, education, and other services. Urging humane policies and practices, the 12-Point Program stated:

> We want an end to the present welfare system; commu-
> nity-worker boards must be established in all welfare cen-
> ters to [e]nsure the protection of women and their needs.[16]

Lawmakers and the corporate media vigorously opposed support to welfare mothers. They characterized African American women and Latinas
as parasites. Their views fed the public clamor for ending social service
programs and promoted the passage of stringent work requirements for
assistance eligibility. Yet, welfare mothers received little support from the
women's movement. Scholar bell hooks writes:

> The most profound betrayal of feminist issues has been the
> lack of mass-based feminist protests challenging the gov-
> ernment's assault on single mothers and the dismantling of
> the welfare system.[17]

In her critique, hooks denounced the privileged white women's movement for not acting against the vicious government attacks on poor
women of color.

The 12-Point Program called attention to state-sanctioned and individual violence against women of color. Point 8 demanded the release
of political prisoners and prisoners of war. It denounced "the sexual brutalization and torture enforced on sisters by prison officials." Point 7
condemned sexual abuse by the military. During this time, the US military occupied 13 percent of Puerto Rico's lands and used the islands of
Vieques and Culebra as naval bombing ranges, testing sites, and training
grounds.[18] WU members gave accounts of US soldiers assaulting women
and facing no consequences. Point 11 asserted a woman's right to self-
defense, declaring, "We believe in the right to defend ourselves against
rapes, beatings, muggings and general abuse."

Echoing the struggles for reproductive justice reviewed in chapter
4, the WU demanded "an end to the experimentation and genocide committed through sterilization, forced abortions, contraceptives, and unnecessary gynecological exams."

Point 10 stated, "We want a true education of our story as women."

Several points mirrored the Young Lords Party's 13-Point Program.
Point 1 declared, "We want the liberation of all Puerto Ricans—liberation on the island and inside the U.S." The last point stated, "We want a
socialist society."

LA LUCHADORA: NEWSPAPER OF THE WOMEN'S UNION

The Women's Union produced a bilingual English/Spanish newspaper, *La Luchadora,* translated as "the fighter." Intended as an educational and organizing tool, the inaugural issue in June 1971 answered the question, "Why a Women's Union?"

> Because as women, we best understand our own oppression and can organize ourselves for our liberation, always remembering that we will not be free until all our people are free.[19]

The articles in *La Luchadora* were written by women of color. Because most writers attended the WU's political education workshops, they brought the conversations taking place among feminist activists of color into the newspaper, reflecting a mix of nationalist, socialist, and feminist perspectives.

Fig 19. *La Luchadora* masthead. 1971.

Many articles referenced "triple oppression," the concept introduced by Black socialist feminists. Women of color readily understood its meaning. In "House Slave," the author explains:

> First, we are oppressed because we are poor. ... Then we are oppressed because of our nationality and/or race. Finally, we suffer because we are women, and women are considered inferior to men.[20]

In "Women Workers," a garment factory worker describes her triple oppression. Hired for the most difficult and lowest-paid jobs, she worked in unsafe and unsanitary conditions while being subjected to racial discrimination, manhandling, and sexual abuse. She criticizes the International Ladies' Garment Workers' Union for not fighting for its 450,000 members, 80 percent of whom were women. At home, her oppression continued, cooking, cleaning, and caring for the family's needs. She writes, "Fathers, husbands, and brothers," who are also "worked like slaves," take out their anger on women. She concludes, "Workers, women and men, must fight united to create a new society that does not exploit anyone." The author of "Machismo" also outlined the oppression of women of color in the home and workplace, reaching a similar conclusion: "Women must educate our men so that they will join us in the struggle to end machismo."[21]

Articles also showed the influence of Friedrich Engels's idea that "the modern individual family is founded on the open or concealed domestic slavery of the wife."[22] "House Slave" emphasizes the drudgery of housework:

> Our role is to deal with the housework like a servant. We live in a world of dishwashing, ironing, cooking, mopping, sweeping, and taking care of children. We do the same jobs over and over again.[23]

Housework is the unpaid domestic work central for all societies to function. Yet the significance of women's role in the home and family is ignored or downplayed. It is not valued because women perform it in their homes and is not considered "real work."

La Luchadora also included stories about Puerto Rico's anticolonial struggle, women patriots, and reproductive rights. Three issues published from June to August 1971 circulated feminist ideas and stimulated discourse about the political concerns of low-income women of color.

WU ACTIVITIES THROUGH MID-1971

The Women's Union facilitated workshops about the herstories of women of color and the impact of oppression on our communities and ourselves. Discussions explored the question: how does colonialism and oppression affect our view of ourselves? Frantz Fanon's concept of "colonized mentality" aided our understanding about how oppressed people accept sexist and racist systems and stereotypes, and how the oppressor perpetuates them. In addition to political education workshops, the WU took part in social justice activities. By mid-1971, WU members were involved in protests against cuts to public assistance, lack of jobs, and unsafe working conditions for women. We supported health-care workers and distributed literature at community venues and hospitals, urging people to attend a "Third World Health Workers' Conference." On International Women's Day, WU members participated in a demonstration at the Women's House of Detention, demanding the rights of detainees. The Women's Union joined coalitions and demonstrations to end the war in Indochina. At a May Day event, WU members marched proudly carrying the "Unión de Mujeres" banner.

Fig 20. Unión de Mujeres banner. *Palante.* 1971.

During 1970, the YLO's Women's Caucus had developed relationships and collaborated with women in the Black Panther Party, the Student Nonviolent Coordinating Committee, the Third World Women's Alliance, the Brown Berets, the Puerto Rican Student Union, and I Wor Kuen. In 1971, the Women's Union sought to build relationships with women in the Puerto Rican Left and invited women activists to attend our meetings. At the time, the main Puerto Rican Left organizations in New York City were Movimiento Pro Independencia, which later became the Puerto Rican Socialist Party; the Puerto Rican Student Union; and El Comité, formed in the summer of 1970 in Manhattan's Upper West Side to fight urban displacement of poor people.[24]

Initially, Puerto Rican women activists from the different organizations met at free Puerto Rico demonstrations and cultural activities. In this way, I first met and developed friendships with El Comité members, Carmen Martell and Diana Caballero. As collaborations among the organizations grew, the exchanges among women revealed similar challenges with male supremacy. As was true throughout the movement, men dominated the leadership of the Puerto Rican Left. Women were primarily rank-and-file members, relegated to administrative and clerical tasks as the "invisible workforce" Chicanas described earlier. Puerto Rican Left leaders were oblivious to feminist concerns or gave them minor importance. According to a male member in the Puerto Rican Socialist Party, "The women were presumed to be responsible for following through on the detailed plans; the men specialized as the ideologues, the strategic thinkers.[25] A prevailing point of view in the Puerto Rican Left maintained it was unnecessary to discuss sexism in a movement that emphasized class and colonialism.[26]

Nevertheless, Puerto Rican women sought to take part in shaping the political agenda. In 1972, El Comité members formed a Women's Commission "to facilitate the participation of women in the organization and in political activism."[27] "Women were encouraged to take leadership roles in the community and the organization to ensure that dialogues on gender oppression were ongoing."[28] The commission pressed for collective childcare during meetings. In 1973, the Puerto Rican Socialist Party (formerly the MPI) established a US branch. Digna Sánchez, the only woman in its Political Commission,[29] led efforts to form a Women's Commission. She ushered in a political education program, explaining that it "reaffirmed feminist principles in support of reproductive rights and challenged the patriarchal underpinnings of our culture."[30] Across the Puerto Rican Left, women activists challenged deeply rooted and widespread male supremacist ideas, and the subjugation of women.

1971 WOMEN'S CONFERENCE AGAINST THE US WAR IN INDOCHINA

In 1971, US feminists from the Black Workers' Congress, El Comité, I Wor Kuen, the Puerto Rican Student Union, and the Young Lords Party took part in the Indochinese Women's Conference in Toronto. President Nixon had escalated the Vietnam War, expanding air and ground operations into Cambodia and Laos to block supply routes along Vietnam's borders. In April, as the North Vietnamese and US governments discussed a cease-fire,[31] six women from Vietnam, Laos, and Cambodia journeyed through war-scarred countries to the conference to build support for the immediate and total US withdrawal from Indochina.[32] The Indochinese women urged attendees to join protests planned in Washington, DC, to oppose the war's expansion.[33] On April 24, 1971, 750,000 thousand people rallied in the capital in "the largest-ever demonstration opposing a U.S. war."[34]

Gloria González and I represented the Young Lords Party at the Toronto conference. When we returned to New York, we gave a full report to the Central Committee. Approximately one thousand North American women attended, representing a microcosm of the US women's liberation movement and its diverse economic classes, races, nationalities, ages, sexual orientations, and political philosophies. Differences sparked acrimonious arguments about racism, classism, and homophobia. Given the significance of the international women's convening, the Central Committee—Gloria González, Juan González, David Pérez, Pablo "Yoruba" Guzmán, and Juan "Fi" Ortiz—responded with an editorial in *Palante* titled "Position on Women's Liberation."

The first part of the editorial summarizes the US women's liberation movement: the different sectors, class interests, and goals. It underlines multiple feminisms. On the right side of the political spectrum were middle- and upper-class white bourgeois feminists who believed that the biggest conflict was the unequal treatment of women by men. Their interest was obtaining power equal to men, not in ending class inequality or racism. In the center "liberals and reformers" sought to improve the status of women. They put their faith in legislation and increasing the representation of women in existing institutions. On the left, socialist feminists asserted that the biggest world conflict was between capitalism and socialism. They focused on issues of class, race, and gender and aimed to reshape society and its institutions. The Young Lords Party supported the anticapitalist and anti-imperialist groups.[35]

The second part of the Central Committee's editorial fell short in its analysis of the liberation struggle of women of color. The article ignores or cherry-picks socialist feminists' ideas, sprinkling them throughout the article but veering off into a discourse about individual male-female attitudes and behavior. The authors focus on what they label "the negative things inside all of us," criticizing men for acting out "macho roles" but accusing women of letting men "mess them over."[36] They conclude that a new society will result from men and women "struggling with each other."[37] However, the Central Committee members failed to specify that male domination is not a sum of individual discriminatory acts but a system that shapes all aspects of life, both collective and individual.[38] An entire system of institutions and individuals perpetuates women's oppression, just as does capitalism and imperialism.

The Central Committee's emphasis on one-dimensional notions of bad male behavior and attitudes echoed past ideas and practices in the Young Lords' history. It was a backward slide to points of view that minimized or dismissed the struggle to end the systemic oppression of women. In hindsight, the editorial's lack of coherence revealed percolating tensions and conflicting ideas, concerning the struggle for the liberation of women of color. On the one hand was the analysis that capitalism, racism, and male supremacy were interrelated and "deadly" systems of domination to be fought together. On the other, was the nationalist position that women's issues were secondary and less important. During 1971, the Central Committee members became increasingly intransigent to the analysis and organizing objectives advanced by socialist feminists of color. The editorial previews the tug-of-war that reemerges in the Young Lords Party's July 1971 retreat.

Fig 21. US Imperialism. *Palante* cover. July 24, 1971.

13.
FROM REVOLUTIONARY
TO NARROW NATIONALISM

a deep remembering of what was,
she survives all.[1]

—Aja Monet, "the ghosts of women once girls," 2017

The Vietnam War continued to dominate US foreign policy in 1971. Antiwar sentiment soared. The 750,000 anti-war protestors who gathered in Washington D.C. on April 24, 1971 registered militant opposition. In June, the release of the Pentagon Papers, a top-secret Department of Defense study, revealed successive presidents had lied about US involvement in Vietnam. Public condemnation surged to record levels.[2] On the US domestic front, economic issues—poverty, high food prices, and inflation—were at the forefront. Unemployment had reached staggeringly high levels, especially in communities of color. The Nixon administration responded with a freeze on wages and an anti-strike order. Thousands of workers took to the streets, demanding, "Freeze War, not Wages." In Puerto Rico, the US carried out operations at major military bases in Vieques, and Culebra (two offshore islands) and in Aguadilla, and other towns. Protests against the US military gained momentum[3] as activists organized to stop the Navy's use of Culebra as a military base. University students demonstrated against the draft and the ROTC presence on campuses. The colonial police, with the backing of US politicians, corporations, and troops, launched a wave of repression against the pro-independence movement, including searches of leaders' homes and arrests.

Against this backdrop, the Young Lords Party had launched "Ofensiva Cadenas," the "Break the Chains Offensive," opening branches in Puerto Rico. The move profoundly impacted every facet of the organization—the leadership, political priorities, structure, and membership. While Juan González, Gloria González, David Pérez, Pablo "Yoruba" Guzmán, and Juan "Fi" Ortiz continued as Central Committee members,

Denise Oliver had resigned in February in disagreement with the decision to move to Puerto Rico. Her absence critically altered the balance of power in the top leadership, leaving Guzmán and Ortiz in the minority position on most issues, and Juan González, Gloria González, and David Pérez as the Central Committee majority in power. Oliver's departure also adversely affected the Young Lords Party's commitment and approach to revolutionary feminist ideals.

From January to July 1971, the Young Lords set up branches in Puerto Rico. Young Lords in the United States developed people's organizations. Members formed activists' collectives in factories, hospitals, and other workplaces, in high schools and colleges, and in Puerto Rican neighborhoods, thus expanding the social justice movement. Among the people's organizations were the HRUM and the PRSU, and the newly formed Workers' Federation, the Community to Defend the Community, and the Women's Union, to name a few. In July, the Central Committee arranged for an organization-wide retreat to evaluate the work of the previous six months. Young Lords assembled in East Harlem, the Bronx, the Lower East Side, Philadelphia, Bridgeport, and in Aguadilla and Santurce, Puerto Rico. Cadres and branch leaders submitted reports, describing their activities and preoccupations. Members expressed enthusiasm for the retreat as an opportunity to weigh in on the Young Lords Party's future.

WHICH DIRECTION FORWARD?

The obvious question facing the retreat was, "Should the organization continue in Puerto Rico?" From the moment, the decision to open branches in the archipelago was announced, it had caused disharmony. The move to Puerto Rico launched an organizational restructuring that weakened the Young Lords Party. The Central Committee members closed US branch offices and abandoned "serve the people" programs. When they opened a national office on 117th Street and Third Avenue in El Barrio, they pulled leading cadres out of local areas to staff it. The move to Puerto Rico depleted resources. Moreover, it triggered a steady stream of resignations, including those of leading women officers such as Denise Oliver, Connie Morales, and Letty Lozano.[4] Hence, most cadre looked forward to the retreat, expecting a thorough report and discussion about the work in Puerto Rico to assess whether to continue with the branches in the archipelago. However, the question about whether to continue in Puerto Rico was not on the agenda.

At the end of the retreat, the Central Committee issued a forty-nine-page document titled the "July 1971 Retreat Paper." It contained three main announcements. First, it praised the YLP's move to Puerto Rico. Second, it declared Puerto Rico's independence struggle as the *main* mission of the Young Lords Party. Third, it outlined plans for a YLP Congress in 1972. About the move to Puerto Rico, the report boasted:

> This [Ofensiva Cadenas or the Break the Chains Offensive] was the most important offensive in our history, beginning the reunification of the Puerto Rican nation. The greatest impact was felt on the front [Puerto Rico].[5]

It was an extravagant and fantastical claim.

In reality, Puerto Ricans watched the Young Lords' arrival in Puerto Rico with curiosity and skepticism. The leading *independentista* organizations—Movimiento Pro Independencia and the Puerto Rican Independence Party—shunned the Young Lords Party, calling the organization arrogant and infantile. They criticized the Young Lords as outsiders unfamiliar with local conditions, language, culture, and the experience of the anticolonial struggle, all which were true. Even the Young Lords cadre sent to organize in Puerto Rico voiced reservations. A few could not speak Spanish well and had never lived in Puerto Rico. As frontline organizers, they lived harsh realities. They shouldered the brunt of severely under resourced branches and went without necessities, at times, even food. Moreover, organizing strategies effective in the United States did not gain traction in this new environment. By July 1971, the cadres in Puerto Rico were fatigued and demoralized.

IMPACT ON GENDER AND RACIAL JUSTICE ORGANIZING

The Central Committee proponents of the Puerto Rico project disregarded the criticisms and hardships. Instead, they unilaterally declared the national liberation of Puerto Rico the Young Lords Party's main mission. Cadres questioned how the shift in political priorities would affect organizing in the United States but received no satisfactory answer. Confusion swelled in the rank and file, and the organizing work deteriorated. The Central Committee blamed the cadres for devoting too much attention to the sexism issue.[6] However, most Young Lords were men not focused on gender discrimination or women's liberation, and the Women's Caucus had been disbanded and was no longer active. Nonetheless, the Central Committee members outlined what they deemed the "correct political priorities":

> The biggest contradictions are the division of the nation and the division between classes. Then come the divisions of sex and race.[7]

The statement exposed a political shift. Just six months earlier, the Central Committee had published the YLP Position Paper on Women, asserting antiracism, antipoverty, and gender justice as equal political priorities. It emphasized that women's emancipation was integral to human liberation and not at odds with Puerto Rico's national liberation struggle.[8] But now they Central Committee ignored the YLP Position Paper.

To reinforce the position that "divisions of sex and race" were secondary, the Central Committee delivered new directives. Heavy criticism fell on the Women's Union. Characterizing the WU's rapid growth as a "political mistake," the Central Committee members halted plans to open the Women's Union in Puerto Rico.[9] "It was incorrect to have put so much emphasis in this organization,"[10] they claimed. Though they did not close the Women's Union in New York, they set forth new priorities as follows: "to organize women workers and lumpen," "to establish day care centers," and to spread *La Luchadora*.[11] These were grandiose goals. Without resources and an action plan, they were not a serious commitment to feminist organizing. Similarly, the Central Committee members failed to address rising homophobia reported by cadres and abolished the homosexual caucuses"[12] without an organizational plan or support to the cadres.

Most astonishing was the order to cease talking about *sexism*.[13] The Central Committee claimed, "Too much time had been given to sexism. This was incorrect."[14] It was another political reversal. The Central Committee had introduced the concept of sexism in the December 1970 retreat paper and published it in the pamphlet *The Ideology of the Young*

Lords Party. It explained, "Sexism is the ideology of a division of the sexes. Male chauvinism and passivity are its results."[15] But the July 1971 Retreat Paper argued that sexism was "too extreme" because there was insufficient understanding of machismo. The Central Committee instructed the Young Lords that discussions with the public (the mass line) should be about "machismo and passivity."[16] As discussed earlier, this idea was more acceptable because it conveyed a false equivalency in the power between men and women and avoided conversations about dismantling the system of male supremacy.

The Central Committee's "correct political priorities" also showed collapsing commitments to racial justice struggles, which had been central to the Young Lords' revolutionary nationalist ideology and activism. When cadres reported in the retreat mounting racism in the Young Lords Party, the Central Committee members blamed it on the cadres' overemphasis on sexism.[17] Still, Young Lords asked, "What does racial justice organizing as secondary to nation and class look like?" African Americans, approximately 20 percent of the membership, sought clarification. They felt the "divided nation" theory and strategy did not represent their interests. However, the Central Committee majority offered no answer, other than to suggest African Americans learn Spanish "to do better organizing."[18] This shocking and patronizing response triggered more resignations. The Health Revolutionary Unity Movement also rejected the "divided nation" strategy, stating the future of the HRUM workers was in the United States, not in Puerto Rico. Last, the Central Committee reneged on its pledge to organize Afro-Puertorriqueños in Puerto Rico, although Gloria González had written that it was one of the reasons for the YLP expansion to Puerto Rico.

Behind the tug-of-war about political priorities and claims the Women's Union had grown too quickly were beliefs that national liberation and women's liberation movements were competitors. The underlying assumption was that if women pursued gender interests, their support for nationalist causes would weaken. Furthermore, nationalists did not consider gender and racial justice struggles as essential to Puerto Rico's anticolonial struggle. They claimed *women's issues* would be addressed when Puerto Rico achieved its national independence. The conflict of ideas between the Central Committee and the Women's Union pointed simultaneously to different futures.

The July 1971 retreat marked a crucial setback. In one fell swoop, the Central Committee members imposed "narrow nationalism." Obsessed with taking leadership in Puerto Rico's independence movement, "Ofensiva Cadenas" or the "Break the Chains Offensive" turned the Young Lords Party in the United States into a base of operations (the base) for the Puerto Rico project (the front). In shifting funds and cadre to open YLP branches in Puerto Rico, the political organizing work suffered. The US branches and sections were floundering. In Puerto Rico, Young Lords grappled with challenges of building an organization from scratch with limited resources, experience, and guidance. Although the Young Lords Party was clearly struggling with the new political direction, the Central Committee majority concluded the biggest problem was lack of funding.[19]

The July 1971 retreat offered a crossroads opportunity to correct mistakes, but the Central Committee squandered it. To be clear, the error was not the opening of branches in Puerto Rico. Rather, it was the flawed analysis, approach, and implementation. The Central Committee majority failed to delineate between conditions in Puerto Rico and the United States and develop organizing plans and strategies relevant to each, as Guzmán had proposed. Furthermore, the Puerto Rico expansionists failed to honestly assess the YLP's capacity, even though cadres and local leaders reported the challenges facing the branches and cadres. Along with the narrow nationalist focus, the Central Committee majority became increasingly authoritarian and arrogant, refusing to listen to the recommendations and advice of Young Lords, and other activists and longtime supporters.

POST–JULY 1971 RETREAT

Though the Central Committee criticized the Women's Union as an example of "incorrect" priorities, we continued to organize in the same manner. We naively thought we could carry out our political work, independently of the July retreat pronouncements and the Central Committee's involvement. From July to December 1971, the WU facilitated political education workshops and produced and distributed *La Luchadora*'s July and August issues. Joining other activists and feminists of color, WU members took part in protests across the city. In September, when more than one thousand prisoners, demanding humane conditions, took over Attica Correctional Facility in upstate New York, WU members marched in support for twenty-five consecutive days. We protested Governor Nelson Rockefeller's assault on prisoners and demanded his indictment for forty-three murders.[20] When New York announced budget cuts, firing teachers, providing fewer funds for supplies, and ending reduced bus and train farecards for students, WU members joined the Third World Students' League and two thousand students at the Board of Education to protest the cutbacks.[21] In November, about four hundred students, including members of the Puerto Rican Student Union and the Women's Union, attended a conference at Princeton University to advocate for Puerto Rican working-class students.[22]

SEXISM AND COLONIALISM

The July retreat paper did not explain why the Central Committee leadership objected so vigorously to speaking about "sexism" with the public. With the benefit of hindsight, several reasons stand out. First, most of the Central Committee members were nationalists who believed gender and racial struggles were not essential to the liberation struggle. Second, ending the systemic oppression of women of color and system of male domination was not a heartfelt cause. Most Central Committee members lacked education and understanding about the herstory of women of color and did not prioritize learning it. Last, the Puerto Rico expansion proponents obsessed with taking leadership in the pro-independence movement assumed that revolutionary socialist feminist ideas regarding the role of gender and racial justice would not be welcomed in the independence movement. On this point, they were not mistaken.

According to feminist scholars in Puerto Rico, the entire political spectrum in the 1970s criticized feminism "as an external, foreign, colonial imposition, and/or a contagion influence" threatening to traditional values and roles.[23] Political parties and ideologies ignored feminist organizations. They demonized Puerto Rican feminists as an outgrowth of the US white women's movement or "an aberration spawned by the yanqui radical Left," as Puerto Rican Socialist Party member Carmen Vivian Rivera observed.[24] They viewed women's rights as a distraction.[25] To speak of women's rights and be accepted by men, it was necessary to affirm heterosexuality and recognize class conflict as the primary social struggle. Many groups were silent on issues of race and racism, and heterosexism and heteronormativity.[26]

Nonetheless, women's rights advocates in Puerto Rico organized to improve education, workplace conditions, and family planning alternatives. They fought for reproductive rights, including abortion and maternity leave. Women mobilized to end domestic violence, sexual harassment, and sexist media representations. Theirs was a dual militancy, as women and as *independentistas* to end US colonialism. According to feminist scholar María I. Bryant, nationalist, socialist, and independence parties in Puerto Rico "privileged the struggle for national liberation and relegated women's and/or feminist activism to secondary status."[27] In a study of *Claridad*, Puerto Rico's main *independentista* newspaper, Bryant found that the "rhetoric of liberation and self-determination rarely made reference to women or addressed the question of the nation from the perspective of women."[28]

The pro-independence organizations in Puerto Rico argued that women's issues would be handled after the success of the anticolonial revolution. Yet, history is full of examples showing that women's struggles in anticolonial and nationalist movements throughout the world, although vital, do not automatically translate into enduring gains for women when the new nation is established.[29] Many studies have examined this theme. For women's political activism to transform into emancipating policies, gender equality must be embedded in the revolutionary demands and struggles from the beginning.[30]

In the article "The Possibility of Nationalist Feminism," scholar Ranjoo S. Herr concludes:

> [E]ven when national independence is achieved, the tension between nationalism and feminism continues. Although male nationalists have encouraged the participation of feminists in nationalist struggles by promising that feminist issues will be addressed once these struggles succeed, feminists have often been betrayed in the end.[31]

The global experiences of feminists affirm that activists in nationalist and anticolonial struggles must pursue feminist and nationalist goals simultaneously.[32] Postcolonial examples show that women's oppression continues even under socialism[33] as does racism. Hence the struggles for gender and racial justice continue so long as the remnants of inequality remain.

THE CENTRAL COMMITTEE SQUASHES APPEALS OF YOUNG LORDS

By the fall of 1971, the Young Lords Party was in disarray. Several Central Committee members were out of New York at the time. Pablo "Yoruba" Guzmán was on a US delegation, representing the Young Lords Party in China. Juan González was on a speaking tour in Hawaii, and Gloria González was in Puerto Rico, supervising the new branches and the Workers' Federation. When Guzmán returned, Central Committee members David Pérez and Juan "Fi" Ortiz reported grave organizational problems, especially the continuing decline in membership. Close to sixty Young Lords left the New York organization during the weeks Guzmán was away.[34]

After meeting with Pérez and Ortiz, Guzmán wrote and circulated a paper titled "Our Present Situation: Statement, Analysis and Suggestions" dated November 10, 1971.[35] He distributed the paper to the Central Committee—Ortiz, David Pérez, Juan González, Gloria González (now using the name Fontanez)—and to the national staff (Richie Pérez, Juan Ramos, Benjy Cruz, Huracán Flores, and me). Inspired by the China trip, Guzmán recommended a full membership discussion regarding the difficulties, a "rectification movement" he called it. It was a call for democracy. Ortiz, Richie Pérez, Ramos, and I supported the rectification movement confident that the cadres were eager for the exchange that never materialized at the July retreat. We favored rethinking and redesigning the Puerto Rico project. On November 14, 1971, Guzmán sent a second report to González and Fontanez[36] emphasizing, "[O]ur situation is bad, both in Puerto Rico and the U.S. … Many departures of important Party people. … Demoralization reigns."

In an initial response to the problems, Guzmán, David Pérez, and Ortiz transferred members out of the Women's Union into the weaker people's organizations to strengthen them. Guzmán reported he had consensus from the New York central and national staffs to do so.[37] Pérez called me to a meeting to inform me of the decision. I did not agree with the shutdown of the Women's Union. Pérez repeated, "The Women's Union was supposed to be the last priority but developed faster than the Workers' Federation, which was supposed to be the first." I replied that I was assigned to organize the Women's Union." He accused me of caring more about women's issues than those of workers. "Women are also workers and face problems of childcare, reproductive rights, sexual violence, and others not fought solely at the workplace," I argued. The WU members are homemakers, working-class students, workers, and welfare mothers," I insisted. Pérez repeated that the Women's Union had grown too rapidly. "We don't have the resources." He ended the conversation, conflating the lack of political vision, commitment, and funds as the rationale to end the Women's Union.

When González and Fontanez returned to New York, they pulled the Central Committee members into a closed-door meeting, not a general membership meeting as proposed. At the end of three weeks, the group distributed a twenty-five-page document titled "Communiqué of Central Committee,"[38] announcing Juan González, Gloria Fontanez, and David Pérez as the "Executive Committee" of the Young Lords Party. With this action, the Central Committee majority became official. They reaffirmed the "divided nation" politics and charged the rectification movement supporters with violating "democratic centralism" for speaking with cadres and "thinking about forming two organizations, one in Puerto Rico and another in the United States."[39]

As punishment for proposing a general members' discussion about the Puerto Rico project, the Executive Committee demoted Guzmán, Ortiz, Richie Pérez, Ramos, and me from the YLP leadership and transferred us out of our home branches. Ramos, cofounder of the Philadelphia branch, was sent to Aguadilla, Puerto Rico; Ortiz to El Caño in Santurce, Puerto Rico; and Guzmán and I to Philadelphia.[40] My transfer also ended my participation and membership in the Women's Union. The Executive Committee actions squashed the rectification movement but lost the respect of veteran cadres and other movement activists for their antidemocratic methods and narrow nationalist politics.

In January 1972, I arrived at the Young Lords storefront office located at Third and Diamond Streets in North Philadelphia and joined the steering committee—Pablo "Yoruba" Guzmán, Michael Rodríguez, and Gloria Rodríguez. For the next two years, we organized with migrant, factory, and hospital workers, and university students. We collaborated with the Black Panther Party and the Yellow Seeds, an Asian organization.[41] Frank Rizzo, the right-wing mayor of Philadelphia and former police commissioner, kept us under constant police surveillance and harassment.

In 1973, Guzmán and Michael Rodríguez were imprisoned. Guzmán was sentenced to two years for refusing induction into the US Army. Michael Rodríguez was convicted of machine gun possession in a frame-up by an agent from the Bureau of Alcohol, Tobacco, and Firearms. Incarcerated in federal prisons in Florida and Virginia, respectively, neither Guzmán nor Rodríguez received a visit from any Executive Committee member. In Philadelphia, Gloria Rodríguez and I were on our own without financial resources or guidance from the national organization. In retrospect, we were better off, away from the Executive Committee's incessant ideological debates, power grabs, and dogmatic politics.

NARROW NATIONALISTS TAKE CONTROL OF THE WOMEN'S UNION

Early in 1972, the Executive Committee members relaunched the Women's Union under the direct control of Gloria Fontanez. They redefined the WU's mission and purpose to mirror the Young Lords Party's political priorities. The Executive Committee actions flagrantly trampled on the revolutionary principle that women as women must organize and lead the fight for their own liberation before, during, and after a socialist revolution.[42] Under Fontanez's direction, the WU's purpose was to recruit women to support Puerto Rico's national liberation struggle. Women's issues, such as reproductive rights and access to birth control, abortion, and health care, ending gender violence, equal pay for women of color, ending institutional discrimination of women of color, among others, were to be addressed when Puerto Rico became an independent nation.

The Women's Union had developed a 12-Point Program, an intersectional feminist agenda. It declared, "We want equality for women—

down with machismo and *sexism*." But the Executive Committee members discarded it and instructed WU members to stop using the term "sexism" and use "machismo and passivity" instead. It was a return to the nationalist ideas that socialist feminist had defeated in the YLP Position Paper on Women in September 1970.

During 1972, the Women's Union ceased to have any independence or autonomy. The Executive Committee specified the tasks to be carried out by the WU members. These were: (1) to set up a childcare center for activists living in the Lower East Side, (2) to produce and distribute *La Luchadora* newspaper, and (3) to work to release Lolita Lebrón from prison.[43] The day-care center project for activists ended within three months[44] due to conflicts with city agencies over permits.[45] *La Luchadora* was never produced again. In March 1971, WU members organized a film screening and talk regarding Lebrón's release, but there were no follow-up activities.[46]

By the end of 1972, the Women's Union no longer existed.

DECLINE OF THE YOUNG LORDS PARTY

March 21, 1972 marked the Young Lords' one-year anniversary in Puerto Rico. Juan González, minister of defense, described its significance in *Palante*:

> We began to make clear that our goals are not just to fight for decent health care, against unemployment, racism, police brutality and indecent housing. We made it clear that we are fighting *principally* for the freedom of the colony of Puerto Rico."[47]

In the article, González admitted the YLP's move to Puerto Rico had caused difficulties: office closings, erratic publication of *Palante*, irregular community programming, and departure of members. He blamed the problems on the "impatience of some leaders, the youthfulness of members, and the lack of working-class consciousness"[48] but did not mention the "divided nation" political line and practice.

González announced the Young Lords Party Congress planned for later in the year. Its purpose, he explained, was "to establish the beginning of *true democracy* in the organization" and articulate "a new step in the struggle for national liberation and socialism for Puerto Rico and the

United States."[49] The lofty goal meant little in practice, as subsequent events illustrate.

A couple of months before the congress, Juan "Fi" Ortiz and Juan Ramos, leaders of the Young Lords Party in Puerto Rico, along with the cadres, recommended closing the branches in the archipelago. They believed the role of the YLP was to fight for the rights of Puerto Ricans in the United States. In a fit of rage, Gloria Fontanez accused them of betraying the Puerto Rican nation and abandoning the Puerto Rican people. Nevertheless, the YLP leaders and most of the cadres in Puerto Rico officially resigned on May 20, 1972, and the Puerto Rico branches closed. Some of us heard from members in Puerto Rico about the arguments with the Executive Committee, but we learned about the resignations through *Palante.* In a full-page attack, the Executive Committee branded the former Young Lords in Puerto Rico as "splitters" and accused them of "factionalism."[50] In this way, the Puerto Rico project came to a bitter and disgraceful end.

About a month later, two nights before the YLP Congress, the Executive Committee held a meeting with Young Lords in the United States and declared the "divided nation" theory was an "error."

> Originally, we felt that the Puerto Ricans in Puerto Rico and the U.S. together made up a divided nation, and that one party must be built to serve the interests of the workers of this divided nation. This was wrong. The Puerto Rican nation is not divided; it is in Puerto Rico.[51]

Veteran cadres like myself and others speculated that the Executive Committee's flip-flop was likely a preemptive maneuver to hold onto their leadership positions in the upcoming party congress.[52]

The Executive Committee's admission that the "divided nation" idea had been an "error" came too late. For two years, Juan González, Gloria Fontanez, and David Pérez refused to heed warnings that it was a mistake. Instead, they became more and more intransigent.[53] González later admitted that he and Fontanez were the principals responsible for continuing the damaging policies and expelling members.[54]

Many Young Lords had sounded the alarm. Pablo "Yoruba" Guzmán, Denise Oliver, and Juan "Fi" Ortiz had opposed the initial proposal to open YLP branches in Puerto Rico. Early in 1971, Carlos Aponte had raised questions, and the Central Committee branded him a police agent. Six months later at the July retreat, numerous members—feminists, African Americans, HRUM workers, and LBGTQ cadres—opposed the "divided nation" politics. By late 1971, with membership in rapid decline, Guzmán, Ortiz, Richie Pérez, Juan Ramos, and I called for a full membership discussion. In retaliation, the Executive Committee demoted us from leadership and transferred us to other branches. More members departed at this time, pushed away by the narrow nationalist and authoritarian politics. The 1972 resignations of Ortiz, Ramos, and other members in Puerto Rico marked the last attempt to rectify the Young Lords Party's biggest political mistake.

From June 30 to July 3, 1972, the Young Lords and members of people's organizations attended the party congress held in the South Bronx. A new crop of activists supported the name change from Young Lords Party to the Puerto Rican Revolutionary Workers Organization (PRRWO). They accepted Gloria Fontanez, Carmen Cruz, and Juan González as the new Executive Committee.[55] The party congress documents published a response to the recurring question, "What is the relationship of Puerto Ricans in the United States to Puerto Rico's national liberation struggle?"

> Revolutionaries who feel their work is primarily the national liberation of Puerto Rico should be there, living among the people, working, raising families, learning the conditions there as they unite with other revolutionaries to build the party of the proletariat in Puerto Rico.[56]

The statement echoed Pablo "Yoruba" Guzmán's proposal made in 1971. However, by mid-1972, the declaration was too late. By then, the Puerto Rico expansionists had dismantled the Young Lords Party. Thousands of members had resigned or drifted away. Yet, despite the zeal for creating an organization in Puerto Rico, none of the Central Committee's proponents of the Puerto Rico expansion followed the resolution. None went to live in Puerto Rico and unite with others to build the party of the proletariat. During the party congress, I was still in Philadelphia. I returned to New York City in late 1974 and resigned from the organization in early January 1975.

In the years that followed, the Puerto Rican Revolutionary Workers Organization turned inward. At the helm, a power-hungry and frenzied Fontanez launched a reign of terror and violence against everyone who disagreed with her. At her side were misinformed and inexperienced youth, opportunists, and undercover police who accompanied her to carry out beatings, torture, and intimidation. Fontanez betrayed the revolutionary movement, the Women's Caucus, and the Women's Union. She was not alone—the corruption of ideals and resort to abuse when a small group in an organization gains too much power is a common story. By 1976, the PRRWO had faded into history.

AFTERMATH OF THE YOUNG LORDS' FEMINIST ORGANIZING

The Young Lords Party represented a new chapter of Puerto Rican militancy in the United States that championed the rights of Puerto Ricans, galvanized a grassroots movement, and inspired a generation. Counterintelligence operations and internal political conflicts played a role in the organization's demise. My earlier book *Through the Eyes of Rebel Women: The Young Lords, 1969–1976* details the conditions and factors behind the decline.[57] Members left at different times and places and in different ways. Each person came to terms with the experience in her or his own way. Some never wanted to speak of revolution again. Others recognized the Young Lords' contributions to the Puerto Rican struggles for social justice and national liberation.

In the aftermath, many former Young Lords pursued new paths to engage in collective struggles for economic and social justice, women's rights, and the decolonization of Puerto Rico. Former women members took part in committees to free Puerto Rican political prisoners and joined activists in the 1977 takeover of the Statue of Liberty, demanding the release of Puerto Rican Nationalists in prison since the 1950s. Similarly, former women members joined committees to free another generation of Puerto Rican political prisoners released in 1999. Many took part in the fight to expel the US navy from Vieques, Puerto Rico. Other assisted in forming and leading the Congress for Puerto Rican Rights. Still others protested and campaigned against police violence, demanding justice, and supporting victims' families.

Former Young Lords entered the labor and the working-class sector as organizers. Sonia Ivany, the first woman member in the New York chapter, went on to become president of the New York City Labor Council for Latin American Advancement; Minerva Solla, a national organizer with 1199 SEIU (United Healthcare Workers East); and Cleo Silvers, a national organizer with the Black Workers' Congress. Many others became educators and college professors such as Denise Oliver, Martha Duarte (Arguello), Gloria Rodríguez, and Diana Caballero, teaching courses in anthropology, women's and gender studies, Caribbean history, psychology, bilingual/multicultural education, and related topics. Others, like Olguie Robles, entered the nonprofit sector, providing counseling services to Puerto Ricans and African Americans in drug rehabilitation programs, and Letty Lozano, working with urban youth programs. Several, like Nydia Mercado, become medical doctors working in local communities. Some became lawyers and judges, like Myrna Martínez, Gloria Colón, Marlin Segarra, and me. Still others, like Elba Saavedra, created organizations dedicated to women's health, or for women's spiritual and personal development, like Gloria Rodríguez, or to produce educational media, like me.

Whatever avenue former women members chose, we continued to engage with Puerto Rican, Latinx, African American, Indigenous, and Asian communities, social justice activists, and young people toward a just and humane society for all oppressed people. We remained committed to the revolutionary principles and ideals we embraced as members of the Young Lords Party.

PART V.
RECKONING WITH THE PAST

A search for keys in past history to help
explain our time—a time that also makes history—
on the basis that the first condition for
changing reality is to understand it.[1]

—Eduardo Galeano, Open Veins of Latin America, 1973

14.
STATE SURVEILLANCE, POLICE VIOLENCE, AND THE ENEMY WITHIN

> By all indications, domestic covert operations
> have become a permanent feature of U.S. politics.
> … [I]n the name of protecting our fundamental
> freedoms, the FBI and the police systematically
> subvert them.[1]
>
> —Brian Glick, preface to *The COINTELPRO Papers*, 1990

To appreciate the challenges of social justice organizing in the United States, it is important to study the intertwined histories of policing, race, and class. Ruling and financial elites are in sharp opposition to those seeking freedom and justice. "Southern slave owners used slave patrols to maintain their 'private property'; the Northern bourgeoisie used the police to repress strikers and send them back to work."[2] During the 1960s and 1970s, the US government and police resorted to all available tactics of violence, surveillance, sabotage, and suppression of democratic and human rights to prevent the furtherance of social justice.

This chapter describes the activities of the FBI's Counterintelligence Program (COINTELPRO) and the New York City police department against the Young Lords Organization and members. Police surveillance, infiltration, harassment, and fabricated criminal charges beset the organization from its inception. The FBI and New York's Red Squad conducted parallel operations. They hired informants, infiltrators, special undercover agents, and provocateurs to destroy the movement. The political police who infiltrated the Young Lords were Puerto Rican, African American, and Latinx, men and women, who showed up at the Young Lords' offices and activities pretending to be friends, revolutionaries, nationalists, and "servants of the people." With smiling faces and disguised purposes, they worked against the aspirations of Puerto Rican activists and revolutionaries.

The full scope of counterintelligence activities directed against the Young Lords is still unknown. Almost fifty years after the organization's demise, the extent of FBI and police involvement remains undocumented. What role did counterintelligence actions have in the Young Lords' move to Puerto Rico, in dismantling the New York organization, and in shutting down racial and gender justice organizing? And what was the role of the political police in the violence and torture of members in the later years?

COINTELPRO: COUNTERINTELLIGENCE PROGRAM

The Counterintelligence Program known as COINTELPRO began in 1956 to destroy the Communist Party of the United States.[3] To stimulate the "red scare," the FBI collaborated with media outlets, publicizing disparaging information about the party[4] and circulating dossiers of alleged communists. By the 1960s, the FBI was focused on destroying the New Left, including anti–Vietnam War activism and the Black Liberation movement. The Chicago Young Lords were close allies of the Black Panther Party and were targeted from the group's inception in 1968. José "Cha Cha" Jiménez, the YLO's founder, and Fred Hampton, leader of the Chicago Black Panther Party, became friends during concurrent stints in jail. Uniting to fight poverty and racism, the Black Panthers, the YLO, and the Young Patriots, an organization of white southerners, formed the Rainbow Coalition. The FBI identified the alliance as a threat and was "quite active in sabotaging it" to "drive a wedge" in the movement.[5]

In 1969, FBI director J. Edgar Hoover declared the Black Panther Party "the greatest threat to the internal security of the United States."[6] Hoover set the foundation to destroy the organization and its members.[7] An earlier memorandum instructed agents in fourteen field offices to "submit imaginative and hard-hitting counter-intelligence measures aimed at crippling the Black Panther Party" within a context of "gang warfare" and "attendant threats of murder and reprisal."[8] FBI tactics ranged "from the petty to the outright murderous," including political assassinations,[9] such as the killings of Black Panther leaders Fred Hampton and Mark Clark as they slept in their beds in Chicago on December 4, 1969.[10]

By the time the Young Lords' chapter formed in New York City on July 26, 1969, the political police had heavily infiltrated the Chicago YLO. Hence, it was not surprising that FBI informants attended the Young Lords' inaugural rally in Tompkins Square Park and submitted reports to their handlers. When the Young Lords Party opened branches in Puerto Rico, COINTELPRO's scrutiny continued. The FBI had a long history of surveilling the anticolonial movement, dating back to the 1930s when the agency devised a program to destroy the Puerto Rican Nationalist Party.[11] In the 1960s, Hoover directed operatives to gather data about pro-independence leaders.[12] Their plan was to exploit factionalism—a fault they identified as endemic within activists' groups.[13]

The FBI kept COINTELPRO activities secret. They only came to public attention in 1971 when a group of anti–Vietnam War activists broke into an FBI office in Pennsylvania. They took more than one thousand classified COINTELPRO documents and mailed them to major newspapers.[14] The documents exposed far-reaching government-sanctioned surveillance and criminal activities against a broad cross section of progressive organizations and individuals.[15]

NYC BUREAU OF SPECIAL SERVICES: "THE RED SQUAD"

The New York City police conducted its own counterintelligence operations. Its undercover agents joined activist organizations, gathered information, and fueled internal conflicts. The department's Bureau of Special Services, "BoSS" or "the Red Squad," operated as a separate political police force trained in undercover surveillance.[16] Between 1968 and 1970, the Red Squad increased its forces from sixty-eight officers to ninety.[17] They fostered illegal activity and stirred up violence.[18] Operatives arranged elaborate frame-ups with fabricated evidence,[19] such as the case of the Panther 21, which accused Black Panther Party members of plotting to blow up department stores and police stations. More than two years after the initial charges, on May 12, 1971, the case went to trial "A jury took just ninety minutes to decide they were not guilty on all 159 counts."[20] Although the verdict acquitted all the defendants, the case took a toll on the Harlem chapter of the Black Panther Party.

POLITICAL POLICE TACTICS AND OBJECTIVES

In a 1967 memo, FBI director Hoover instructed agents to "expose, disrupt, misdirect, discredit, or otherwise neutralize" the social justice movement.[21] The mission was to destroy revolutionary organizations by any means. Undercover agents in the Young Lords Organization gathered information, collecting reports, news clippings, copies of speeches, flyers, transcripts of the *Palante* radio program, articles, letters and other correspondence, bank account records, and photographs. Some conducted wiretapping, bugging, and mail tampering. Others broke into offices, ransacked members' homes, and conducted warrantless searches. Still others used data gathering as a tool to intimidate, contacting employers, landlords, and teachers. Political police agents went to the homes of Young Lords. They visited their family members and knocked on neighbors' doors to frighten and threaten them. There was no consideration of constitutional rights.[22] The *Palante* newspaper documented police fire bombings of Young Lords offices in the Bronx, Newark, Philadelphia, Bridgeport, and El Caño, Puerto Rico. Seeking to raise awareness about political police operations, Young Lords provided instruction in "security consciousness" and published information about "bugging" devices"[23] and other police methods.

Hoover's goal was to "divide, conquer, and weaken" the progressive and revolutionary movements, immobilize organizations, demoralize members, and distort the public image of activists' groups. Police agents identified points of conflict. Their job was to sow dissension among leaders and members. Infiltrators fueled conflicts and preyed on personal and political weaknesses. They fanned jealousies among leaders or stole organizational funds and steered suspicion to others.[24] Agents filed the information they gathered about the organization or individual members by case numbers. The files on an individual contained a detailed political history, personal information, physical description, and facts about family members, creating a profile that assessed the person's weaknesses and vulnerabilities. The FBI targeted leaders, intending to discredit, isolate, or eliminate them.

FBI documents show that agents shared reports among multiple agencies and locations across the United States and Puerto Rico.[25] Federal and local police agencies cooperated with each other. Eager for information to augment their written reports, informants scoured newspapers. I learned this detail from a copy of my FBI file, which I obtained through the Freedom of Information Act. It included articles and stories from *Palante* and other newspapers. The report had more clippings and redacted pages than readable text. I learned that the file was opened in "Mexico City" when I was on a trip to Cuba. The file indicated that ten copies had been distributed to various US agencies, including the FBI field office in New York City. Last, I learned that the opening date of the file was seven months before the Young Lords opened the New York chapter in July 1969.

Fig 22. Philadelphia Young Lords at New York protest.
(Courtesy: Michael Abramson)

COINTELPRO implemented a program of aggressive harassment and violence against the Young Lords. In February 1971, *Palante* published a report titled "Repression against the Young Lords," documenting a long list of arrests in the organization's first eighteen months.[26] Agents approached members any time of day or night. They routinely stopped members in the street or riding the subways. Police harassed Young Lords passing out flyers or selling copies of *Palante*. At demonstrations and protests, police assaulted and beat up Young Lords. They made petty arrests, and members faced recurring charges of felonious assault, obstructing government administration, flight to avoid prosecution, resisting arrest, inciting to riot, arson, and carrying a deadly weapon. The government arrested and detained several members for refusing induction into the US army.

Bogus criminal arrests and charges were a tactic to busy the organization with legal challenges and fundraising activities for bail to get members released from jail. Frivolous arrests had as their purpose to punish and deter people from exercising the fundamental right to protest. Repeated arrests exhausted and detoured members from community organizing activities. The undercover police who arrested Julio Roldán and Bobby Lemus in East Harlem charged them with arson, alleging they had set a fire in the building's vestibule where they lived. As described earlier, the two men were arraigned and locked up in the Tombs. Within days, prison officials reported that Roldán was found hanged in his cell. The police claimed suicide, although there was evidence of a beating.

The FBI's "fingerprints" are all over the Young Lords Party's debates about the move to Puerto Rico. This period in the organization's evolution presented perfect conditions for FBI operatives. Discussions about shifting political priorities were fertile ground to generate chaos and sow dissension. A fractured leadership dismantled the Young Lords Party and accelerated the decline of members, discussed in chapters 11 and 13. The YLP's centralized hierarchical structure afforded little room for the exchange of ideas, and authoritarian rule took control. Throughout the organization's history, some Central Committee members falsely and unjustly accused members who expressed political differences with them of being police agents. While the rank and file were led to believe the allegations, it is likely that real agents and opportunists remained in-cognito and unexposed.

COINTELPRO used physical violence and psychological warfare. Because of the enduring mental and physical impact of these experiences, former YLO members suffered post-traumatic stress disorder (PTSD) from the chronic and acute stress. Unrelenting police and FBI harass-ment caused fatigue and paranoia. The internal dissension and name calling caused mistrust and demoralization. The killing of comrades in-censed us. Beatings and arrests of members enraged us. They exasperated and depressed us. As the movement declined and Young Lords resigned, those who remained suffered the loss of comrades and friends. Our spir-its were wounded.

ACTIVISTS CHALLENGE POLICE SURVEILLANCE

In 1971, a class-action lawsuit challenged the New York Police Depart-ment's practice of keeping dossiers on activists and infiltrating political organizations. The city settled the lawsuit by a consent decree known as the Handschu Agreement. It prohibited police "from investigating polit-ical and religious organizations and groups unless there was 'specific in-formation'" linking the group to a crime.[27] After September 11, 2001, however, the police intensified surveillance against Muslims and sought to expand their powers to scrutinize groups and individuals. Two law-suits challenged these encroachments and won "minimum safeguards" for Muslims.[28]

Another lawsuit in 2016 produced 520 boxes of surveillance files and photographs that the New York Police Department claimed they had lost. The boxes contained records of African American leaders such as Malcolm X and Martin Luther King Jr.; of organizations like the Black Panthers, the Nation of Islam, the Congress of Racial Equality, the Young Lords, and others; and of Vietnam protests and other demonstrations. Responding to this "discovery," Pablo "Yoruba" Guzmán, former minis-ter of information of the Young Lords Party, wrote,

> We would be most interested in discovering who they sent
> in to infiltrate us—who were the undercovers and who was
> subverting what we were doing. But we're not going to find

out who the turncoats were, who the agents were. They're going to redact all that.[29]

Guzmán was correct. The 520 boxes of sanitized files disclosed nothing new. For decades, Young Lords have speculated about the identity of paid agents in the organization. The boxes gave no new clues about the political police's role in orchestrating the demise of the Young Lords Party. COINTELPRO did its job. At the end, only a couple of self-designated "leaders" remained, using gangster tactics and violence against anyone who disagreed with them.

The US government's systematic program and campaign aided the destruction of the late sixties and seventies' political movements. Despite the severe setback, activists have continued to organize people's movements fighting for economic, racial, and gender justice.

15.
"THE PAST DOES NOT EXIST INDEPENDENTLY FROM THE PRESENT"

> We have to keep walking, even if we are short of breath, even if we are tired, even if there are stones in the road, even if we do not see the end. Because a revolution is precisely that. It is to climb as high as you can to touch the clouds in your hand.[1]
>
> —Zuleica Romay Guerra, Director of Afro-American Studies at Casa de las Américas, Havana, 2021

History is often depicted as moving seamlessly from one set of events and ideas to another. The experiences of women members of the Young Lords Organization tell a different story. Histories of colonialism and migration, racism, sexism, and poverty intertwined, collided, ebbed, and flowed. Women joined the organization to fight for the rights of Puerto Ricans in the United States and the national liberation of Puerto Rico. From 1969 through 1972, feminist members brought attention to struggles for gender justice, insisting they were essential to revolutionary change. Our activism sprang from the realities and experiences of marginalized and working-class Puerto Rican, Latina, and African American women and conditions in our communities. We understood our struggles as part of a historical continuum, dating back to slavery and colonialism in the Americas. We believed in the collective power of oppressed people to improve society and collaborated with African American, Chicana, Latina, Asian, and Native feminists, learning from their histories, philosophies, and practices. We understood there were victories and setbacks in the battle for justice and liberation. Though we advocated for short-term reforms, we did not tie our activism to one campaign's success. Our long-term goal was a structural transformation of society. We believed in socialism.

The Young Lords Organization identified as revolutionary nationalist. Socialist feminist ideas and practices developed in the interaction with the nationalist ideology. The exchange shaped the rise and decline of feminism in the organization. Women's struggles proceeded in phases; each had successes and setbacks that offered lessons. It was a battle of ideas, resulting in different consequences and realities for women. Most women members had not studied nationalist or feminist theories or been involved with the white women's liberation movement when they joined the Young Lords. We gained ideological understanding about social movements in the course of our collective organizing activities, specifically in 1970 and 1971. We led campaigns that seeded feminist ideas, organizing approaches and practices that influenced socialist feminist politics later in the decade.[2]

THE WOMEN'S CAUCUS

Early in 1970, women members formed a caucus to end male supremacist practices in the Young Lords Organization and bring attention to the oppression and exploitation of Puerto Rican and other women of color. We challenged the discrepancy between theory and practice. The contradiction between "liberating all oppressed people" stated in the 13-Point Program and the discriminatory treatment of women ignited our demands. The organization's commitment to liberate the Puerto Rican nation and people preserved gender inequality. Although the 13-Point Program stated, "we want equality for women," it described gender oppression as a problem of bad male attitudes and behavior. It showed reluctance to declare an end to patriarchy. The Central Committee's endorsement of "revolutionary machismo," proposed to tinker with male frustrations not to end the "system of social structures and practices in which men dominate and exploit women."[3]

Like Black and other US feminists of color, the Women's Caucus embraced the concept of "triple oppression," analyzing the multiple dominations of women by class, gender, and race. We expected the Young Lords, as a revolutionary group, to fight institutional gender discrimination and advocate for *"women's issues,"* such as reproductive rights and access to birth control, abortion, quality health care, and childcare. However, the leaders of the Young Lords argued that feminist ideas and struggles were a detour from "real political work." As a result of the exchanges and debates, revolutionary socialist feminist ideas and practices ascended. Women members assumed leadership in social justice and reproductive rights campaigns. Debates about gender paved the way for LGBTQ members to join the organization. The YLP published a Position Paper on Women that advanced a socialist feminist analysis, asserting that capitalism, racism, and machismo were interrelated systems of domination. The phrase "the revolution within the revolution" emphasized the struggle for gender justice was ongoing.

Gender studies scholar Kristie Soares sums up the contributions of the Women's Caucus:

> [T]he feminist restructuring of 1970 was one of the most successful examples of feminist organizing within the decolonial movements of the time, in that it introduced a focus on gender rather than a distraction from it.[4]

The Women's Caucus sought to expand the Young Lords' revolutionary nationalist ideology to make it inclusive of women's concerns and interests. Caucus members debunked the idea that women were inferior and brought a focus to the oppression and struggles of Puerto Rican and other women of color. The caucus moved the Young Lords Party to ban gender discrimination in the organization, in words if not always in deeds. Despite progress on these issues, the struggle to uplift women's rights and gender justice campaigns continued. When the Central Committee disbanded the Women's Caucus at the end of 1970, it raised concerns about the YLP's continuing commitment to the liberation struggle of women of color.

THE WOMEN'S UNION

In 1971, feminist struggles in the Young Lords Party entered a second phase. The exchange between nationalist and feminist ideologies deepened when the Central Committee shifted political priorities, declaring Puerto Rico's fight against colonialism as the organization's main mission. In the United States, the YLP developed the Women's Union as a people's organizations to expand the social justice movement. Building on the experiences of the Women's Caucus, the Women's Union was formed as a women-led mass organization with its own steering committee, political priorities, and members. It focused on the interests and concerns of Puerto Rican and African American women in low-income communities, and advocated for *women's issues*, the decolonization of

Puerto Rico, and a socialist society. Members developed an intersectional feminist agenda and collaborated with US feminists of color and other activists for social justice and women's rights.

As revolutionary socialist feminists successfully challenged sexism and advanced revolutionary ideas, the Young Lords Party was exhibiting signs of decline. Narrow nationalist ideas consolidated in the Central Committee with dire consequences. Though the Women's Union had been established as a women-led organization, the Central Committee, made up primarily of males, denied the WU its autonomy. The Central Committee set the WU's political priorities, assigned women their political tasks, and ordered them not to speak publicly about sexism. Taking direct control, the Central Committee members subverted the WU's original ideals and practices. They recruited women for Puerto Rico's national liberation struggle, but not to organize around women-specific concerns, maintaining these would be tackled after the anticolonial revolution was won. These actions were brazen violations of the right of women to self-determination. They illustrate why many women in the revolutionary nationalist movements of the 1960s and 1970s split off to form feminist-led, autonomous, and independent organizations. The Central Committee's pursuit of narrow nationalist politics derailed the struggle for revolutionary socialist feminism.

AFTERMATH OF THE YOUNG LORDS' FEMINIST ORGANIZING

From the 1960s through the mid-1970s, the activism of African American, Latina, Chicana, Puerto Rican, Asian, and Native women created a vital bridge, linking past herstories and struggles to future gender and racial justice movements. In 1974, Black feminist lesbian socialists formed the Combahee River Collective. The "Combahee River Collective Statement," published in 1977, remains central to Black and feminist socialist politics and organizing. Also in 1974, women in the Puerto Rican Socialist Party played important roles in establishing the Committee to End Sterilization Abuse and in passing federal guidelines to protect low-income women from coerced sterilization procedures. In 1975, members of El Comité–MINP (Movimiento de Izquierda Nacional Puertorriqueño), formed the Latin Women's Collective. Chicana feminists sparked a wealth of writings in the 1980s that inspired interest in women of color feminism. Among them was the groundbreaking anthology *This Bridge Called My Back: Writings by Radical Women of Color*, edited by Cherríe Moraga and Gloria Anzaldúa and published in 1981. The shared critique of feminists of color regarding racism, sexism, capitalism, and imperialism laid a theoretical and practical foundation connecting past, present, and future generations.

RECKONING WITH THE PRESENT

Today, feminist organizing must contend with the impact of COVID-19. The pandemic severely exacerbated already existing structural inequalities across the world and within countries. As a result of COVID, millions died, and even more lost their livelihoods and experienced deepening poverty. Meanwhile, billionaires saw their wealth soar. The male capitalist elites who own most of the planet's wealth further enriched themselves from the pandemic and women's labor.[5] COVID-19 made visible women's compounding burdens and society's dependence on women as essential workers, on the front lines and at home:

> [Women] are over-represented working in health systems, continue to do the majority of unpaid care work in households, face high risks of economic insecurity, and face increased risks of violence, exploitation, abuse, or harassment during times of crisis and quarantine.[6]

Although women were already doing most of the world's unpaid care work, the pandemic dramatically increased this burden.[7] It magnified the crisis of socially reproductive work and put a spotlight on the range of unpaid activities women engage in that are essential to the functioning of society, such as childcare, domestic housework, taking care of elderly family members, among others.

In the United States, official reports declared Latina, Black, Indigenous, and immigrant women the biggest pandemic victims, especially women without college degrees.[8] Health disparities heaped on top of other inequities, such as workplace discrimination, rollbacks in reproductive rights, high rates of incarceration, attacks on immigrant families, to name a few. These are the enduring legacy of racial and ethnic inequalities instituted during the first phases of European imperialism and colonization in the Americas.[9]

In Puerto Rico, COVID worsened the humanitarian crisis facing the archipelago under US colonialism. The oppression of Puerto Rican women "cannot be separated from the colonial experience."[10] The relation between colonialism, capitalism, and patriarchy presumes control over both the archipelago and women's bodies.[11] Under the pandemic, gender violence skyrocketed, including state-sanctioned violence, domestic violence, and sexual harassment in the streets and workplaces. The conditions exacerbated by COVID intensified one of the highest femicide rates in the Americas.[12] The battle against gender-based violence is "part of a larger constellation of structural forces that harm women and limit life chances,"[13] as feminist scholar Marisol LeBrón explains. Colonialism is a women's issue. The fight to end gender and racial oppression and violence is intertwined with the struggle against poverty and colonialism.

Despite the world's greatest public health challenge in over a century, the global response to COVID-19 showed possibilities and strategies for creating social justice movements. The pandemic, climate crisis, extreme economic disparities, racial injustice, and gender violence moved millions to question existing power structures and governments. When institutions failed to respond, people acted in solidarity, caring for each other. During 2020, people engaged in extraordinary activism, grassroots organizing, and collaborative efforts. Among the many examples, young people led protests to recognize the human right to a healthy environment. They sought to make the deliberate destruction of nature a crime.[14] Black Lives Matter demonstrations protested systemic anti-Black racism and state-sanctioned killings of Black people in every continent and elevated racial justice demands. A resurgence in global feminist organizing responded to gender violence and advanced demands for reproductive justice and economic and racial equality.[15] Women's organizing efforts, for example, brought about the legalization of abortion in Argentina, Mexico, and Colombia, "three of the four most populous countries in Latin America."[16]

Still, the extreme concentration of wealth and power brings the world's population to a historic crossroads. It calls for demands to redirect wealth and capital to people's needs, human values, and structural changes that promote different ways of living and organizing societies.

Women are central to the societal transformation that is necessary. Human rights lawyer and feminist Erika Guevara Rosas elaborates:

> Solutions can be found only through collective and connected efforts at community, national and global levels. The voices of women and girls must be central to shaping the post-pandemic future. It is not about system recovery after COVID-19, it must be system redesign and transformation, eliminating all forms of gender-based violence and discrimination, while addressing their root causes.[17]

"System redesign and transformation" calls for reimagining and reinventing. It cannot be business as usual. Transforming society must address the intersecting oppressions of class, race, gender, colonialism, and environmental destruction. The voices and strategies of historically excluded peoples and communities, especially low-income Black and marginalized women of color in every part of the world, must be central to action plans.

Revisiting Herstories: The Young Lords Party focuses on the organizing ideas, strategies, and activities of US feminists of color in the late 1960s and early 1970s. As Puerto Rican women activists, we were part of a worldwide movement for societal change in which working class and marginalized Black and women of color played leading roles. The legacies of resistance and collective organizing remind us that people committed to revolutionary principles and actions have the power to achieve change that moves society forward and benefits humanity. Our experiences in the US revolutionary nationalist movements and struggles to end colonialism in Puerto Rico affirm that ending poverty, women's oppression and exploitation, and anti-Black racism must be essential goals and demands of *all* progressive movements. Our struggle continues.

Fig 23. Former members of the Young Lords Party. 2015.
L to R: Wilma, Denise, Minerva, Olguie, Gloria Rodríguez, Iris,
Cookie, and Martha

Fig 24. Fiftieth Anniversary of the Young Lords Party. July 2019.
(Photos courtesy: José Angel Figueroa)

Acknowledgments

T he 2019 uprising in Puerto Rico moved me to write this book. Inspired by the actions of feminists and other activists to remove the corrupt governor and fight for gender and racial justice, led me to revisit the herstories of the Young Lords Party. When COVID-19 put the world on lockdown, I began writing in earnest.

The Young Lords emerged to demand justice and human rights during the worldwide movements of the 1960s and 1970s. I'm honored to have participated alongside amazing Black, Latina, Indigenous, and Asian feminists who performed the day-to-day work of revolutionary change and whose convictions, courage, and compassion formed bonds of comradeship. Women were the heart of the Young Lords Party, and I'm deeply grateful for the experiences we shared. I thank and acknowledge the dedication and commitment of the women with whom I worked most closely: Mecca Adai, Micky Agrait, Marta Arguello, Bernadette Baken, Iris Benítez, Diana Caballero, Lulu Carreras, Gloria Colón, Carmen Copeland, Aida Cruset, Yolanda DeJesus, Yvonne Dominguez, Jenny Figueroa, Elena González, Mirta González, Beverly Kruset, Elsie López, Lulu Limardo, Letty Lozano, Doleza Miah, Myrna Martínez, Nydia Mercado, Carmen Mercado, Connie Morales, Elsie Morales, Denise Oliver, Isa Ríos, Olguie Robles, Gloria Rodríguez, Miriam Rodríguez, Elba Saavedra, Marlin Segarra, Lydia Silva, Cleo Silvers, and Becky Serrano.

I acknowledge all the Young Lords who joined the struggles for social justice, Puerto Rican rights, and the national liberation of Puerto Rico in the late 1960s and early 1970s and who remained true to revolutionary principles and practices, despite the obstacles placed in our way from within and without the organization. The members strong convictions and commitments reflected in the community organizing work and sparked a people's movement. The Young Lords contributed an important chapter to the history/herstory of the Puerto Rican diaspora in the United States.

While there are many who aided me through this project, I would like to acknowledge those without whom completion of this book would not have been possible.

First, I thank my mother Almida Roldan for her guiding spirit and perseverance in the face of adversities.

I thank my compañero José Angel Figueroa for his faithful support. He was my anchor. He believed in the book from day one and his consistent reassurance and belief encouraged me to write and keep writing. I'm grateful for his reading of many drafts. His comments, insights, and poetic reflections led me to dig deeper and uncover forgotten stories.

I thank my dear friend Dr. Deborah Paredez who read an early version and whose enthusiasm gave me confidence to see the project through to the end. I'm grateful for her encouragement, words of support, and friendship.

I owe a debt of gratitude to Dr. Edna Acosta-Belén who graciously accepted my request to read a complete draft of an early manuscript. Her comments and notes prompted me to do further research, enriching the content. I'm thankful for her guidance, patience, and scholarship.

I extend a special thank you to Dr. Barbara Ransby, historian, scholar, and activist. As a long-time admirer and student of her work concerning social justice movements and Black women activists and freedom fighters, I'm grateful to have her support of this book.

Several scholars, colleagues, and friends read drafts of sections or chapters along the way and offered ideas and recommendations that aided my historical exploration and narrative. My heartfelt thanks to Dr. Ujju Aggawal, Dr. Nicole Burrows, Dr. Claudia Sofía Garriga-López, Dr. Rebeca Hey-Colón, Dr. Vanessa Valdes, Dr. Wilson Valentin Escobar, and activist and filmmaker Karina Hurtado-Ocampo. Their probing questions, literature suggestions, and technical comments helped develop and shape the project. Dr. Ariana Mangual read an early proposal and offered wise counsel and support. Dr. Jillian Baez and Dr. Claudine Taffee provided early encouragement. Thank you to Felicitas N. Nunez, Carmen Rivera, and Carmen Vivian Rivera for reading sections and Wendy Barrales and Maya García for conducting preliminary research.

I thank my friend Michael Abramson for allowing me to include his iconic photographs in this book. It's been a pleasure to collaborate on many projects over the years.

Craig Wilse provided a meticulous editorial review of the manuscript. His analysis and observations encouraged me to find the bigger picture in the details.

I thank Norman Ware for his thorough and careful final editing.

Writing during the isolation of the pandemic, communication with family and friends was vital to my spirit and mental health. My son Adrien was a good and thoughtful friend. My grandson Lorenzo made me laugh, often and loudly. My sister Yolanda shared reminiscences. My friends, Vernon Douglas, Patricia Leonard, Anna Gyorgy, Francia Castro, Lori Salmon, sent texts, pictures, and caring messages. Thank you to Angel Antonio Ruiz. DK Dyson, Magdalena Gomez, Lisa Jones, and Betsy Salas for their check-ins.

I extend a special acknowledgement to Dr. Darrel Enck-Wanzer for *The Young Lords: A Reader*, which was a main resource for the Young Lords' documents referenced in the book.

JT Tagaki and Roselly Torres deserve special recognition for their outstanding work, promoting and distributing the documentary, *¡Palante Siempre Palante! The Young Lords*. My thanks to Dr. Yarimar Bonilla, Director of the Center for Puerto Rican Studies, and Dr. Frances Negrón-Muntaner for hosting a commemoration of the film's 25th anniversary and to Edgardo Miranda Rodríguez, Vanessa Roman, and Patria Rodríguez for their participation.

Newsreel and Third World Newsreel deserve special credit for the production and distribution of *¡El Pueblo Se Levanta!* The People Rise Up! Since 1971, the documentary has kept alive a visual history of the Young Lords Party and the anti-colonial struggle of the Puerto Rican people.

APPENDIX

- Thirteen Point Program & Platform (Written October 1969)
- Thirteen Point Program & Platform, (Revised, December 1970)
- Young Lords Party Position Paper on Women (September 1970)
- Why a Women's Union? (June 1971)
- Women's Union 12-Point Program (June 1971)

THE YOUNG LORDS ORGANIZATION IS A REVOLUTIONARY POLITICAL PARTY FIGHTING FOR THE LIBERATION OF ALL OPPRESSED PEOPLE

1. WE WANT SELF-DETERMINATION FOR PUERTO RICANS—LIBERATION ON THE ISLAND AND INSIDE THE UNITED STATES

For 500 years, first spain and then the united states have colonized our country. Billions of dollars in profits leave our country for the united states every year. In every way we are slaves of the gringo. We want liberation and the Power in the hands of the People, not Puerto Rican exploiters.
QUE VIVA PUERTO RICO LIBRE!

2. WE WANT SELF-DETERMINATION FOR ALL LATINOS

Our Latin Brothers and Sisters, inside and outside the united states, are oppressed by amerikkkan business. The Chicano people built the Southwest, and we support their right to control their lives and their land. The people of Santo Domingo continue to fight against gringo domination and its puppet generals. The armed liberation stuggles in Latin America are part of the same war of Latinos against imperialism.
QUE VIVA LA RAZA!

3. WE WANT LIBERATION OF ALL THIRD WORLD PEOPLE

Just as Latins first slaved under spain and then the yanquis, Black people, Indians, and Asians slaved to build the wealth of this country. For 400 years they have fought for freedom and dignity against racist Babylon (decadent empire). Third World people have led the fight for freedom. All the colored and oppressed peoples of the world are one nation under oppression.
NO PUERTO RICAN IS FREE UNTIL ALL PEOPLE ARE FREE!

4. WE ARE REVOLUTIONARY NATIONALISTS AND OPPOSE RACISM

The Latin, Black, Indian and Asian people inside the u.s. are colonies fighting for liberation. We know that washington, wall street, and city hall will try to make our nationalism into racism; but Puerto Ricans are of all colors and we resist racism. Millions of poor white people are rising up to demand freedom and we support them. These are the ones in the u.s. that are stepped on by the rulers and the government. We each organize our people, but our fights are the same against oppression and we will defeat it together.
POWER TO ALL OPPRESSED PEOPLE!

5. WE WANT COMMUNITY CONTROL OF OUR INSTITUTIONS AND LAND

We want control of our communities by our people and programs to guarantee that all institutions serve the needs of our people. People's control of police, health services, churches, schools, housing, transportation and welfare are needed. We want an end to attacks on our land by urban removal, highway destruction, universities and corporations.
LAND BELONGS TO ALL THE PEOPLE!

6. WE WANT A TRUE EDUCATION OF OUR CREOLE CULTURE AND SPANISH LANGUAGE

We must learn our history of fighting against cultural, as well as economic genocide by the yanqui. Revolutionary culture, culture of our people, is the only true teaching.
LONG LIVE BORICUA!   LONG LIVE EL JIBARO!

7. WE OPPOSE CAPITALISTS AND ALLIANCES WITH TRAITORS

Puerto Rican rulers, or puppets of the oppressor, do not help our people. They are paid by the system to lead our people down blind alleys, just like the thousands of poverty pimps who keep our communities peaceful for business, or the street workers who keep gangs divided and blowing each other away. We want a society where the people socialistically control their labor.
VENCEREMOS!

8. WE OPPOSE THE AMERIKKKAN MILITARY

We demand immediate withdrawal of us military forces and bases from Puerto Rico, Vietnam, and all oppressed communities inside and outside the us. No Puerto Rican should serve in the u.s. army against his Brothers and Sisters, for the only true army of oppressed people is the people's army to fight all rulers.
U.S. OUT OF VIETNAM, FREE PUERTO RICO!

9. WE WANT FREEDOM FOR ALL POLITICAL PRISONERS

We want all Puerto Ricans freed because they have been tried by the racist courts of the colonizers, and not by their own people and peers. We want all freedom fighters released from jail.
FREE ALL POLITICAL PRISONERS!

10. WE WANT EQUALITY FOR WOMEN. MACHISMO MUST BE REVOLUTIONARY...NOT OPPRESSIVE

Under capitalism, our people have been oppressed by both the society and our own men. The doctrine of machismo has been used by our men to take out their frustrations against their wives, sisters, mothers, and children. Our men must support their women in their fight for economic and social equality, and must recognize that our women are equals in every way within the revolutionary ranks.
FORWARD, SISTERS, IN THE STRUGGLE!

11. WE FIGHT ANTI-COMMUNISM WITH INTERNATIONAL UNITY.

Anyone who resists injustice is called a communist by "the man" and condemned. Our people are brainwashed by television, radio, newspapers, schools, and books to oppose people in other countries fighting for their freedom. No longer will our people believe attacks and slanders, because they have learned who the real enemy is and who their real friends are. We will defend our Brothers and Sisters around the world who fight for justice against the rich rulers of this country.
VIVA CHE!

12. WE BELIEVE ARMED SELF-DEFENSE AND ARMED STRUGGLE ARE THE ONLY MEANS TO LIBERATION

We are opposed to violence—the violence of hungry children, illiterate adults, diseased old people, and the violence of poverty and profit. We have asked, petitioned, gone to courts, demonstrated peacefully, and voted for politicians full of empty promises. But we still ain't free. The time has come to defend the lives of our people against repression and for revolutionary war against the businessman, politician, and police. When a government oppresses our people, we have the right to abolish it and create a new one.
BORICUA IS AWAKE!   ALL PIGS BEWARE!

13. WE WANT A SOCIALIST SOCIETY

We want liberation, clothing, free food, education, health care, transportation, utilities, and employment for all. We want a society where the needs of our people come first, and where we give solidarity and aid to the peoples of the world, not oppression and racism.
HASTA LA VICTORIA SIEMPRE!

Fig 25. Thirteen-Point Program. October 1969.

YOUNG LORDS PARTY

13 POINT PROGRAM

AND PLATFORM

THE YOUNG LORDS PARTY IS A REVOLUTIONARY POLITICAL PARTY FIGHTING FOR THE LIBERATION OF ALL OPPRESSED PEOPLE

1. WE WANT SELF-DETERMINATION FOR PUERTO RICANS, LIBERATION ON THE ISLAND AND INSIDE THE UNITED STATES.

For 500 years, first spain and then the united states have colonized our country. Billions of dollars in profits leave our country for the united states every year. In every way we are slaves of the gringo. We want liberation and the Power in the hands of the People, not Puerto Rican exploiters. QUE VIVA PUERTO RICO LIBRE!

2. WE WANT SELF-DETERMINATION FOR ALL LATINOS.

Our Latin Brothers and Sisters, inside and outside the united states, are oppressed by amerikkkan business. The Chicano people built the Southwest, and we support their right to control their lives and their land. The people of Santo Domingo continue to fight against gringo domination and its puppet generals. The armed liberation struggles in Latin America are part of the war of Latinos against imperialism. QUE VIVA LA RAZA!

3. WE WANT LIBERATION OF ALL THIRD WORLD PEOPLE.

Just as Latins first slaved under spain and the yanquis, Black people, Indians, and Asians slaved to build the wealth of this country. For 400 years they have fought for freedom and dignity against racist Babylon. Third World people have led the fight for freedom. All the colored and oppressed peoples of the world are one nation under oppression. NO PUERTO RICAN IS FREE UNTIL ALL PEOPLE ARE FREE!

4. WE ARE REVOLUTIONARY NATIONALISTS AND OPPOSE RACISM.

The Latin, Black, Indian and Asian people inside the u.s. are colonies fighting for liberation. We know that washington, wall street, and city hall will try to make our nationalism into racism; but Puerto Ricans are of all colors and we resist racism. Millions of poor white people are rising up to demand freedom and we support them. These are the ones in the u.s. that are stepped on by the rulers and the government. We each organize our people, but our fights are the same against oppression and we will defeat it together. POWER TO ALL OPPRESSED PEOPLE!

5. WE WANT EQUALITY FOR WOMEN. DOWN WITH MACHISMO AND MALE CHAUVANISM.

Under capitalism, women have been oppressed by both society and our men. The doctrine of machismo has been used by men to take out their frustrations on wives, sisters, mothers, and children. Men must fight along with sisters in the struggle for economic and social equality and must recognize that sisters make up over half of the revolutionary army: sisters and brothers are equals fighting for our people. FORWARD SISTERS IN THE STRUGGLE!

6. WE WANT COMMUNITY CONTROL OF OUR INSTITUTIONS AND LAND.

We want control of our communities by our people and programs to guarantee that all institutions serve the needs of our people. People's control of police, health services, churches, schools, housing, transportation and welfare are needed. We want an end to attacks on our land by urban renewal, highway destruction, and university corporations. LAND BELONGS TO ALL THE PEOPLE!

7. WE WANT A TRUE EDUCATION OF OUR AFRO-INDIO CULTURE AND SPANISH LANGUAGE.

We must learn our long history of fighting against cultural, as well as economic genocide by the spaniards and now the yanquis. Revolutionary culture, culture of our people, is the only true teaching. JIBARO SI, YANQUI NO!

8. WE OPPOSE CAPITALISTS AND ALLIANCES WITH TRAITORS.

Puerto Rican rulers, or puppets of the oppressor, do not help our people. They are paid by the system to lead our people down blind alleys, just like the thousands of poverty pimps who keep our communities peaceful for business, or the street workers who keep gangs divided and blowing each other away. We want a society where the people socialistically control their labor. VENCEREMOS!

9. WE OPPOSE THE AMERIKKKAN MILITARY.

We demand immediate withdrawal of all u.s. military forces and bases from Puerto Rico, VietNam, and all oppressed communities inside and outside the u.s.. No Puerto Rican should serve in the u.s. army against his Brothers and Sisters, for the only true army of oppressed people is the People's Liberation Army to fight all rulers. U.S. OUT OF VIETNAM, FREE PUERTO RICO NOW!

10. WE WANT FREEDOM FOR ALL POLITICAL PRISONERS AND PRISONERS OF WAR.

No Puerto Rican should be in jail or prison, first because we are a nation, and amerikkka has no claims on us; second, because we have not been tried by our own people (peers). We also want all freedom fighters out of jail, since they are prisoners of the war for liberation. FREE ALL POLITICAL PRISONERS AND PRISONERS OF WAR!

11. WE ARE INTERNATIONALISTS.

Our people are brainwashed by television, radio, newspapers, schools and books, to oppose people in other countries fighting for their freedom. No longer will we believe these lies, because we have learned who the real enemy is and who our real friends are. We will defend our sisters and brothers around the world who fight for justice and are against the rulers of this country. QUE VIVA CHE GUEVARA!

12. WE BELIEVE ARMED SELF-DEFENSE AND ARMED STRUGGLE ARE THE ONLY MEANS TO LIBERATION

We are oppose to violence - the violence of hungry children, illiterate adults, diseased old people, and the violence of poverty and profit. We have asked, petitioned, gone to courts, demonstrated peacefully, and voted for politicians full of empty promises. But we still ain't free. The time has come to defend the lives of our people against repression and for revolutionary war against the businessmen, politicians, and police. When a government oppresses the people, we have the right to abolish it and create a new one. ARM OURSELVES TO DEFEND OURSELVES!

13. WE WANT A SOCIALIST SOCIETY.

We want liberation, clothing, free food, education, health care, transportation, full employment and peace. We want a society where the needs of the people come first, and where we give solidarity and aid to the people of the world, not oppression and racism. HASTA LA VICTORIA SIEMPRE!

Fig 26. Thirteen-Point Program. (Revised, December 1970.)

YOUNG LORDS PARTY POSITION PAPER ON WOMEN
CENTRAL COMMITTEE

Puerto Rican, Black, and other Third World (colonized) women are becoming more aware of their oppression in the past and today. They are suffering three different types of oppression under capitalism. First, they are oppressed as Puerto Ricans or Blacks. Second, they are oppressed as women. Third, they are oppressed by their own men. The Third World woman becomes the most oppressed person in the world today.

Economically, Third World women have always been used as a cheap source of labor and as sexual objects. Puerto Rican and Black women are used to fill working class positions in factories, mass assembly lines, hospitals, and all other institutions. Puerto Rican and Black women are paid lower wages than whites and kept in the lowest positions within society. At the same time, giving Puerto Rican and Black women jobs means that the Puerto Rican and Black man is kept from gaining economic independence, and the family unit is broken down. Capitalism defines manhood according to money and status; the Puerto Rican and Black man's manhood is taken away by making the Puerto Rican and Black woman the breadwinner. This situation keeps the Third World man divided from his woman. The Puerto Rican and Black man either leaves the household, or he stays and becomes economically dependent on the woman, undergoing psychological damage. He takes out all of his frustrations on his woman, beating her, repressing, and limiting her freedom. Because this society produces these conditions, our major enemy is capitalism rather than our oppressed men.

Third World Women have an integral role to play in the liberation of all oppressed people as well as in the struggle for the liberation of women. Puerto Rican and Black women make up over half of the revolutionary army, and in the struggle for national liberation they must press for the equality of women. The woman's struggle is the revolution within the revolution. Puerto Rican women will be neither behind nor in front of their brothers but always alongside them in mutual respect and love.

In the past women were oppressed by several institutions, one of which was marriage. When a woman married a man, she became his property and lost her last name. A man could have several wives in order to show other men what wealth he had and enhance his position in society. In Eastern societies men always had several wives and a number of women who were almost prostitutes, called concubines, purely sexual objects. Women had no right to own anything, not even their children; they were owned by her husband. This was true in places all over the world. In many societies, women had no right to be divorced, and in India it was the custom of most of the people that when the husband died, all his wives became the property of his brother.

In Latin America and Puerto Rico, the man had a wife and another woman called la corteja. This condition still exists today. The wife was there to be a homemaker, to have children and to maintain the family name and honor. She had to be sure to be a virgin and remain pure for the rest of her life, meaning she could never experience sexual pleasure. The wife had to have children in order to enhance the man's concept of virility and his position within the Puerto Rican society. La corteja became his sexual instrument. The man could have set her up in another household, paid her rent, bought her food, and paid her bills. He could have children with this woman, but they are looked upon as by-products of a sexual relationship. Both women had to be loyal to the man. Both sets of children grew up very confused and insecure and developed negative attitudes about the role.

Women have always been expected to be wives and mothers only. The community respects them for being good cooks, good housewives, and good mothers but never for being intelligent, strong, educated, or militant. In the past, women were not educated, only the sons got an education, and mothers were respected for the number of sons they had, not daughters. Daughters were worthless, and the only thing they could do was marry early to get away from home. At home, the role of the daughter was to be a nursemaid for the other children and kitchen help for her mother.

The daughter was guarded like a hawk by her father, brothers, and uncles to keep her a virgin. In Latin America, the people used dueñas or old lady watchdogs to guard the purity of the daughters. The husband must be sure that his new wife never has been touched by another man because that would ruin the "merchandise." When he marries her, her purpose is to have sons and keep his home but not to be a sexual partner.

Sex was a subject that was never discussed, and women were brainwashed into believing that the sex act was dirty and immoral, and its only function was for the making of children. In Africa, many tribes performed an operation on young girls to remove the clitoris so they would not get any pleasure out of sex and would become better workers.

THE DOUBLE STANDARD, MACHISMO, AND SEXUAL FASCISM

Capitalism sets up standards applied differently to Puerto Rican and Black men from the way they are applied to Puerto Rican and Black women. These standards are also applied differently to Third World people than they are applied to whites. These standards must be understood since they are created to divide oppressed people in order to maintain an economic system that is racist and oppressive.

Puerto Rican and Black men are looked upon as rough, athletic, and sexual, but not as intellectuals. Puerto Rican women are not expected to know anything except about the home, kitchen, and bedroom. All that they are expected to do is look pretty and add a little humor. The Puerto Rican man sees himself as superior to his woman, and his superiority, he feels, gives him license to do many things—curse, drink, use drugs, beat women, and run around with many women. As a matter of fact these things are considered natural for a man to do and he must do them to be considered a man. A woman who curses, drinks, and runs around with a lot of men is considered dirty scum, crazy, and a whore.

Today Puerto Rican men are involved in a political movement. Yet the majority of their women are home taking care of the children. The Puerto Rican sister that involves herself is considered aggressive, castrating, hard, and unwomanly. She is viewed by the brothers as sexually accessible because what else is she doing outside of the home. The Puerto Rican man tries to limit the woman's role because he feels the double standard is threatened; he feels insecure without it as a crutch.

Machismo has always been a very basic part of Latin American and Puerto Rican culture. Machismo is male chauvinism and more. Machismo means "mucho macho" or a man who puts himself selfishly at the head of everything without considering the woman. He can do whatever he wants because his woman is an object with certain already defined roles: wife, mother, and good woman.

Machismo means physical abuse, punishment, and torture. A Puerto Rican man will beat his woman to keep her in place and show her who's boss. Most Puerto Rican men do not beat women publicly because in the eyes of other men that is a weak thing to do. So, they usually wait until they're home. All the anger and violence of centuries of oppression that should be directed against the oppressor is directed at the woman. The aggression is also directed at daughters. The daughters hear their fathers saying, "the only way a woman is going to do anything, or listen is by hitting her." The father applies this to the daughter, beating her so that she can learn *respeto*. The daughters grow up with messed-up attitudes about their role as women and about manhood. They grow to expect that men will always beat them.

Sexual fascists are very sick people. Their illness is caused in part by this system, which mouths puritanical attitudes and laws and yet exploits the human body for profit.

Sexual Fascism is tied closely to the double standard and machismo. It means that a man or woman thinks of the opposite sex solely as sexual objects to be used for gratification and then discarded. Sexual fascists do not consider people's feelings; all they see everywhere is a pussy or a dick. They will use any rap, especially political, to get sex.

PROSTITUTION

Under capitalism, Third World women are forced to compromise themselves because of their economic situation. The facts that her man cannot get a job and that the family is dependent on her for support means she hustles money by any means necessary. Black and Puerto Rican sisters are put into a situation where jobs are scarce or nonexistent and are forced to compromise body, mind, and soul; they are then called whores or prostitutes. Puerto Rican and Black sisters are made to prostitute themselves in many other ways. The majority of these sisters on the street are also hard-core drug addicts, taking drugs as an escape from oppression. These sisters are subjected to sexual abuse from dirty old men who are mainly white racists who view them as the ultimate sexual objects. Also, he has the attitude that he cannot really prove his manhood until he has slept with a Black or Puerto Rican woman. The sisters also suffer abuse from the pimps, really small-time capitalists, who see the woman as private property that must produce the largest possible profit.

Because this society controls and determines the economic situation of Puerto Rican and Black women, sisters are forced to take jobs at the lowest wages, and at the same time take insults and other indignities in order to keep the job. In factories, our men are worked like animals and cannot complain because they will lose their jobs—their labor is considered abundant and cheap. In hospitals, our women comprise the majority of the nurses' aides, kitchen workers, and clerks. These jobs are unskilled; the pay is low, and there is no chance for advancement. In offices, our positions are usually as clerks, typists, and no-promotion jobs. In all of these jobs, our sisters are subjected to racial slurs, jokes, and other indignities such as being leered at, manhandled, propositioned, and assaulted. Our sisters are expected to prostitute themselves and take abuse of any kind or lose these subsistence jobs.

Everywhere our sisters are turned into prostitutes. The most obvious example is the sisters hustling their bodies on the streets, but the other forms of prostitution are also types of further exploitation of the Third World woman. The only way to eliminate prostitution is to eliminate this society, which creates the need. Then we can establish a socialist society that meets the economic needs of all the people.

BIRTH CONTROL, ABORTION, STERILIZATION-GENOCIDE

We have no control over our bodies, because capitalism finds it necessary to control the woman's body to control population size. The choice of motherhood is being taken out of the mother's hands. She is sterilized to prevent her from having children, or she has to have a child because she cannot get an abortion.

Third World sisters are caught up in a complex situation. On one hand, we feel that genocide is being committed against our people. We know that Puerto Ricans will not be around very long if Puerto Rican women are sterilized at the rate they are being sterilized now. . ... Part of this genocide is also the use of birth control pills, which were tested for 15 years on Puerto Rican sisters (guinea pigs) before being sold in the US market. Even now many doctors feel that these pills cause cancer and death from blood clotting.

Abortions in hospitals that are butcher shops are little better than the illegal abortions our women used to get. The first abortion death in NYC under the new abortion law was Carmen Rodríguez, a Puerto Rican sister who died in Lincoln Hospital. Her abortion was legal, but the conditions in the hospital were deadly. On the other hand, we believe that abortions should be legal if they are community controlled, if they are safe, if our people are educated about the risks, and if doctors do not sterilize our sisters while performing abortions. We realize that under capitalism our sisters and brothers cannot support large families and the more children we have, the harder it is to support them. We say, change the system so that women can freely be allowed to have as many children as they want without suffering any consequences.

DAY CARE CENTERS

One of the main reasons why many sisters are tied to the home and cannot work or become revolutionaries is the shortage of day care centers for children. The centers that already exist are overcrowded, expensive, and are only super-baby-sitting centers. Day care centers should be free, should be open 24 hours a day, and should be centers where children are taught their revolutionary history and culture. Many sisters leave their children with a neighbor, or the oldest child is left to take care of the younger ones. Sometimes they are left alone, and all of us have read the tragic results in the newspapers of what happens to children left alone—they are burned to death in fires, or they swallow poison, or fall out of windows to their death.

REVOLUTIONARY WOMEN

Throughout history, women have participated and been involved in liberation struggles. But the writers of history have never given full acknowledgment to the role of revolutionary women.

MARIANA BRACETTI was a Puerto Rican woman who together with her husband fought in the struggle for independence in Lares. She was called "El Brazo de Oro" because of her unlimited energy. For her role in the struggle, she was imprisoned. She sewed the first flag of El Grito de Lares.

Another nationalist woman was LOLA RODRÍGUEZ DE TIÓ, a poet who expressed the spirit of liberty and freedom in "La Borinqueña" in 1867. Besides being a nationalist, she was a fighter for women's rights. She refused to conform to the traditional customs concerning Puerto Rican women and at one point cut her hair very short.

BLANCA CANALES was a leader of the revolution in Jayuya in 1950.

LOLITA LEBRÓN, together with three other patriots, opened fire on the House of Representatives [in Washington, DC] in an armed attack in 1954 bringing the attention of the world to Puerto Rico's colonial status. She emptied a .45 automatic from the balcony of the Congress onto the colonial legislators. She then draped herself in the Puerto Rican flag and cried, "Viva Puerto Rico Libre." The result was five legislators [were] shot, and one critically wounded. She was imprisoned in a federal penitentiary and sentenced to 50 years and is still in prison for this heroic act.

Only recently, a 19-year-old coed, ANTONIA MARTÍNEZ, was killed in Puerto Rico in a demonstration against the presence of amerikkkan military recruiting centers. She was murdered when she yelled, "Viva Puerto Rico Libre!"

SOJOURNER TRUTH was born a slave in New York around 1800. She traveled in the north speaking out against slavery and for women's rights. She was one of the most famous Black orators in history.

KATHLEEN CLEAVER is a member of the Central Committee of the Black Panther Party. The Black Panthers are the vanguard of the Black liberation struggle in the United States. Another Panther sister, ERICKA HUGGINS, is imprisoned in Connecticut for supposedly being a member of a conspiracy. She was forced to have her child in prison and was given no medical attention while she was pregnant. Her child was later taken away from her because of her political beliefs.

ANGELA DAVIS is a Black revolutionary sister who is being hunted by the f.b.i. and is on their 10 most wanted list because she has always defended her people's right to armed self-defense and because of her Marxist-Leninist philosophy.

In other parts of the world, women are fighting against imperialism and foreign invasion. Our sisters in Vietnam have struggled alongside their brothers for 26 years; first against the french colonizer, then against the japanese invaders, and now against the amerikkkan aggressors. Their military capability and efficiency has been demonstrated in so many instances that a women's brigade was formed in the National Liberation Front of the North Vietnamese Army.

LA THI THAM was born in a province constantly bombarded by US planes. After her fiancé was killed in action, she sought and got a job with a time bomb detecting team. She scanned the sky with field glasses and when the enemy dropped bombs along the countryside, she would locate those that had not yet exploded, and her teammates would open them and clear the road for traffic.

KAN LICH, another Vietnamese sister, fought under very harsh and dangerous conditions. She became a brilliant commander, decorated many times for her military ability. Her practice to "hit at close quarters, hit hard, withdraw quickly" proved to be valid.

The Central Committee of the Young Lords Party has issued this position paper to explain and to educate about the role of sisters in the past and how we see sisters in the struggle now and in the future. We criticize those brothers who are "machos" and who continue to treat our sisters as less than equals. We criticize sisters who remain passive, who do not join in the struggle against our oppression. We are fighting every day within our party against male chauvinism because we want to make a revolution of brothers and sisters, together, in love and respect for each other.

Palante, vol. 2, no. 12, September 25, 1970

WHY A WOMEN'S UNION?

June 1971

The Third World Woman is exploited in many ways.

First, we are used as a source of cheap labor. As workingwomen, we get the dirtiest jobs at the lowest wages. We get paid less than men and less than white women for the same amount of work. Because we work out of necessity, we have to put up with abuse and manhandling from the bosses to keep our jobs. We are worked like animals in factories, especially in the garment industry where we spend most of our lives making clothes for other people while we can barely clothe ourselves. Our labor is considered abundant and cheap. If we speak up against the mistreatment, the boss fires us and gets himself another "girl." In the hospitals, we make up the majority of the workers as nurses' aides, kitchen workers, and clerks. In offices, we work as clerks and typists. They squeeze out our sweat and blood and still we don't make enough for a decent life.

Second, we are the women that are forced to prostitute ourselves in order to survive within a system that excludes us because there are no jobs. We sell our bodies like merchandise in order to stay alive. We are forced into a situation where we depend on the streets for our survival. Most of us are the street hustlers selling our bodies and barely making a living at it. A lot of us are prostituting because we depend on drugs that the rich pushers bring into our communities, and the government doesn't do anything because it benefits them. Or we're on welfare taking government handouts that are not enough to support ourselves and our children.

Third, as women our bodies are used for experimentation. Puerto Rican women have been sterilized to stop us from having "too many babies." This kind of murder leaves ⅓ of Puerto Rican women sterile today. The birth control pill was tested on Puerto Rican women for 15 years before it was sold in the u.s. Puerto Rican women have the highest death rate from butcher performed abortions, like the case of Carmen Rodríguez who was killed at Lincoln Hospital in New York City when she went for an abortion.

This government also uses us as sexual objects. We have always been portrayed as very exotic and sexual, but with no brains. We are used as objects with which to sell different things, which we then are brainwashed into buying. Women buy the most products. We are taught from the time we are born to look at ourselves negatively. Puerto Ricans refer to a baby girl as a *chancleta*—a slipper. Consciously and non-consciously, we believe we are inferior. So, then businessmen make products promising us that we will look better and be happier. Things like padded bras, girdles, false eyelashes, wigs, make-up, vaginal sprays, and crash diets are just a few examples. We are taught to look pretty, get married, have children, take care of them, do the housekeeping, and serve the husband as his slave. Depending on how well we do these things, determines how good a woman we are. A good woman does all the housework alone, even if she works [outside the home as well]. A good woman obeys her husband and never talks back to him. We're not supposed to have the brains to think, and we're supposed to remain passive and conform to the role of being shy, timid. Women aren't supposed to be fighters.

Yet our history has always had women fighters. . ..

Why a Women's Union?

Because as women we can best organize other women for the liberation of Puerto Rico and for the self-determination of all oppressed people. Because as women, we best understand our own oppression and can organize ourselves for our liberation, always remembering that we will not be free until all our people are free.

We don't want to be cheap labor horses anymore. We don't want to be used as guinea pigs anymore. We want to be respected and treated as human beings by our men. We want all our people to be treated like human beings, and if not, we will fight till we are.

La Luchadora, vol. 1, no. 1, June 1971

WOMEN'S UNION
12-POINT PROGRAM

1) We believe in the liberation of all Puerto Ricans—liberation on the island and inside the U.S.

2) We believe in the self-determination of all third world people.

3) We want equality for women—down with machismo and sexism.

4) We want full employment and equal pay for all women with day care facilities provided by the work institution.

5) We want an end to the present welfare system; community-worker boards must be established in all welfare centers to [e]nsure the protection of women and their needs.

6) We want an end to the particular oppression of prostitutes and drug-addict sisters.

7) We want the withdrawal of the American military force from our communities and an end to their sexual abuse of women.

8) We want freedom for all political prisoners and prisoners of war and an end to the sexual brutalization and torture enforced on sisters by prison officials.

9) We want an end to the experimentation and genocide committed on sisters through sterilization, forced abortions, contraceptives, and unnecessary gynecological exams.

10) We want a true education of our story as women.

11) We believe in the right to defend ourselves against rapes, beatings, muggings, and general abuse.

12) We want a socialist society.

La Luchadora, vol. 1, no. 1, June 1971

Endnotes

PREFACE

[1] Nicole Acevedo, Gabe Gutierrez, and Annie Rose Ramos, "Puerto Ricans Flood Streets, Demand Resignation of Governor in Huge Protest," NBC News, last modified July 23, 2019, https://www.nbcnews.com/news/latino/march-people-puerto-rico-mobilizes-largest-protest-gov-rossell-s-n1032286.

[2] Sandra Guzmán, "Meet the Women Leading Puerto Rico's Feminist Revolution," Shondaland, August 9, 2019, https://www.shondaland.com/change-makers/a28653844/puerto-rico-protests-feminist-revolution.

[3] "Boricua" means Puerto Rican.

[4] Thirteen-Point Program and Platform, in Darrel Enck-Wanzer, ed., *The Young Lords: A Reader* (New York: New York University Press, 2010), 9.

[5] Patricia Hill Collins, *Black Feminist Thought: Knowledge, Consciousness, and the Politics of Empowerment* (New York: Routledge, 2000), ix.

[6] Andrés Torres, "Introduction: Political Radicalism in the Diaspora—The Puerto Rican Experience," in *The Puerto Rican Movement: Voices from the Diaspora*, ed. Andrés Torres and José E. Velázquez (Philadelphia: Temple University Press, 1998), 4.

[7] Audre Lorde, *Sister Outsider: Essays and Speeches* (1984; Berkeley, CA: Crossing Press, 2007), 138.

[8] Timofei Gerber, "A Decolonial Feminism: In Conversation with Françoise Vergès," *Epoché*, no. 28 (January 23, 2020), https://epochemagazine.org/a-decolonial-feminism-in-conversation-with-fran%C3%A7oise-verg%C3%A8s-9cf3bec9aa14.

[9] Edna Acosta-Belén, "Introduction: Unveiling and Preserving a Puerto Rican Historical Memory," in *Through the Eyes of Rebel Women: The Young Lords, 1969–1976*, by Iris Morales (New York: Red Sugarcane Press, 2016), 1.

[10] Elizabeth Fee and Michael Wallace, "The History and Politics of Birth Control," *Feminist Studies* 5, no. 1 (Spring 1979): 202.

[11] Michel-Rolph Trouillot, *Silencing the Past: Power and the Production of History* (Boston: Beacon Press, 1995), 22.

[12] Maylei Blackwell, *¡Chicana Power! Contested Histories of Feminism in the Chicano Movement* (Austin: University of Texas Press, 2011), 102.

[13] Trouillot, *Silencing the Past,* 22.

[14] Lucille Clifton, "Why Some People Be Mad at Me Sometimes," The Dewdrop, June 10, 2020, https://thedewdrop.org/2020/06/10/lucille-clifton-why-some-people-be-mad-at-me-sometimes/.

PART I. ANOTHER CYCLE OF GRASSROOTS MILITANCY

[1] Zuleica Romay Guerra, "New World Coming: Race in Socialist Cuba," YouTube, November 19, 2021, https://www.youtube.com/watch?v=5jJQBtPTPks.

CHAPTER 1. HUMAN RIGHTS, NOT JUST CIVIL RIGHTS

[1] Kym Klass, "Gwen Patton, Lifelong Civil Rights Activist, Dies," *Washington Times*, May 21, 2017, https://www.washington-times.com/news/2017/may/21/gwen-patton-lifelong-civil-rights-activist-dies/.

[2] Raquel M. Ortiz and Iris Morales, *Vicki and a Summer of Change! ¡Vicki Y Un Verano de Cambio!* (New York: Red Sugarcane Press, Inc. 2021). The first children's book about the Young Lords.

[3] Judy Klemesrud, "Young Women Find a Place in High Command of Young Lords," *New York Times*, November 11, 1970, 78.

[4] Edna Acosta-Belén and Carlos E. Santiago, *Puerto Ricans in the United States: A Contemporary Portrait* (Boulder, CO: Lynne Rienner, 2006), 81.

[5] Acosta-Belén and Santiago, *Puerto Ricans in the United States*, 75-80.

[6] Pedro Caban, "Puerto Rico, Colonialism in," Scholars Archive, University at Albany, State University of New York, 2005, https://scholarsarchive.library.albany.edu/cgi/viewcontent.cgi?article=1018&context=lacs_fac_scholar: 517.

[7] Maura Toro-Morn and Ivis García Zambrano, "Gendered Fault Lines: A Demographic Profile of Puerto Rican Women in the United States," *Centro Journal* 29, no. 3 (Fall 2017): 17.

[8] "35% of Puerto Rican Women Sterilized," Chicago Women's Liberation Union, Herstory Project, September 19, 2016, https://www.cwluherstory.org/health/35-of-puerto-rican-women-sterilized.

[9] Puerto Rico is an archipelago comprising various islands—Puerto Rico proper, Vieques, Mona, Desecheo, and Culebra.

[10] Acosta-Belén and Santiago, *Puerto Ricans in the United States*, 81.

[11] Matthew Gandy, "Between Borinquen and the *Barrio*: Environmental Justice and New York City's Puerto Rican Community, 1969–1972," *Antipode* 34, no. 4 (September 2002): 732.

[12] Lorrin Thomas, *Puerto Rican Citizen: History and Political Identity in Twentieth-Century New York City* (Chicago: University of Chicago Press, 2010), 56–59.

[13] Komozi Woodward, "Rethinking the Black Power Movement," *Africana Age*, Schomburg Center for Research in Black Culture, New York Public Library, http://exhibitions.nypl.org/africanaage/essay-black-power.html.

[14] NewsOne Staff, "Malcolm X's Most Iconic Speeches," NewsOne, last modified May 19, 2022, https://newsone.com/3903093/malcolm-x-most-iconic-speeches/.

[15] Barbara Ransby, *Ella Baker and the Black Freedom Movement: A Radical Democratic Vision* (Chapel Hill: University of North Carolina Press, 2003), 344.

[16] Ransby, *Ella Baker*, 344.

[17] "Achieving the Dream: Death of a Panther," WTTW Digital Archives, http://www.wttw.com/main.taf?p=76,4,6,1.

[18] Erin Blakemore, "Why People Rioted after Martin Luther King Jr.'s Assassination," History, April 2, 2018; last modified, December 13, 2021, https://www.history.com/news/mlk-assassination-riots-occupation.

[19] Karen A. Secrist, "Occupy Lincoln Park: The Militant Drama of the Young Lords Organization," *Journal of African American Studies* 23, no. 4 (December 2019): 393, doi:10.1007/s12111-019-09449-3.

[20] Secrist, "Occupy Lincoln Park," 394.

[21] Frank Browning, "From Rumble to Revolution: The Young Lords," *Ramparts*, October 1970, 20.

[22] "Cosmoe Speaks," *Y.L.O.* (newspaper of the Chicago Young Lords Organization) 1, no. 4 (1969).

[23] Ella Turney, "Human Rights vs Civil Rights," US Institute of Diplomacy and Human Rights, March 17, 2021, https://usidhr.org/human-rights-vs-civil-rights.

[24] Terence McArdle, "The 'Law and Order' Campaign That Won Richard Nixon the White House 50 Years Ago," *Washington Post*, November 5, 2018, https://www.washingtonpost.com/history/2018/11/05/law-order-campaign-that-won-richard-nixon-white-house-years-ago/.

[25] "Nixon Adviser Admits War on Drugs Was Designed to Criminalize Black People," Equal Justice Initiative, last modified March 25, 2016, https://eji.org/news/nixon-war-on-drugs-designed-to-criminalize-black-people/.

[26] "People in Jail and Prison in 2020," Vera Institute of Justice, January 25, 2021, https://www.vera.org/publications/people-in-jail-and-prison-in-2020.

[27] Vincent Browne, "Richard Nixon Committed Far Greater Crimes Than the Watergate Break-In," *Irish Times*, June 19, 2013, https://www.irishtimes.com/news/politics/richard-nixon-committed-far-greater-crimes-than-the-watergate-break-in-1.1433510.

[28] Taylor Owen and Ben Kiernan, "Making More Enemies Than We Kill? Calculating U.S. Bomb Tonnages Dropped on Laos and Cambodia, and Weighing Their Implications," *Asia-Pacific Journal*, April 27, 2015, https://apjjf.org/Ben-Kiernan/4313.html.

[29] "Richard Nixon," Encyclopedia Britannica, https://www.britannica.com/biography/Richard-Nixon.

[30] "Nixon Insists That He Is 'Not a Crook,'" History, November 16, 2009; last modified, November 14, 2019, https://www.history.com/this-day-in-history/nixon-insists-that-he-is-not-a-crook.

[31] According to 1970 census data, 817,712 Puerto Ricans lived in New York, or roughly 10 percent of the city's population. "On Arrival: Puerto Ricans in Post-World War II New York," Teachers College - Columbia University, n.d. https://www.tc.columbia.edu/che/projects/past-projects/blog-posts/on-arrival-puerto-ricans-in-post-world-war-ii-new-york/.

[32] Mark Schmitt, "Liberalism's Mayor," *American Prospect*, May 21, 2010, https://prospect.org/article/liberalism-s-mayor/.

[33] Seymour P. Lachman and Robert Polner, *The Man Who Saved New York: Hugh Carey and the Great Fiscal Crisis of 1975* (Albany: State University of New York Press, 2010), 58.

[34] Stephen Brier, "Why the History of CUNY Matters: Using the CUNY Digital History Archive to Teach CUNY's Past," *Radical Teacher* 108, no. 1 (Spring 2017): 30.

[35] Puerto Rican Forum, *A Study of Poverty Conditions in the New York Puerto Rican Community* (New York: Puerto Rican Forum, 1970).

[36] Acosta-Belén and Santiago, *Puerto Ricans in the United States*, 73.

[37] "The Fight for Survival During the 50s," *Palante* 5, no. 9 (October 30–November 20, 1973): 5.

[38] Alice Colón-Warren, "The Feminization of Poverty among Women in Puerto Rico and Puerto Rican Women in the Middle Atlantic Region of the United States," *Brown Journal of World Affairs* 5, no. 2 (Summer–Fall 1998): 272, https://www.jstor.org/stable/24590326?read-now=1&seq=15.

[38] Colón-Warren, "The Feminization of Poverty," 272.

[39] Colón-Warren, "The Feminization of Poverty," 264.

[40] "New York School Boycott," Civil Rights Digital Library, December 17, 2020, https://crdl.usg.edu/events/ny_school_boycott/?Welcome.

[41] Felipe Hinojosa, *Apostles of Change: Latino Radical Politics, Church Occupations, and the Fight to Save the Barrio* (Austin: University of Texas Press, 2021), 98.

[42] Brier, "Why the History of CUNY Matters," 31–32. Brier describes rallies and confrontations in the spring of 1969, culminating in student strikes and building occupations at the City College of New York, Brooklyn College, Queens College, Bronx Community College, and the Borough of Manhattan Community College. Administrators called police on several campuses to retake the occupied buildings. Students of color led class boycotts and were supported by many white students and faculty.

[43] Tia Tenopia, "Latinopia Event 1969 Denver Youth Conference," Latinopia, March 4, 2012, https://latinopia.com/latino-history/latinopia-event-1969-denver-youth-conference/.

[44] Luis Aponte-Parés, "The East Harlem Real Great Society, a Puerto Rican Chapter in the Fight for Self-Determination," Planners Network, March 12, 1999, https://www.plannersnetwork.org/1999/03/the-east-harlem-real-great-society-a-puerto-rican-chapter-in-the-fight-for-self-determination/.

[45] Anne Garland Mahler, *From the Tricontinental to the Global South: Race, Radicalism, and Transnational Solidarity* (Durham, NC: Duke University Press, 2018), 121.

[46] Roxanne Dunbar-Ortiz, *An Indigenous Peoples' History of the United States* (Boston: Beacon Press, 2014), 2.

[47] Alan Maass, *The Case for Socialism*, 3rd ed. (Chicago: Haymarket Books, 2010), 5.

[48] Van Gosse, *Rethinking the New Left: An Interpretive History* (New York: Palgrave Macmillan, 2005), 2.

[49] Rose Muzio, *Radical Imagination, Radical Humanity: Puerto Rican Political Activism in New York* (Albany: State University of New York Press, 2017), 3.

CHAPTER 2. SERVING THE PEOPLE. WE ARE REVOLUTIONARY NATIONALISTS

[1] Mao Tse-tung, *Quotations from Chairman Mao Tse-tung*, Marxists Internet Archive, https://www.marxists.org/ebooks/mao/Quotations_from_Chairman_Mao_Tse-tung.pdf. *The Little Red Book* explains the meaning of "Serving the People:" "Our point of departure is to serve the people whole-heartedly and never for a moment divorce ourselves from the masses, to proceed in all cases from the interests of the people and not from one's self-interest or from the interests of a small group."

[2] Subcommander Marcos, *The Zapatistas' Dignified Rage: Final Public Speeches of Subcommander Marcos*, ed. Nick Henck, trans. Henry Gales (Chico, CA: AK Press, 2018), 52.

[3] Gary Eidsvold, Anthony Mustalish, and Lloyd F. Novick, "The New York City Department of Health: Lessons in a Lead Poisoning Control Program," *American Journal of Public Health* 64, no. 10 (October 1974): 956–62, https://ajph.aphapublications.org/doi/pdf/10.2105/AJPH.64.10.956.

[4] Theresa Horvath, "The Health Initiatives of the Young Lords Party: How a Group of 1960s Radicals Made Health a Revolutionary Concern," Hofstra University, 5, https://www.hofstra.edu/pdf/community/culctr/culctr_events_healthcare0310_%20horvath_paper.pdf.

[5] Eidsvold, Mustalish, and Novick, "The New York City Department of Health," 957.

[6] Horvath, "The Health Initiatives of the Young Lords Party," 6.

[7] Eidsvold, Mustalish, and Novick, "The New York City Department of Health," 957.

[8] Browning, "From Rumble to Revolution," 23.

[9] Iris Benítez, *Y.L.O*, January 1970, 20.

[10] "Young Lords Defy Take-Over Order," *New York Times*, January 3, 1970.

[11] "*¡Palante Radio!* Latin Liberation News and the Young Lords Organization of New York," Down and to the Left, December 2, 2013, https://downandtotheleft.wordpress.com/2013/12/02/palante-radio-liberation-news-and-the-new-york-young-lords-organization/.

[12] Felipe Luciano, New York State deputy chairman, in Enck-Wanzer, *The Young Lords: A Reader*, 133.

[13] Mahler, *From the Tricontinental to the Global South*, 96.

[14] Mahler, *From the Tricontinental to the Global South*, 121–22. The phrase "within the belly of the beast" is from a writing by Cuban poet and political exile José Martí about his time living in New York City.

[15] Felipe Luciano, "On Revolutionary Nationalism," in Enck-Wanzer, *The Young Lords: A Reader*, 133.

[16] Jorge Duany, "Nation on the Move: The Construction of Cultural Identities in Puerto Rico and the Diaspora," *American Ethnologist* 27, no. 1 (February 2000): 7, doi:10.1525/ae.2000.27.1.5.

[17] Edna Acosta-Belén, email correspondence, September 8, 2021.

[18] Felipe Luciano, "On Revolutionary Nationalism," in Enck-Wanzer, *The Young Lords: A Reader*, 134.

[19] MerriCatherine, "Huey P. Newton's Interview with The Movement (1968)," Medium, January 13, 2018, https://medium.com/@merricatherine/huey-p-newtons-interview-with-the-movement-magazine-1968-a328e6b78c32.

[20] Margaret Power, "Seeing the U.S. Empire through the Eyes of Puerto Rican Nationalists Who Opposed It," *Modern American History* 2, no. 2 (July 2019): 190, doi:10.1017/mah.2019.18.

[21] Edgardo Pratts, "A 85 años de la masacre de Río Piedras," 80 Grados, November 13, 2020, https://www-80grados-net.translate.goog/a-85-anos-de-la-masacre-de-rio-pie-dras/?_x_tr_sl=es&_x_tr_tl=en&_x_tr_hl=en&_x_tr_pto=sc.

[22] Pratts, "A 85 años de la masacre de Río Piedras."

[23] Pratts, "A 85 años de la masacre de Río Piedras."

[24] Charles R. Venator Santiago, "The Other Nationalists: Marcus Garvey and Pedro Albizu Campos" (master's thesis, University of Massachusetts Amherst, 1996), 33, https://scholarworks.umass.edu/cgi/viewcontent.cgi?article=3676&context=theses.

[25] Yenica Cortes, "Remembering Puerto Rico's Ponce Massacre," *Liberation*, March 1, 2007, https://www.liberationnews.org/07-03-01-remembering-puerto-ricos-ponce-html/.

[26] Jose Colon, "Estado Libre Asociado: The Constitutionality of Puerto Rico's Legal Status," Chicana/o Latina/o Law Review 7, no. 0 (1984): 105, doi:10.5070/c770020957.

[27] Venator Santiago, "The Other Nationalists," 33.

[28] Margaret Pour, "Puerto Rican Women Nationalist vs. U.S. Colonialism: An Exploration of Their Conditions and Struggles in Jail and Court," *Chicago-Kent Law Review* 87, no. 2 (April 2012): 465, https://scholarship.kent-law.iit.edu/cklawreview/vol87/iss2/9.

[29] "Utuado Uprising," Military Wiki, https://military-history.fan-dom.com/wiki/Utuado_Uprising.

[30] Pedro Caban, "Puerto Rican Nationalist Uprising," Latin American, Caribbean, and U.S. Latino Studies Faculty Scholarship 22 (2005), Scholars Archive, University at Albany, State University of New York, https://scholarsarchive.library.albany.edu/lacs_fac_scholar/22.

[31] Pedro A. Malavet, *America's Colony: The Political and Cultural Conflict between the United State and Puerto Rico* (New York: New York University Press, 2004) 92.

[32] Antonia Darder, "Pedro Albizu Campos," Encyclopedia Britannica, n.d.https://www.britannica.com/biography/Pedro-Albizu-Campos.

[33] Malavet, *America's Colony*, 92.

[34] Venator Santiago, "The Other Nationalists," 36.

[35] Antonia Darder, "Pedro Albizu Campos," Encyclopedia Britannica, n.d.https://www.britannica.com/biography/Pedro-Albizu-Campos.

[36] Manuel Maldonado-Denis, "Prospects for Latin American Nationalism: The Case of Puerto Rico," *Latin American Perspectives* 3, no. 3 (Summer 1976): 39.

[37] Maldonado-Denis, "Prospects for Latin American Nationalism," 41.

[38] Felipe Luciano, "On Revolutionary Nationalism," in Enck-Wanzer, *The Young Lords: A Reader*, 134.

[39] MerriCatherine, "Huey P. Newton's Interview."

[40] Loretta Ross, "Fighting White Supremacy and White Privilege to Build a Human Rights Movement," *Understanding and Dismantling Privilege* 6, no. 1 (April 2016): 3.

[41] Elizabeth "Betita" Martínez, "What Is White Supremacy?" Catalyst Project, 2013, https://collectiveliberation.org/wp-content/uploads/2013/01/What_Is_White_Supremacy_Martinez.pdf.

[42] Young Lords Party, Michael Abramson, and Iris Morales, *Palante: Voices and Photographs of the Young Lords, 1969–1971* (Chicago: Haymarket Books, 2011), 67.

[43] Report of Central Committee Evaluation and Retreat, December 21–23, 1970, 20. Recap of activities from July to December 1970 and goals for 1971. Iris Morales files.

[44] Mahler, *From the Tricontinental to the Global South*, 124–25.

[45] Iris Morales, "Puerto Rican Racism" ("Racismo borincaño"), in Enck-Wanzer, *The Young Lords: A Reader*, 136.

[46] Marta I. Cruz-Janzen, "Out of the Closet: Racial Amnesia, Avoidance, and Denial; Racism among Puerto Ricans." *Race, Gender and Class* 10, no. 3 (2003): 71.

[47] Marilisa Jiménez García, *Side by Side: US Empire, Puerto Rico, and the Roots of American Youth Literature and Culture* (Jackson: University Press of Mississippi, 2021), 17.

[48] Vanessa K. Valdés, *Diasporic Blackness: The Life and Times of Arturo Alfonso Schomburg* (Albany: State University of New York Press, 2017), 8.

[49] Young Lords Party Central Committee, *The Ideology of the Young Lords Party* (pamphlet), 1971, 4. Afro-Boricuas are defined as a "mixture of mostly Spanish and African who developed in the sugarcane plantations and coasts of Puerto Rico, … and whose ancestors were slaves. … [T]he culture and customs [of Puerto Ricans] are mostly African, and the racist societies of Spain and Amerikkka treat them as though they are inferior."

[50] Carlos Aponte, "Loiza Aldea," *Palante* 2, no. 9 (1970): 6.

[51] Jorge Duany, "Neither White nor Black: The Politics of Race and Ethnicity among Puerto Ricans on the Island and in the U.S. Mainland," paper presented at the Conference on the Meaning of Race and Blackness in the Americas: Contemporary Perspectives, Providence, Rhode Island, February 10–12, 2000, 4, http://maxweber.hunter.cuny.edu/eres/docs/eres/SOC217_PIMENTEL/duany.pdf.

[52] Anne McClintock, "Family Feuds: Gender, Nationalism and the Family," *Feminist Review*, no. 44 (Summer 1993), 63, doi:10.2307/1395196.

[53] McClintock, "Family Feuds," 77.

[54] Thirteen-Point Program and Platform, in Enck-Wanzer, *The Young Lords: A Reader*, 9–10.

[55] Young Lords Party, Abramson, and Morales, *Palante*, 13.

[56] McClintock, "Family Feuds," 77.

CHAPTER 3. THE RISE OF THE WOMEN'S CAUCUS

[1] Ana Lydia Vega, "Cloud Cover Caribbean," in *Short Stories by Latin American Women: The Magic and the Real*, ed. Celia Correas de Zapata (New York: Modern Library, 2003), 223.

[2] Browning, "From Rumble to Revolution," 23.

[3] Young Lords Party, Abramson, and Morales, *Palante*, 40.

[4] Santa Cruz Feminist of Color Collective, "Building on 'the Edge of Each Other's Battles': A Feminist of Color Multidimensional Lens." *Hypatia* 29, no. 1 (Winter 2014): 28-29.

[5] María Lugones, "Indigenous Movements and Decolonial Feminism," Department of Women's, Gender, and Sexuality Studies, Ohio State University, 2, https://wgss.osu.edu/sites/wgss.osu.edu/files/LugonesSeminarReadings.pdf.

[6] Santa Cruz Feminist of Color Collective, "Building on 'the Edge of Each Other's Battles,'" 27.

[7] Santa Cruz Feminist of Color Collective, "Building on 'the Edge of Each Other's Battles,'" 24.

[8] Carole Boyce Davies, *Left of Karl Marx: The Political Life of Black Communist Claudia Jones* (Durham, NC: Duke University Press, 2008), 23.

[9] Kathryn Blackmer Reyes and Julia E. Curry Rodríguez, "*Testimonio*: Origins, Terms, and Resources," *Equity and Excellence in Education* 45, no. 3 (2012): 525, doi:10.1080/10665684.2012.698571. The authors link the use of *testimonio* to liberation efforts and anti-imperialist movements in Third World nations.

[10] Lisa Gail Collins, "Activists Who Yearn for Art That Transforms: Parallels in the Black Arts and Feminist Art Movements in the United States," *Signs: Journal of Women in Culture and Society* 31, no. 3 (Spring 2006): 727, doi:10.1086/498991.

[11] Kristie Soares, "Joy, Rage, and Activism: The Gendered Politics of Affect in the Young Lords Party," *Signs: Journal of Women in Culture and Society* 46, no. 4 (Summer 2021): 940, doi:10.1086/713295.

[12] Isabel Allende, *The Soul of a Woman* (New York: Ballantine Books, 2021), 13.

[13] Young Lords Organization, "13-Point Program and Platform," *Palante* 2, no. 2 (1970): 19.

[14] BlackPast, "(1981) Audre Lorde, 'The Uses of Anger: Women Responding to Racism,'" August 12, 2012, https://www.blackpast.org/african-american-history/speeches-african-american-history/1981-audre-lorde-uses-anger-women-responding-racism/.

[15] *Women in the Colonies*, episode 2 of 3, Pacifica Radio Archives, March 1970, https://www.pacificaradioarchives.org/recording/bb383502.

[16] Young Lords Party, Abramson, and Morales, *Palante*, 13.

[17] Ernesto Che Guevara, *Man and Socialism in Cuba* (Havana: Guairas Book Institute, 1967).

[18] Young Lords Party, Abramson, and Morales, *Palante*, 48.

[19] BlackPast, "(1970) Huey P. Newton, 'The Women's Liberation and Gay Liberation Movements,'" April 17, 2018, https://www.blackpast.org/african-american-history/speeches-african-american-history/huey-p-newton-women-s-liberation-and-gay-liberation-movements/.

[20] BlackPast, "(1970) Huey P. Newton."

[21] Enck-Wanzer, *The Young Lords: A Reader*, 23.

[22] Firuzeh Shokooh Valle, "Getting into the Mainstream: The Virtual Strategies of the Feminist Movement in Puerto Rico" (master's thesis, Northeastern University, 2010), 58.

[23] María I. Bryant, "Puerto Rican Women's Roles in Independence Nationalism: Unwavering Women" (PhD diss., American University, 2011), 216.

[24] Becky Serrano, "Ana Roqué," *Palante* 3, no. 1 (1971): 11.

[25] Sojourner Truth, "Ain't I a Woman?," December 1851, Modern History Sourcebook, Fordham University, https://sourcebooks.fordham.edu/mod/sojtruth-woman.asp.

PART II. FEMINISTS OF COLOR AND GENDER JUSTICE MOVEMENTS

[1] "Women Who Disagree," in *Mujer en pie de lucha*, ed. Dorinda Moreno (Mexico City: Espina del Norte, 1973), 29.

[1] Diane Feeley, "Antoinette Konikow: Marxist and Feminist," in *Revolutionary Traditions of American Trotskyism*, ed. Paul Le Blanc (New York: Fourth Internationalist Tendency, 1988), 5. Reprinted from *International Socialist Review* 33 (January 1972): 19–23.

CHAPTER 4. STERILIZATION POLITICS AND STRUGGLES FOR REPRODUCTIVE JUSTICE

[1] Natasha Lennard, "The Long, Disgraceful History of American Attacks on Brown and Black Women's Reproductive Systems," The Intercept, September 17, 2020, xx, https://theintercept.com/2020/09/17/forced-sterilization-ice-us-history/.

[2] Enck-Wanzer, *The Young Lords: A Reader*, 165. See also Iris Morales, "Sterilized Puerto Ricans," *Palante* 2, no. 2 (1970): 8. Reprinted in *Palante* 2, no. 10 (1970): 5.

[3] Jennifer A. Nelson, "'Abortions under Community Control': Feminism, Nationalism, and the Politics of Reproduction among New York City's Young Lords," *Journal of Women's History* 13, no. 1 (Spring 2001): 157, doi:10.1353/jowh.2001.0031.

[4] Ranjani Chakraborty, "The US Medical System Is Still Haunted by Slavery," *Vox*, December 7, 2017, https://www.vox.com/health-care/2017/12/7/16746790/health-care-black-history-inequality.

[5] Sylviane A. Diouf, "Remembering the Women of Slavery," Schomburg Center for Research in Black Culture, New York Public Library, March 27, 2015, https://www.nypl.org/blog/2015/03/27/remembering-women-slavery.

[6] Liz Barnes, review of *When Rape Was Legal: The Untold History of Sexual Violence during Slavery*, by Rachel A. Feinstein, Reviews in History, October 2019, https://reviews.history.ac.uk/review/2344.

[7] Stephanie E. Jones-Rogers, *They Were Her Property: White Women as Slave Owners in the American South* (New Haven: Yale University Press, 2019).

[8] Isabel Wilkerson, *Caste: The Origins of Our Discontents* (New York: Random House, 2020), 79.

[9] Laura Briggs, *Reproducing Empire: Race, Sex, Science, and U.S. Imperialism in Puerto Rico* (Berkeley: University of California Press, 2003), 83.

[10] Briggs, *Reproducing Empire*, 87.

[11] Elizabeth Fee and Michael Wallace, "The History and Politics of Birth Control," *Feminist Studies* 5, no. 1 (Spring 1979): 202.

[12] Blanca Noelle Martínez, "Puertorriqueña Power and *Testimonio*: Puerto Rican Women's Fight for Reproductive Freedom in the 1930s through the 1970s" (master's thesis, University of California, San Diego, 2018), 8.

[13] This reference is to the Puerto Rican Socialist Party founded in 1899 by Santiago Iglesias Pantín.

[14] Carlos Sanabria, *Puerto Rican Labor History, 1898–1934: Revolutionary Ideals and Reformist Politics* (Lanham, MD: Lexington Books, 2018), 92

[15] Martínez, "Puertorriqueña Power and *Testimonio*," 8.

[16] Briggs, *Reproducing Empire*, 90.

[17] Annette B. Ramírez de Arellano and Conrad Seipp, *Colonialism, Catholicism, and Contraception: A History of Birth Control in Puerto Rico* (Chapel Hill: University of North Carolina Press, 2017), 28–29.

[18] Briggs, *Reproducing Empire*, 76.

[19] César J. Ayala and Rafael Bernabe, *Puerto Rico in the American Century: A History since 1898* (Chapel Hill: University of North Carolina Press, 2017), 207.

[20] Briggs, *Reproducing Empire*, 77.

[21] Ruth Arroyo, Rafael Bernabe, and Nancy Herzig, "Confronting Anti-Choice Forces in Puerto Rico," Marxists Internet Archive, https://www.marxists.org/history/etol/newspape/atc/4725.html.

[22] "35% of Puerto Rican Women Sterilized," Chicago Women's Liberation Union, Herstory Project.

[23] Iris Ofelia López, *Matters of Choice: Puerto Rican Women's Struggle for Reproductive Freedom* (New Brunswick, NJ: Rutgers University Press, 2008), 13.

[24] Briggs, *Reproducing Empire*, 80.

[25] Nick Thimmesch, "Puerto Rico and Birth Control," *Journal of Marriage and Family* 30, no. 2 (May 1968): 257.

[26] "Puerto Rico," Eugenics Archives, https://eugenicsarchive.ca/discover/tree/530ba18176f0db569b00001b.

[27] Erin Blakemore, "The First Birth Control Pill Used Puerto Rican Women as Guinea Pigs," History, May 9, 2018; last modified, March 11, 2019, https://www.history.com/news/birth-control-pill-history-puerto-rico-enovid.

[28] Martínez, "Puertorriqueña Power and *Testimonio*," 24.

[29] Olivia Kinnear, "Sterilization: The Untold Story of Puerto Rico," Pasquines, September 1, 2015, https://pasquines.us/2015/09/01/sterilization-the-untold-story-of-puerto-rico/.

[30] López, *Matters of Choice*, 15.

[31] Briggs, *Reproducing Empire*, 102.

[32] Briggs, *Reproducing Empire*, 104.

[33] "Puerto Rico," Eugenics Archives.

[34] Briggs, *Reproducing Empire*, 108.

[35] Bianca González, "Eugenics and Contraceptives in Puerto Rico: A History of Manipulation and Unethical Experimentation," *Liberal Currents*, May 22, 2020, https://www.liberalcurrents.com/eugenics-and-contraceptives-in-puerto-rico-a-history-of-manipulation-and-unethical-experimentation/.

[36] Katherine Andrews, "The Dark History of Forced Sterilization of Latina Women," Panoramas, October 30, 2017, https://www.panoramas.pitt.edu/health-and-society/dark-history-forced-sterilization-latina-women.

[37] Ella Jordan-Smith, "A Historical Analysis of U.S. Imperialism on Women in Puerto Rico" (honors thesis, State University of New York at New Paltz, 2019), 10, https://soar.suny.edu/bitstream/handle/20.500.12648/1329/Jordan-Smith_Honors.pdf?sequence=1&isAllowed=y.

[38] Kathryn Krase, "The History of Forced Sterilization in the United States," *Our Bodies Ourselves,* last modified September 21, 2020, https://www.our-bodiesourselves.org/book-excerpts/health-article/forced-sterilization.

[39] Ana María García, dir., *La operación*, Cinema Guild, 1982. The film documents the 1950s and 1960s sterilization campaign in Puerto Rico.

[40] Rodríguez Trías advocated for health services for poor and working-class women and children and served as director of the Lincoln Hospital Pediatrics Department in the Bronx. She was the first Latina president of the American Public Health Association, a founding member of its women's caucus, and a recipient of the Presidential Citizens Medal.

[41] Alexandra Minna Stern, "Forced Sterilization Policies in the US Targeted Minorities and Those with Disabilities—and Lasted into the 21st Century," Institute for Healthcare Policy and Innovation, September 23, 2020, https://ihpi.umich.edu/news/forced-sterilization-policies-us-targeted-minorities-and-those-disabilities-and-lasted-21st.

[42] Alexandra Minna Stern, "That Time the United States Sterilized 60,000 of Its Citizens," *Huffington Post*, January 7, 2016, https://www.huffpost.com/entry/sterilization-united-states_n_568f35f2e4b0c8beacf68713.

[43] Nicole L. Novak and Natalie Lira, "California Once Targeted Latinas for Forced Sterilization," *Smithsonian Magazine*, March 22, 2018, https://smithsonianmag.com/history/california-targeted-latinas-forced-sterilization-180968567/.

[44] The Student Nonviolent Coordinating Committee, "Genocide in Mississippi," Tulane University Digital Library, last modified 1964, https://digitallibrary.tulane.edu/islandora/object/tulane%3A21196.

[45] Paola Alonso, "Autonomy Revoked: The Forced Sterilization of Women of Color in 20th Century America," Texas Woman's University, n.d., https://twu.edu/media/documents/history-government/Autonomy-Revoked-The-Forced-Sterilization-of-Women-of-Color-in-20th-Century-America.pdf.

[46] Alonso, "Autonomy Revoked."

[47] Blake T. Hilton, "Frantz Fanon and Colonialism: A Psychology of Oppression," *Journal of Scientific Psychology*, December 2011, 54, https://www.psyencelab.com/uploads/5/4/6/5/54658091/frantz_fanon_and_colonialism.pdf.

[48] Sandra Knispel, "Coerced Sterilization of Native Women Occurred in the 70s," *Futurity*, October 24, 2019, https://www.futurity.org/sterilizations-native-american-women-2192722-2/. See also Beth Adams, "'Reproduction on the Reservation': The History of Forced Sterilization of Native American Women," WXXI News, Rochester, New York, October 28, 2019, https://www.wxxinews.org/post/reproduction-reservation-history-forced-sterilization-native-american-women.

[49] J. Nelson, "Abortions under Community Control," 167.

[50] José E. Velázquez, Carmen V. Rivera, and Andres Torres, eds., *Revolution Around the Corner: Voices from the Puerto Rican Socialist Party in the United States* (Philadelphia: Temple University Press, 2021), 148.

[51] Sue Davis, "A Doctor Who Fought Sterilization Abuse," *Workers World*, April 20, 2005, http://www.workers.org/2005/us/rakow-0428.

[52] Renee Tajima-Peña, dir., *No más bebés*, PBS, 2015. Mothers involved in the *Madrigal v. Quilligan* trial recount the day they were sterilized.

[53] Juliana Jiménez J., "California Compensates Victims of Forced Sterilizations, Many of Them Latinas," NBC News, July 23, 2021, https://www.nbcnews.com/news/latino/california-compensates-victims-forced-sterilizations-many-latinas-rcna1471.

[54] Briggs *Reproducing Empire*, 124.

[55] Sharon Smith, "Women's Liberation: The Marxist Tradition," *International Socialist Review*, no. 93 (Summer 2014), https://isreview.org/issue/93/womens-liberation-marxist-tradition/index.html.

[56] Drew C. Pendergrass and Michelle Y. Raji, "The Bitter Pill: Harvard and the Dark History of Birth Control," *Harvard Crimson*, September 28, 2017, https://www.thecrimson.com/article/2017/9/28/the-bitter-pill/.

[57] Pendergrass and Raji, "The Bitter Pill."

[58] "The Puerto Rico Pill Trials," PBS, January 4, 2018, https://www.pbs.org/wgbh/americanexperience/features/pill-puerto-rico-pill-trials/.

[59] Blakemore, "The First Birth Control Pill."

[60] Chana Gazit, "The Pill," PBS, 2007, https://www.pbs.org/wgbh/amex/pill/index.html.

[61] Theresa Vargas, "Guinea Pigs or Pioneers? How Puerto Rican Women Were Used to Test the Birth Control Pill," *Washington Post*, May 9, 2017, https://www.washingtonpost.com/news/retropolis/wp/2017/05/09/guinea-pigs-or-pioneers-how-puerto-rican-women-were-used-to-test-the-birth-control-pill/.

[62] Amanda Brownlee, "A Virtue Ethics Analysis of the Puerto Rico Birth Control Trials," April 24, 2020, STS Research Paper, 13.

[63] Brownlee, "A Virtue Ethics Analysis," 14.

[64] Vargas, "Guinea Pigs or Pioneers?"

[65] Pendergrass and Raji, "The Bitter Pill."

CHAPTER 5. UNITIES WITH BLACK AND CHICANA FEMINISTS

[1] Angela Davis, quoted in Max Peterson, "The Revolutionary Practice of Black Feminisms," National Museum of African American History and Culture, Smithsonian Institution, March 4, 2019, https://nmaahc.si.edu/explore/stories/revolutionary-practice-black-feminisms.

[2] Yuderkys Espinosa Miñoso, "Why We Need Decolonial Feminism: Differentiation and Co-Constitutional Domination in Western Modernity," Afterall, July 1, 2020, https://www.afterall.org/article/why-we-need-decolonial-feminism-differentiation-and-co-constitutional-domination-of-western-modernit.

[3] Karen Vieira Powers, *Women in the Crucible of Conquest: The Gendered Genesis of Spanish American Society, 1500–1600* (Albuquerque: University of New Mexico Press, 2005), 178.

[4] Angela Y. Davis, *Women, Race and Class* (New York: Vintage Books, 1983), 21.

[5] "Overview Essay: Women in Resistance," Slave Resistance: A Caribbean Study, n.d., http://scholar.library.miami.edu/slaves/womens_resistance/womens.html.

[6] Powers, *Women in the Crucible of Conquest*, 178.

[7] Sharon Smith, *Women and Socialism: Class, Race, and Capital* (Chicago: Haymarket Books, 2015), xii.

[8] Davies, *Left of Karl Marx*, 39.

[9] Claudia Jones, "An End to the Neglect of the Problems of the Negro Woman!," University of Central Florida Digital Library, June 1949, 4, http://purl.flvc.org/FCLA/DT/1927554.

[10] Erik S. McDuffie, *Sojourning for Freedom: Black Women, American Communism, and the Making of Black Left Feminism* (Durham, NC: Duke University Press, 2011), 3.

[11] Jones, "An End to the Neglect," 15–17.

[12] "Kimberlé Crenshaw on Intersectionality, More Than Two Decades Later," Columbia Law School, June 8, 2017, https://www.law.columbia.edu/news/archive/kimberle-crenshaw-intersectionality-more-two-decades-later.

[13] Ashley Bohrer, "Intersectionality and Marxism: A Critical Historiography," *Historical Materialism* 26, no. 2 (June 2018): 49, doi:10.1163/1569206x-00001617.

[14] Benita Roth, *Separate Roads to Feminism: Black, Chicana, and White Feminist Movements in America's Second Wave* (Cambridge: Cambridge University Press, 2004), 12.

[15] Kimberly Springer, *Living for the Revolution: Black Feminist Organizations, 1968–1980* (Durham, NC: Duke University Press, 2006), 3.

[16] Kathleen A. Laughlin, Julie Gallagher, Dorothy Sue Cobble, Eileen Boris, Premilla Nadasen, Stephanie Gilmore, and Leandra Zarnow, "Is It Time to Jump Ship? Historians Rethink the Waves Metaphor," *Feminist Formations* 22, no. 1 (Spring 2010): 76–78, doi:10.1353/nwsa.0.0118.

[17] Laughlin et al., "Is It Time to Jump Ship?," 77–81.

[18] Jasmin A. Young, "Strapped: A Historical Analysis of Black Women and Armed Resistance, 1959–1979" (PhD diss., Rutgers University, 2018), 209.

[19] Young, "Strapped," 209.

[20] Linda Burnham, "The Wellspring of Black Feminist Theory," Women of Color Resource Center, Working Paper Series, no. 1, 2001, 5, https://solidarity-us.org/pdfs/cadreschool/fws.burnham.pdf.

[21] Ransby, *Ella Baker*, 352.

[22] Ransby, *Ella Baker*, 352.

[23] "Dr. Gwen Patton: A Long Time Movement Activist," Civil Rights Movement Archive, 2017, https://www.crmvet.org/vet/patton.htm.

[24] Ashley D. Farmer, "Remembering Gwen Patton, Activist and Theorist," June 14, 2017, https://www.ashleydfarmer.com/blog/2017/6/14/remembering-gwen-patton-activist-and-theorist.

[25] Patricia Romney, *We Were There: The Third World Women's Alliance and the Second Wave* (New York: Feminist Press, 2021), 47.

[26] Frances M. Beal, "Double Jeopardy: To Be Black and Female," *Meridians* 8, no. 2 (2008): 166, https://www.jstor.org/stable/40338758.

[27] Beal, "Double Jeopardy," 166.

[28] Young, "Strapped," 210–11.

[29] Beal, "Double Jeopardy," 174–75.

[30] BlackPast, "The Black Panthers' Ten Point Program," https://www.blackpast.org/african-american-history/primary-documents-african-american-history/black-panther-party-ten-point-program-1966/.

[31] Kathleen Neal Cleaver, "Women, Power, and Revolution (1998)," History Is a Weapon, https://www.historyisaweapon.com/defcon1/cleaverwomen-powerrev.html.

[32] Mary Phillips, "The Feminist Leadership of Ericka Huggins in the Black Panther Party," *Black Diaspora Review* 4, no. 1 (Winter 2014): 200.

[33] Salamishah Tillet, "The Panthers' Revolutionary Feminism," *New York Times*, October 2, 2015, 12, https://www.nytimes.com/2015/10/04/movies/the-panthers-revolutionary-feminism.html.

[34] Phillips, "The Feminist Leadership of Ericka Huggins," 200.

[35] Phillips, "The Feminist Leadership of Ericka Huggins," 190–93.

[36] Meera White, "Seeing Black Women in Power," National Museum of African American History and Culture, Smithsonian Institution, July 28, 2017, https://nmaahc.si.edu/explore/stories/collection/seeing-black-women-power.

[37] Nicole Martin, "Women Were Key in the Black Panther Party," Clayman Institute for Gender Research, Stanford University, January 6, 2014, https://gender.stanford.edu/news-publications/gender-news/women-were-key-black-panther-party.

[38] Tracye A. Matthews, "'No One Ever Asks What a Man's Role in the Revolution Is': Gender Politics and Leadership in the Black Panther Party, 1966–71," in *Sisters in the Struggle: African American Women in the Civil Rights–Black Power Movement*, ed. Bettye Collier-Thomas and V. P. Franklin (New York: New York University Press, 2001), 246, https://libcom.org/files/No%20one%20ever%20asks%20what%20a%20man's%20role%20in%20the%20revolution%20is.pdf.

[39] Springer, *Living for the Revolution*, 27.

[40] Young, "Strapped," 213. It is unclear if the Puerto Rican activists who requested membership in the BWA were members of other nationalist, socialist, or feminist organizations.

[41] Springer, *Living for the Revolution*, 48.

[42] Frances Beal, interviewed by Loretta J. Ross, Oakland, March 18, 2005, Voices of Feminism Oral History Project, Sophia Smith Collection, Smith College, 5, https://www.smith.edu/libraries/libs/ssc/vof/transcripts/Beal.pdf.

[43] Patricia Romney, *We Were There: The Third World Women's Alliance and the Second Wave* (New York: Feminist Press, 2021).

[44] Springer, *Living for the Revolution*, 78.

[45] Lee Bebout, *Mythohistorical Interventions: The Chicano Movement and Its Legacies* (Minneapolis: University of Minnesota Press, 2011); Blackwell, *¡Chicana Power!*; and Maria E. Cotera, review of *Mythohistorical Interventions* by Lee Bebout and *¡Chicana Power!* by Maylei Blackwell, *Signs: Journal of Women in Culture and Society* 38, no. 3 (Spring 2013), https://www.journals.uchicago.edu/doi/10.1086/668556.

[46] Rodolfo Gonzales and Alurista, "El Plan Espiritual de Aztlán," *El Grito del Norte* 2, no. 9 (July 6, 1969): 5, https://icaa.mfah.org/s/en/item/803398#?c=&m=&s=&cv=1&xywh=793%2C2029%2C1029%2C576.

[47] Amy D. Rublin, "'Though All Women Are Women, No Woman Is Only a Woman': Black, White, and Chicana Feminist Consciousness Development from 1955 to 1985" (honors thesis, University of Pennsylvania, 2007), 52.

[48] Rublin, "Though All Women Are Women," 42.

[49] Alma M. García, ed., *Chicana Feminist Thought: The Basic Historical Writings* (New York: Routledge, 1997), 29.

[50] Tia Tenopia, "Latinopia Event 1969 Denver Women's Caucus," Latinopia, March 3, 2013, https://latinopia.com/latino-history/latinopia-event-1969-denver-womens-caucus/.

[51] García, *Chicana Feminist Thought*, 1.

[52] Clarissa Dominguez, "Emergence of the Chicana Movement," Feminist Poetry Movement, December 10, 2018, https://sites.williams.edu/engl113-f18/dominguez/emergence-of-the-chicana-movement/.

[53] García, *Chicana Feminist Thought*, 6.

[54] Alma M. García, "The Development of Chicana Feminist Discourse, 1970–1980," *Gender and Society* 3, no. 2 (June 1989): 223, http://www.jstor.org/stable/189983.

[55] Miroslava Chávez-García, "A Genealogy of Chicana History, the Chicana Movement, and Chicana Studies," in *Routledge Handbook of Chicana/o Studies*, ed. Francisco A. Lomelí, Denise A. Segura, and Elyette Benjamin-Labarthe (Abingdon, Oxon., England: Routledge, 2019), Academia.edu - Share Research, https://www.academia.edu/410638736.

[56] García, "The Development of Chicana Feminist Discourse," 220.

[57] Mirta Vidal, "Chicanas Speak Out—Women: New Voice of La Raza," Duke University Libraries, Repository Collections and Archives, October 1971, 3, https://repository.duke.edu/dc/wlmpc/wlmms01005.

[58] García, *Chicana Feminist Thought*, 3.

[59] Dionne Espinoza "'Revolutionary Sisters': Women's Solidarity and Collective Identification among Chicana Brown Berets in East Los Angeles, 1967–1970," *Aztlán* 26, no. 1 (Spring 2001): 18.

[60] Elvira Rodríguez, "Covering the Chicano Movement: Examining Chicano Activism through Chicano, American, African American, and Spanish-Language Periodicals, 1965–1973" (PhD diss., University of California, Riverside, 2013), 30.

[61] Espinoza, "Revolutionary Sisters," 19.

[62] Sonia A. López, "The Role of the Chicana within the Student Movement," in *Chicana Feminist Thought: The Basic Historical Writings*, ed. Alma M. García (New York: Routledge, 2007), 103.

[63] Blackwell, *¡Chicana Power!*, 68.

[64] Espinoza "Revolutionary Sisters," 17.

[65] Espinoza "Revolutionary Sisters," 17.

[66] Blackwell, *¡Chicana Power!*, 8.

[67] Blackwell, *¡Chicana Power!*, 68.

[68] Blackwell, *¡Chicana Power!*, 30.

[69] Blackwell, *¡Chicana Power!*, 31.

[70] García, "The Development of Chicana Feminist Discourse," 226.

[71] García, "The Development of Chicana Feminist Discourse," 227.

[72] Vidal, "Chicanas Speak Out," 21.

[73] Vicki L. Ruíz, *From Out of the Shadows: Mexican Women in Twentieth-Century America* (New York: Oxford University Press, 2008), 107.

CHAPTER 6. DEMANDS OF THE WOMEN'S CAUCUS

[1] Audre Lorde, *A Burst of Light and Other Essays* (Ithaca, NY: Firebrand Books, 1988).

[2] McClintock, "Family Feuds," 77.

[3] "The Long Feminist History of Fighting for Universal Childcare," Bitch Media, September 4, 2020, https://www.bitchmedia.org/article/universal-childcare-feminist-history.

[4] "Young Lords Council Removes Luciano as National Chairman," *New York Times*, September 5, 1970. See also "Press Release on Felipe," *Palante 2*, no.11 (1970): 2.

[5] Enck-Wanzer, *The Young Lords: A Reader*, 175. See also Jenny Figueroa, "World of Fantasy," *Palante* 3, no. 2 (1971): 4.

[6] Lulu Rovira, "Makeup and Beauty," *Palante* 3, no. 12 (1971): 9.

[7] "YLP Editorial," *Palante* 2, no. 4 (1970): 11.

[8] "Contract for the Murder of Chairman Felipe," *Palante* 2, no. 8 (1970): 2.

[9] "Young Lords Council Removes Luciano," *New York Times*, 21.

[10] Young Lords Party Central Committee, "On Felipe Luciano," *Palante* 2, no. 11 (1970): 2.

[11] "Young Lords Council Removes Luciano," *New York Times*, 21.

[12] Nydia Mercado, "Revolutionary Wedding," *Palante* 2, no. 9 (1970): 9.

[13] Erica González, "Mujeres of the Young Lords," Colorlines, August 19, 2009, https://www.colorlines.com/articles/mujeres-young-lords.

[14] Young Lords Party, Abramson, and Morales, *Palante*, 48.

[15] Young Lords Party, Abramson, and Morales, *Palante*, 50.

[16] Enck-Wanzer, *The Young Lords: A Reader*, 169. See also Young Lords Party Central Committee, "Young Lords Party Position on Women," *Palante* 2, no. 12 (1970): 12.

[17] "La posición del Partido de los Young Lords cuanto a las Mujeres." Spanish-language version of "Young Lords Party Position on Women," *Palante* 2, no. 13 (1970): 11.

[18] "Women in Cuba: The Revolution within the Revolution," in *Anthropology for the Nineties: Introductory Readings*, ed. Johnnetta B. Cole (New York: Free Press, 1988), 533.

[19] Debra Evenson, "Women's Equality in Cuba: What Difference Does a Revolution Make?," *Minnesota Journal of Law and Inequality* 4, no. 2 (June 1986): 309, https://scholarship.law.umn.edu/cgi/viewcontent.cgi?article=1328&context=lawineq.

[20] Klemesrud, "Young Women Find a Place," 78.

CHAPTER 7. QUEER LIBERATION AND THE YOUNG LORDS PARTY

[1] Princess Harmony, "Queer People and the U.S. Communist Movement, 1969–1979," *Workers World*, January 14, 2022, https://www.workers.org/2022/01/61137/?utm_source=rss&utm_medium=rss&utm_campaign=queer-people-and-the-u-s-communist-movement-1969-1979.

[2] Emily K. Hobson, *Lavender and Red: Liberation and Solidarity in the Gay and Lesbian Left* (Oakland: University of California Press, 2016), 25–26.

[3] "Gay Liberation in New York City," Out History, Page One, n.d., https://outhistory.org/exhibits/show/gay-liberation-in-new-york-cit/3rd-world/pg-1.

[4] "Third World Gay Liberation Statement, 1970," in *Dear Sisters: Dispatches from the Women's Liberation Movement*, ed. Rosalyn Baxandall and Linda Gordon (New York: Basic Books, 2000), 64.

[5] "Gay Liberation in New York City," Out History.

[6] BlackPast, "(1970) Huey P. Newton."

[7] Ronald K. Porter, "A Rainbow in Black: The Gay Politics of the Black Panther Party," in *Sexualities in Education: A Reader*, ed. Erica R. Meiners and Therese Quinn, special issue, *Counterpoints* 367 (2012): 364–75.

[8] Hobson, *Lavender and Red*, 32.

[9] BlackPast, "(1970) Huey P. Newton."

[10] BlackPast, "(1970) Huey P. Newton."

[11] BlackPast, "(1970) Huey P. Newton."

[12] BlackPast, "(1970) Huey P. Newton."

[13] Joshua Bloom and Waldo E. Martin Jr., *Black against Empire: The History and Politics of the Black Panther Party* (Oakland: University of California Press, 2013), 306.

[14] Black Panther Party, "*Black Panther* Newspaper Insert on People's Revolutionary Constitutional Convention, June 11, 1970," Roz Payne Sixties Archive, https://rozsixties.unl.edu/items/show/667.

[15] George Katsiaficas, "Organization and Movement: The Case of the Black Panther Party and the Revolutionary People's Constitutional Convention of 1970," in *1963–2013: A Civil Rights Retrospective*, ed. Richard Cambridge, special issue, *About Place Journal* 2, no. 4 (February 2014), https://aboutplacejournal.org/issues/civil-rights/future-perfect/george-katsiaficas/#notes.

[16] Porter, "A Rainbow in Black," 364–75.

[17] Jared E. Leighton, "Freedom Indivisible: Gays and Lesbians in the African American Civil Rights Movement" (PhD diss., University of Nebraska–Lincoln, 2013), 372.

[18] Leighton, "Freedom Indivisible," 364.

[19] Leighton, "Freedom Indivisible," 366.

[20] Third World Gay Revolution, "Sixteen Point Platform and Program," Pinko, last modified October 15, 2019, https://pinko.online/pinko-1/third-world-gay-revolution-archive.

[21] Greta Olson and Mirjam Horn-Schott, "Introduction: Beyond Gender—Toward a Decolonized Queer Feminist Future," in *Beyond Gender: An Advanced Introduction to Futures of Feminist and Sexuality Studies*, ed. Greta Olson, Daniel Hartley, Mirjam Horn-Schott, and Leonie Schmidt (Abingdon, Oxon., England: Routledge, 2018), 14.

[22] Gillian Brockell, "The Transgender Women at Stonewall Were Pushed Out of the Gay Rights Movement. Now They Are Getting a Statue in New York," *Washington Post*, June 12, 2019, https://www.washingtonpost.com/history/2019/06/12/transgender-women-heart-stonewall-riots-are-getting-statue-new-york/.

[23] Sylvia Rivera, "I'm Glad I Was in the Stonewall Riot," interview by Leslie Feinberg, *Workers World*, July 2, 1998, https://www.solidarity-us.org/files/SylviaRiveraInterview.pdf.

[24] Samuel Galen Ng, "Trans Power! Sylvia Lee Rivera's STAR and the Black Panther Party," *Left History* 17, no. 1 (Spring–Summer 2013): 22, doi:10.25071/1913-9632.39213.

[25] Rivera, "I'm Glad I Was in the Stonewall Riot."

[26] Young Lords Party, Abramson, and Morales, *Palante*, 40.

[27] Young Lords Party, Abramson, and Morales, *Palante*, 40.

[28] Ross, "Fighting White Supremacy."

[29] Young Lords Party Central Committee, July 1971 Retreat Paper, 6. It summarizes activities from January 1 to June 3, 1971. It announces the national liberation of Puerto Rico as the organization's political priority and gender and racial justice struggles as secondary. Iris Morales Files.

[30] Young Lords Party Central Committee, "Communiqué of Central Committee, Meeting of December 7–28, 1971," 1. It reviews activities from Sep-

tember to December 1971, including the rectification movement, the demotions of leading members, the Women's Union, and the YLP Party Congress. Iris Morales files.

PART III. "WE DO NOT LIVE SINGLE-ISSUE LIVES"

[1] Audre Lorde, *Sister Outsider: Essays and Speeches* (New York: Ten Speed Press, 2007), 138.

CHAPTER 8. POVERTY IS A HEALTH ISSUE

[1] Enck-Wanzer, *The Young Lords: A Reader*, 188.

[2] Lloyd Ultan and Barbara Unger, *Bronx Accent: A Literary and Pictorial History of the Borough* (New Brunswick, NJ: Rutgers University Press, 2000), 192.

[3] "Empire Roundup: Caught in the Squeeze," *Health/PAC Bulletin*, Health Policy Advisory Center, October 1970, https://www.healthpacbulletin.org/wp-content/uploads/1970/10/1970-October_Corrected.pdf.

[4] Michael T. Kaufman, "Lincoln Hospital: Case History of Dissension That Split Staff," *New York Times*, December 21, 1970, 1.

[5] "Lincoln History: A Bronx Legacy," NYC Health + Hospitals, n.d., https://www.nychealthandhospitals.org/lincoln/about-lincoln-hospital/history/.

[6] Kaufman, "Lincoln Hospital: Case History of Dissension," 1.

[7] Merlin Chowkwanyun, "The New Left and Public Health, the Health Policy Advisory Center, Community Organizing, and the Big Business of Health, 1967–1975," *American Journal of Public Health* 101, no. 2 (February 2011): 242, doi:10.2105/ajph.2009.189985.

[8] Chowkwanyun, "The New Left and Public Health."

[9] Interview with Cleo Silvers, March 12, 2007, Bronx African American History Project, BAAHP Digital Archive, Fordham University.

[10] "Editorial: Institutional Organizing," *Health/PAC Bulletin*, no. 37, Health Policy Advisory Center, January 1972, https://www.healthpacbulletin.org/healthpac-bulletin-january-1972/.

[11] Interview with Cleo Silvers, March 12, 2007.

[12] Fitzhugh Mullan, *White Coat, Clenched Fist: The Political Education of an American Physician* (Ann Arbor: University of Michigan Press, 2006), 139.

[13] Richard Fleming, "Could It Ever Happen Here? Lincoln Hospital Making Unprecedented Changes in Health Care," UCSF Synapse Archive, University of California, San Francisco, November 15, 1973, https://synapse.library.ucsf.edu/?a=d&d=ucsf19731115-01.2.13&e=-------en--20--1--txt------txIN--.

[14] Mullan, *White Coat, Clenched Fist*, 141.

[15] Mullan, *White Coat, Clenched Fist*, 142.

[16] Carl Pastor, "Socialism at Lincoln," *Palante* 2, no. 8 (1970): 5.

[17] Stephen Torgoff, "HRUM Sums Up Hospital Organizing," Marxists Internet Archive, December 27, 1972, https://www.marxists.org/history/erol/ncm-1/hrum.htm.

[18] "Your Asian Wasn't Quiet," Tumblr, n.d., https://asianamericanactivism.tumblr.com/post/68946140266/i-wor-kuen-12-point-party-platform-i-wor-kuen.

[19] "Empire Roundup: Caught in the Squeeze," *Health/PAC Bulletin*.

[20] Bella August, "El Barrio: A People's Health Movement," *Health/PAC Bulletin*, Health Policy Advisory Center, February 1970, http://www.healthpacbulletin.org/healthpac-bulletin-february-1970-2/.

[21] Health Revolutionary Unity Movement, *"Ideology,"* 4.

[22] Health Revolutionary Unity Movement, "Ideology, History, Patients' and Workers' Rights," 10.

[23] "Editorial: Institutional Organizing," *Health/PAC Bulletin*.

[24] Health Revolutionary Unity Movement, *"Ideology,"* 8.

[25] Health Revolutionary Unity Movement, *"Ideology,"* 9.

[26] Health Revolutionary Unity Movement, *"Ideology,"* 11–12.

[27] Ritch Whyman, "How Do We Fight Racism and Capitalism?," Socialist.ca, International Socialists, February 1, 2012, https://www.socialist.ca/node/745.

[28] Health Revolutionary Unity Movement, *"Ideology,"* 8.

[29] Health Revolutionary Unity Movement, *"Ideology,"* 6–7.

[30] Merlin Chowkwanyun, "Have You Heard of the Lincoln Collective?," History of Medicine and Public Health, New York Academy of Medicine Library Blog, May 17, 2016, https://nyamcenterforhistory.org/2016/05/17/have-you-heard-of-the-lincoln-collective/.

[31] Pastor, "Socialism at Lincoln," 5.

[32] Alfonso A. Narvaez, "Young Lords Seize Lincoln Hospital Building," *New York Times*, July 15, 1970, 34, https://www.nytimes.com/1970/07/15/archives/young-lords-seize-lincoln-hospital-building-offices-are-held-for-12.html.

[33] Mullan, *White Coat, Clenched Fist*, 146.

[34] Mullan, *White Coat, Clenched Fist*, 146.

[35] Pastor, "Socialism at Lincoln," 5.

[36] "Editorial: Institutional Organizing," *Health/PAC Bulletin*.

[37] Willard Cates Jr., David A. Grimes, and Kenneth F. Schulz, "The Public Health Impact of Legal Abortion: 30 Years Later," *Perspectives on Sexual and Reproductive Health* 35, no. 1 (January–February 2003): 25, doi:10.1363/3502503.

[38] Julia Jacobs, "Remembering an Era before Roe, When New York Had the 'Most Liberal' Abortion Law," *New York Times*, July 19, 2018,

https://www.nytimes.com/2018/07/19/us/politics/new-york-abortion-roe-wade-nyt.html.

[39] Martin Gansberg, "Abortion Death Reported by City," *New York Times*, July 21, 1970, 32.

[40] Charlayne Hunter, "Community Dispute Cuts Service at City Hospital," *New York Times*, August 26, 1970, 1.

[41] Mullan, *White Coat, Clenched Fist*, 148–49.

[42] Kaufman, "Lincoln Hospital: Case History of Dissension," 1.

[43] Edward Hudson, "Doctors Stay Out at Hospital Here," *New York Times*, August 28, 1970, 24, https://www.nytimes.com/1970/08/28/archives/doctors-stay-out-at-hospital-here-injunction-fails-to-influence-27.html.

[44] Hudson, "Doctors Stay Out."

[45] Jennifer Nelson, *Women of Color and the Reproductive Rights Movement* (New York: New York University Press, 2003), 102.

[46] Nelson, Women of Color and the Reproductive Rights Movement, p. 108.

[47] Le Pioufle, "Feminism and the Puerto Rican Independence Movement."

[48] Enck-Wanzer, *The Young Lords: A Reader*, 178. See also Gloria Colón, "Abortions," *Palante* 3, no. 5 (1971): 12.

[49] See generally J. Nelson, "Abortions under Community Control," 157–80.

[50] Enck-Wanzer, *The Young Lords: A Reader*, 178.

[51] J. Nelson, "Abortions under Community Control," 170, and Nelson's interview with Olguie Robles, New York City, April 18, 2000, in the same article.

[52] Enck-Wanzer, *The Young Lords: A Reader*, 169.

[53] Sean Gardiner, "Heroin: From the Civil War to the 70s, and Beyond," *City Limits*, July 5, 2009, https://citylimits.org/2009/07/05/heroin-from-the-civil-war-to-the-70s-and-beyond/.

[54] Joseph Lelyveld, "Obituary of a Heroin User Who Died at 12," New York Times, January 12, 1970, 1.

[55] Viola H. Huang, "Between Protest, Compromise, and Education for Radical Change: Black Power Schools in Harlem in the Late 1960s," (PhD diss., Columbia University, 2019).

[56] Thomas F. Brady, "St. Luke's Yields on Drug Facility," *New York Times*, January 18, 1970, 56.

[57] Alondra Nelson, "'Genuine Struggle and Care': An Interview with Cleo Silvers," *American Journal of Public Health* 106, no. 10 (October 2016), doi:10.2105/AJPH.2016.303407.

[58] Merlin Chowkwanyun, "On Fitzhugh Mullan's *White Coat, Clenched Fist*," *Social Medicine* 2, no. 2 (April 2007): 103, https://www.socialmedicine.info/index.php/socialmedicine/article/download/124/238.

[59] "Editorial: Institutional Organizing," *Health/PAC Bulletin.*

[60] "N.Y.C. Human Rights Commission Releases Report on Einhorn Case; Blames All Parties," Jewish Telegraphic Agency, July 16, 1971, https://www.jta.org/1971/07/16/archive/n-y-c-human-rights-commission-re-leases-report-on-einhorn-case-blames-all-parties.

[61] A. Nelson, "Genuine Struggle and Care."

[62] Chowkwanyun, "The New Left and Public Health," 242.

[63] "Editorial: The Medical Industrial Complex," *Health/PAC Bulletin*, Health Policy Advisory Center, November 1969, https://www.healthpacbulle-tin.org/healthpac-bulletin-november-1969/.

CHAPTER 9. UPRISINGS AGAINST THE NEW YORK CITY CRIMINAL JUSTICE SYSTEM

[1] Assata Shakur, *Assata: An Autobiography* (Chicago: Lawrence Hill, 2001), 1.

[2] Sarah Childress, "Michelle Alexander: 'A System of Racial and Social Control,'" Frontline, April 29, 2014, https://www.pbs.org/wgbh/frontline/arti-cle/michelle-alexander-a-system-of-racial-and-social-control/.

[3] Wendy Sawyer and Peter Wagner, "Mass Incarceration: The Whole Pie, 2020," Prison Policy Initiative, March 24, 2020, https://www.prisonpol-icy.org/re-ports/pie2020.html?c=pie&gclid=CjwKCAiA1uKMBhAGEiwAxzvX96qz7gc nuY4urRqElLQlx7DegMV2ZO7NnC1nkgwVjmF.

[4] Willie Mack, "'Traitors in Our Midst': Race, Corrections, and the 1970 Tombs Uprising," Gotham Center for New York City History, October 1, 2020, https://www.gothamcenter.org/blog/traitors-in-our-midst-race-correc-tions-and-the-1970-tombs-uprising.

[5] Orisanmi Burton, "Organized Disorder: The New York City Jail Rebellion of 1970," *Black Scholar* 48, no. 4 (October 2018): 30, doi:10.1080/00064246.2018.1514925.

[6] Heather Ann Thompson, "How a Series of Jail Rebellions Rocked New York—and Woke a city," *The Nation*, March 21, 2019, https://www.thena-tion.com/article/archive/new-york-jail-rebellion-1970-tombs-mdc/.

[7] William J. vanden Heuvel, interviewed by Jeffrey A. Kroessler, February 2, 2011, Justice in New York: An Oral History no. 12, Lloyd Sealy Library Digi-tal Collections, http://dc.lib.jjay.cuny.edu/index.php/Detail/Object/Show/ob-ject_id/657.

[8] Emily L. Thuma, *All Our Trials: Prisons, Policing, and the Feminist Fight to End Violence* (Urbana: University of Illinois Press, 2019), 24.

[9] Thompson, "How a Series of Jail Rebellions Rocked New York."

[10] "The House of D: A Panel on the Women's House of Detention," Village Preservation, August 27, 2020, https://www.villagepreservation.org/event/the-house-of-d/.

11 Olga Jiménez de Wagenheim, *Nationalist Heroines, Puerto Rican Women History Forgot, 1930s to 1950s* (Princeton: Markus Wiener Publishers, 2016), 228.

12 Wagenheim, Nationalist Heroines, 230.

13 "Smith Act," Wikipedia, last modified September 13, 2022, https://en.wikipedia.org/wiki/Smith_Act.

14 Wagenheim, *Nationalist Heroines*, 232-233.

15 Hobson, *Lavender and Red*, 25–26.

16 Hugh Ryan, "The Queer History of the Women's House of Detention," *Activist History Review*, May 31, 2019, https://activisthistory.com/2019/05/31/the-queer-history-of-the-womens-house-of-detention/. Daughters of Bilitis, founded in San Francisco in 1955, took its name from a poetry collection called *Songs of Bilitis.* Bilitis was the female character romantically associated with Sappho, the female Greek lyric poet. https://www.britannica.com/topic/Daughters-of-Bilitis

17 Ryan, "The Queer History of the Women's House of Detention."

18 For a discussion of the history of International Women's Day, see Temma Kaplan, "On the Socialist Origins of International Women's Day," *Feminist Studies* 11, no. 1 (Spring 1985): 163–71, doi:10.2307/3180144.

19 Minnie Bruce Pratt, "1970: Reviving the Fighting Spirit of Int'l Women's Day," *Workers World*, February 23, 2005, https://www.workers.org/2005/us/womens-day-0303/.

20 Pratt, "1970: Reviving the Fighting Spirit."

21 Pratt, "1970: Reviving the Fighting Spirit."

22 Hobson, *Lavender and Red*, 46.

23 Hobson, *Lavender and Red*, 6.

24 "Prison Struggle 1970–71," *Critical Resistance*, last modified March 9, 2012, https://criticalresistance.org/resources/prison-struggle-1970-1-5/.

25 Thompson, "How a Series of Jail Rebellions Rocked New York."

26 Burton, "Organized Disorder," 34.

27 Thompson, "How a Series of Jail Rebellions Rocked New York."

28 Thompson, "How a Series of Jail Rebellions Rocked New York."

29 Burton, "Organized Disorder," 32.

30 Burton, "Organized Disorder," 32.

31 Thompson, "How a Series of Jail Rebellions Rocked New York."

32 Burton, "Organized Disorder," 34.

33 Thompson, "How a Series of Jail Rebellions Rocked New York."

34 Burton, "Organized Disorder," 36.

35 Burton, "Organized Disorder," 37.

36 Burton, "Organized Disorder," 39.

[37] Bruce Jackson, *Law and Disorder: Criminal Justice in America* (Urbana: University of Illinois Press, 1984), 85.

[38] Philip Quarles, "An Unexplained Death and an Unacceptable System," WNYC, New York Public Radio, September 21, 2017, https://www.wnyc.org/story/unexplained-death-and-unacceptable-system/.

[39] I Wor Kuen translates as "Fist of Harmony"; the phrase originates from the Chinese fight to overthrow imperialism and colonialism during the Boxer Rebellion of 1900.

[40] Los Siete de la Raza were seven young Latinos from San Francisco's Mission District accused of murdering a policeman in 1969. The men were acquitted in 1970.

[41] Michael T. Kaufman, "200 Armed Young Lords Seize Church after Taking Body There," *New York Times*, October 19, 1970, 26.

[42] Kaufman, "200 Armed Young Lords Seize Church," 26.

[43] Mecca Adai, "Free Our Sisters," *Palante* 2, no. 17 (December 1970): 19.

[44] Adai, "Free Our Sisters," 19.

[45] Adai, "Free Our Sisters," 19.

[46] Afeni Shakur, "Women's House of Detention," *Palante* 2, no. 17 (1970): 3.

[47] Shakur, "Women's House of Detention," 3.

[48] Shakur, "Women's House of Detention," 3.

[49] Angela Y. Davis, *Are Prisons Obsolete?* (New York: Seven Stories Press, 2003), 60–83.

[50] Davis, *Are Prisons Obsolete?*, 83.

[51] Ellen Pierce, "Demonstration at the House of D," Wisconsin Historical Society, GT Press Collection, 1964–1977, https://content.wisconsinhistory.org/digital/collection/p15932coll8/id/62636.

[52] Adai, "Free Our Sisters," 19.

[53] Adai, "Free Our Sisters," 19.

[54] Adai, "Free Our Sisters," 19.

[55] Pierce, "Demonstration at the House of D."

[56] Tony Platt, quoted in "Organizing the Prisons in the 1960s and 1970s: Part One, Building Movements," Process: A Blog for American History, September 20, 2016, https://www.processhistory.org/prisoners-rights-1/.

[57] Thuma, *All Our Trials*, 4.

[58] "Words from Prison—Did You Know …?" American Civil Liberties Union, https://www.aclu.org/other/words-prison-did-you-know.

[59] Michele Goodwin, "The New Jane Crow: Women's Mass Incarceration," tJust Security, July 20, 2020, https://www.justsecurity.org/71509/the-new-jane-crow-womens-mass-incarceration/.

[1] Puerto Rican Student Union, "Somos Puertorriqueños y estamos desper-tando," pamphlet, New York, 1970, 1. Iris Morales files.

[2] Brier, "Why the History of CUNY Matters," 30.

[3] Sean Molloy, "SEEK's Fight for Racial and Social Justice at CUNY (1965–1969)," CUNY Digital History Archive, June 23, 2017, https://cdha.cuny.edu/secondary-sources/seek.

[4] Zita Dixon, "Creating, Passing, and Protecting a Racially Equitable Higher Education Social Policy Program: A Critical Historical Case Study of a State's Policymaking Process and Its Participants" (PhD diss., Brandeis University, 2021), 10.

[5] Danny Shaw, "NYC Ruling Class Targets Black, Latino City University Students," *Liberation*, November 1, 2006, https://www.liberationnews.org/06-11-01-nyc-ruling-class-targets-black-html/#.XzcFPPJ7kSI.

[6] "Minutes from 4/8/1965 CCNY Faculty Council Meeting · CUNY Digital History Archive," Home · CUNY Digital History Archive, last modified April 8, 1965, https://cdha.cuny.edu/items/show/6982.

[7] Frederick Douglass Opie, *Upsetting the Apple Cart: Black-Latino Coali-tions in New York City from Protest to Public Office* (New York: Columbia University Press, 2014), 74.

[8] Christopher Gunderson, "The Struggle for CUNY: A History of the CUNY Student Movement, 1969–1999," 7, https://eportfolios.macau-lay.cuny.edu/hainline2014/files/2014/02/Gunderson_The-Struggle-for-CUNY.pdf.

[9] Gunderson, "The Struggle for CUNY," 8.

[10] In 1971, the MPI became the Puerto Rican Socialist Party (Partido Social-ista Puertorriqueño).

[11] Ashley Leane Black, "From San Juan to Saigon: Shifting Conceptions of Puerto Rican Identity during the Vietnam War" (master's thesis, University of British Columbia, 2012), 40–42, https://central.bac-lac.gc.ca/.item?id=TC-BVAU-42499&op=pdf&app=Library&oclc_number=1032917918.

[12] Mirta González, "Free Puerto Rico," *Y.L.O.*, January 1970, 8.

[13] L.U.C.H.A. (Latinos Unidos Con Honor Y Amistad), student organization formed at New York University in 1969.

[14] Frederick D. Opie, *Upsetting the Apple Cart: Black-Latino Coalitions in New York City from Protest to Public Office* (New York: Columbia University Press, 2014), 74-75.

[15] "La historia de la Unión Estudiantil Boricua, movimiento estudiantil revo-lucionario," pamphlet. Iris Morales files.

[16] Richie Pérez, "Puerto Rican Student Union," *Palante* 3, no. 3 (1971): 7.

[17] "Proposal for Unifying the Puerto Rican Student Movement," document from the student section of the Puerto Rican Revolutionary Workers Organization. Iris Morales files.

[18] Ben Lieber, "Latins Demand 'Free Puerto Rico,'" Marxists Internet Archive, September 24, 1970, https://www.marxists.org/history/erol/ncm-8/pl-latins.htm. First published in the *Columbia Daily Spectator* 115, no. 2 (September 24, 1970).

[19] Lieber, "Latins Demand 'Free Puerto Rico.'"

[20] Olga Jiménez de Wagenheim, "Remembering March 1, 1954," 80 Grados, March 9, 2019, https://www.80grados.net/remembering-march-1-1954/

[21] Marisol LeBrón, "Puerto Rico and the Colonial Circuits of Policing," North American Congress on Latin America, September 27, 2017, https://nacla.org/news/2017/09/27/puerto-rico-and-colonial-circuits-policing.

[22] "Jayuya Uprising," Military Wiki, https://military-history.fandom.com/wiki/Jayuya_uprising.

[23] The Associated Press, "Revolt Flares in Puerto Rico; Soon Quelled With 23 Dead," The New York Times, October 31, 1950, 1.

[24] "La Revolución Nacionalista," YouTube, October 6, 2007, https://www.youtube.com/watch?v=RfOJj0nmGEU.

[25] Olivia Kinnear, "Women in Puerto Rican History: Blanca Canales," Pasquines, June 15, 2015, https://pasquines.us/2015/06/15/women-in-the-history-of-puerto-rico-blanca-canales/.

[26] Davies, *Left of Karl Marx*, 141.

[27] Davies, Left of Karl Marx, xxiv-xxvii.

[28] Davies, Left of Karl Marx, 110–11.

[29] Davies, *Left of Karl Marx*, 110–13.

[30] Olivia Kinnear, "Women in Puerto Rican History: Blanca Canales," Pasquines, June 15, 2015, https://pasquines.us/2015/06/15/women-in-the-history-of-puerto-rico-blanca-canales/.

PART IV. NATIONALISMS AND FEMINISMS

[1] Skyler Gomez, "On Love and Identity: 6 Poems by Julia de Burgos," Literary Ladies Guide, June 14, 2019, https://www.literaryladiesguide.com/classic-women-authors-poetry/poems-julia-de-burgos-puerto-rican-poet/.

CHAPTER 11. REBELLION RUSHIN' DOWN THE WRONG ROAD

[1] This line from "Five Nights of Bleeding," published by poet-musician Linton Kwesi Johnson in 1973, resonates as a metaphor for the Young Lords' move to Puerto Rico. At eleven years old, Johnson emigrated from Jamaica to South London to join his mother. In his final year of secondary school, he joined the Black Panther Party of England. See Johnson's work at: Robert J.

Stewart, "Linton Kwesi Johnson: Poetry Down a Reggae Wire," New West Indian Guide/Nieuwe West-Indische *Gids* 67, nos. 1–2 (1993): 69–89.

[2] Young Lords Party, Abramson, and Morales, *Palante*, 72.

[3] Pablo "Yoruba" Guzmán, "Why the Young Lords Party," *Palante* 2, no. 17 (1970).

[4] Report of Central Committee Evaluation and Retreat, December 21–23, 1970, 15.

[5] Gloria González, "Rompe Cadenas," *Palante* 3, no. 2 (1971): 12–13.

[6] Report of Central Committee Evaluation and Retreat, 13.

[7] Juan González and Juan "Fi" Ortiz, "Letter from Puerto Rico," *Palante* 2, no. 11 (1970): 4.

[8] Report of Central Committee Evaluation and Retreat, 14.

[9] The Young Lords defined "lumpen" or lumpenproletariat as the unemployable—people on drugs or in jail, sex workers, and welfare mothers. A jibaro was an agricultural worker.

[10] Report of Central Committee Evaluation and Retreat, 12–15.

[11] Roberto P. Rodríguez-Morazzani, "Political Cultures of the Puerto Rican Left in the United States," in *The Puerto Rican Movement: Voices from the Diaspora*, ed. Andrés Torres and José E. Velázquez (Philadelphia: Temple University Press, 1998), 42.

[12] Report of Central Committee Evaluation and Retreat, 2–5.

[13] Report of Central Committee Evaluation and Retreat, 5.

[14] Report of Central Committee Evaluation and Retreat, 5.

[15] Report of Central Committee Evaluation and Retreat, 5.

[16] Report of Central Committee Evaluation and Retreat, 11.

[17] Report of Central Committee Evaluation and Retreat, 5.

[18] Report of Central Committee Evaluation and Retreat, 3.

[19] YLP Ministry of Defense, "Beware of What You Say (Bugging)," *Palante* 3, no. 3 (1971): 14.

[20] Young Lords Party, "Police Agents," *Palante*, 3, no. 3 (1971): Defense Supplement, 14.

[21] Young Lords Party Central Committee, July 1971 Retreat Paper, 2.

[22] Juan González Papers, Box 29, Folders 10 and 11, Center for Puerto Rican Studies Library and Archives at Hunter College, New York City.

[23] Young Lords Party, Abramson, and Morales, *Palante*, 72.

[24] "Pig of the Year," *Palante* 3, no. 1 (1971): 14.

[25] Marisabel Brás, "The Changing of the Guard: Puerto Rico in 1898," World of 1898: The Spanish-American War, Hispanic Division, Library of Congress, https://www.loc.gov/rr/hispanic/1898/bras.html.

[26] Acosta-Belén and Santiago, *Puerto Ricans in the United States*, 57.

[27] Report of Central Committee Evaluation and Retreat, 20.

[28] Young Lords Party Central Committee, "Two Years of Struggle," *Palante* 3, no. 13 (1971): 10.

[29] Michael Staudenmaier, "Puerto Rican Independence Movement, 1898–Present," Marxists Internet Archive, 2798, https://www.marxists.org/history/erol/ncm-8/history-independence-movement.pdf.

[30] Andrés Torres, "A Brief History of the Puerto Rican Socialist Party in the United States," in *Revolution around the Corner: Voices from the Puerto Rican Socialist Party in the United States*, ed. José E. Velázquez, Carmen V. Rivera, and Andrés Torres (Philadelphia: Temple University Press, 2021), 29.

[31] Torres, "Introduction: Political Radicalism in the Diaspora," 7.

[32] Torres, "A Brief History of the Puerto Rican Socialist Party," 28.

CHAPTER 12. THE WOMEN'S UNION AND THE 12-POINT PROGRAM

[1] The Women's Union, *La Luchadora* 1, no.1. (June 1971)

[2] Report of Central Committee "Evaluation and Retreat," 17.

[3] Report of Central Committee "Evaluation and Retreat," 17.

[4] Report of Central Committee Evaluation and Retreat, 19.

[5] Report of Central Committee Evaluation and Retreat, 18. In the lumpen group, Pérez identified "prostitutes, drug addicts, welfare mothers, hustlers, the street people, unemployed, and prisoners in jail and all political prisoners."

[6] BlackPast, "(1965) The Moynihan Report: The Negro Family, the Case for National Action," January 21, 2007, https://www.blackpast.org/african-american-history/moynihan-report-1965/.

[7] Susan Greenbaum, "Opinion: Where's the Obituary for the Moynihan Report?" Al Jazeera America, October 10, 2015, http://america.aljazeera.com/opinions/2015/10/wheres-the-obituary-for-the-moynihan-report.html.

[8] Chong Chon-Smith, *East Meets Black: Asian and Black Masculinities in the Post–Civil Rights Era* (Jackson: University Press of Mississippi, 2015), 17.

[9] Chon-Smith, *East Meets Black*, 16–18.

[10] Kay S. Hymowitz, "The Black Family: 40 Years of Lies," *City Journal*, Summer 2005, https://www.city-journal.org/html/black-family-40-years-lies-12872.html.

[11] Daniel Geary, "Moynihan's Anti-Feminism," *Jacobin*, July 1, 2015, https://www.jacobinmag.com/2015/07/moynihans-report-fiftieth-anniversary-black-family/.

[12] Geary, "Moynihan's Anti-Feminism."

[13] Greenbaum, "Opinion: Where's the Obituary?"

[14] Springer, *Living for the Revolution*, 17.

[15] Young Lords Party Central Committee, July 1971 Retreat Paper, 20.

[16] Women's Union 12-Point Program and Platform. See appendix.

17 bell hooks, *Feminism Is for Everybody: Passionate Politics* (Cambridge, MA: South End Press, 2000), 42.

[18] Matthew Yarrow, "Colonial Legacy and Military Strategy: The U.S. Military in Puerto Rico," Latin America/Caribbean Program, American Friends Service Committee Peacebuilding Unit, n.d., https://www.afsc.org/sites/default/files/documents/2000%20Colonial%20Legacy%20and%20Military%20Strategy%20The%20US%20Military%20in%20Puerto%20Rico.pdf.

[19] Women's Union, *La Luchadora*, centerfold, 1971.

[20] Women's Union, "Esclava de casa," *La Luchadora* 1, no. 1 (July 1971): 2.

[21] Women's Union, "Machismo," *La Luchadora* 1, no. 2 (August 1971): 4.

[22] Friedrich Engels, *Origins of the Family, Private Property, and the State*, II. The Family, 4. The Monogamous Family, Marxists Internet Archive, https://www.marxists.org/archive/marx/works/1884/origin-family/ch02d.htm.

[23] Women's Union, "Esclava de casa," 2.

[24] Muzio, *Radical Imagination, Radical Humanity*, 1.

[25] Torres, "A Brief History of the Puerto Rican Socialist Party," 71.

[26] Carmen Vivian Rivera, "Our Movement: One Woman's Story," in *The Puerto Rican Movement: Voices from the Diaspora*, ed. Andrés Torres and José E. Velázquez (Philadelphia: Temple University Press, 1998), 204.

[27] Muzio, *Radical Imagination, Radical Humanity*, 38.

[28] Muzio, *Radical Imagination, Radical Humanity*, 88.

[29] Torres, "A Brief History of the Puerto Rican Socialist Party," 69.

[30] Zoilo Torres, "What the Puerto Rican Socialist Party Nurtured in Me," in *Revolution around the Corner: Voices from the Puerto Rican Socialist Party in the United States*, ed. José E. Velázquez, Carmen V. Rivera, and Andrés Torres (Philadelphia: Temple University Press, 2021), 282.

[31] "U.S. Withdraws from Vietnam," History, November 24, 2009; last modified May 25, 2022, https://www.history.com/this-day-in-history/u-s-withdraws-from-vietnam.

[32] Ruth Robinett, "Report on Canadian Conference with Indochinese Women," May 3, 1971, Marxists Internet Archive, https://www.marxists.org/history/etol/document/youth/ysa/ysa-docs-min-1971/04-AWWP-women-con-NEC-mins-07.pdf.

[33] Robinett, "Report on Canadian Conference," 2.

[33] Stephen Zunes and Jesse Laird, "The US Anti-Vietnam War Movement (1964–1973)," International Center on Nonviolent Conflict, January 2010, https://www.nonviolent-conflict.org/us-anti-vietnam-war-movement-1964-1973/.

[35] Enck-Wanzer, The Young Lords: A Reader, 181.

[36] Enck-Wanzer, The Young Lords: A Reader, 180.

[37] Enck-Wanzer, The Young Lords: A Reader, 182

[38] Denise Comanne, "How Patriarchy and Capitalism Combine to Aggravate the Oppression of Women," Committee for the Abolition of Illegitimate Debt, May 28, 2020, https://www.cadtm.org/How-Patriarchy-and-Capitalism-Combine-to-Aggravate-the-Oppression-of-Women.

CHAPTER 13. FROM REVOLUTIONARY TO NARROW NATIONALISM

[1] Aja Monet, *My Mother Was a Freedom Fighter* (Chicago: Haymarket Books, 2017), 3.

[2] "Pentagon Papers," History, August 2, 2011; last modified June 9, 2021, https://www.history.com/topics/vietnam-war/pentagon-papers.

[3] Katherine T. McCaffrey, Military Power and Popular Protest: The U.S. Navy in Vieques, Puerto Rico (Chicago: Rutgers University Press, 2002), 68.

[4] Young Lords Party Central Committee, July 1971 Retreat Paper, 6.

[5] Central Committee, July 1971 Retreat Paper, 3.

[6] Central Committee, July 1971 Retreat Paper, 5.

[7] Central Committee, July 1971 Retreat Paper," 5.

[8] Iris Morales, *Through the Eyes of Rebel Women: The Young Lords, 1969–1976* (New York: Red Sugarcane Press, 2016), 183; see also Palante 2, no. 12 (1970): 11.

[9] Central Committee, July 1971 Retreat Paper, 14.

[10] Central Committee, July 1971 Retreat Paper, 5.

[11] Central Committee, July 1971 Retreat Paper, 15.

[12] Central Committee, July 1971 Retreat Paper, 6.

[13] Central Committee, July 1971 Retreat Paper, 4.

[14] Central Committee, July 1971 Retreat Paper, 6.

[15] Young Lords Party Central Committee, *The Ideology of the Young Lords Party*, 31.

[16] Central Committee, July 1971 Retreat Paper, 6.

[17] Central Committee, July 1971 Retreat Paper, 6.

[18] Central Committee, July 1971 Retreat Paper, 6.

[19] Central Committee, July 1971 Retreat Paper, 3.

[20] Young Lords Party Central Committee, "Communiqué," 1.

[21] Third World Students' League, "United We Stand, Divided We Walk," *Palante* 3, no. 19 (1971): 5.

[22] Puerto Rican Student Union, "The Puerto Rican Studies Conference," *Palante* 3, no. 20 (1971): 9.

[23] Bryant, "Puerto Rican Women's Roles," 130.

[24] Rivera, "Our Movement: One Woman's Story," 205.

[25] Bryant, "Puerto Rican Women's Roles," 64.

[26] Bryant, "Puerto Rican Women's Roles," 67.

[27] Bryant, "Puerto Rican Women's Roles," 69.

[28] Bryant, "Puerto Rican Women's Roles," 77.

[29] Lina Sunseri, "Moving Beyond the Feminism Versus National Dichotomy: An Anti-Colonial Feminist Perspective on Aboriginal Liberation Struggles," *Canadian Woman Studies/Le Cahiers de la Femme* 20, no. 2 (2000), https://cws.journals.yorku.ca/index.php/cws/article/view/7621.

[30] Radwa Saad and Sara Soumaya Abed, "A Revolution Deferred: Sexual and Gender-Based Violence in Egypt," in *Gender, Protests and Political Change in Africa*, ed. Awino Okech (Cham, Switzerland: Palgrave Macmillan, 2020), 81–106.

[31] Ranjoo Seodu Herr, "The Possibility of Nationalist Feminism," *Hypatia* 18, no. 3 (August 2003): 137, doi:10.1111/j.1527-2001.2003.tb00825.

[32] Herr, "The Possibility of Nationalist Feminism," 142.

[33] Camille Le Pioufle, "Feminism and the Puerto Rican Independence movement since the 1950s: From Unrequited Love to a Matching pair?" Dumas - Dépôt Universitaire De Mémoires Après Soutenance, last modified 2019, https://dumas.ccsd.cnrs.fr/dumas-02172215/ file/2018_MM2_Le_Pioufle C. pdf. 92.

[34] Pablo "Yoruba" Guzmán, "Report to Central Committee, December 7, 1971," 13. In this forty-five-page report, Guzmán discusses his trip to China and presents ideas for the future of the Young Lords Party. Iris Morales files.

[35] Pablo "Yoruba" Guzmán, "Our Present Situation: Statement, Analysis, Suggestions, Draft Paper for Discussion," November 10, 1971, 1. Iris Morales files.

[36] Pablo "Yoruba" Guzmán, "Report #1 to Juan González and Gloria Fontanez, November 14, 1971," 1–2. This two-page report describes the YLP's deteriorating conditions and Guzmán's meetings with national staff members. Iris Morales files.

[37] Guzmán, "Report to the Central Committee, December 7, 1971," 17–18.

[38] Central Committee, "Communiqué," 1.

[39] Central Committee, "Communiqué," 5.

[40] Central Committee, "Communiqué," 23–24.

[41] Yellow Seeds broadside, Balch Institute for Ethnic Studies, Historical Society of Pennsylvania, http://www2.hsp.org/exhibits/Balch%20exhibits/chinatown/yellowseeds.html.

[42] Jean Tepperman, "The Material Basis of Women's Oppression in Capitalist Society," Marxists Internet Archive, last modified July 1981, https://www.marxists.org/history/erol/ncm-8/19812302.htm.

[43] Central Committee, "Communiqué," 17.

[44] Lulu Rovira, "Children's Center Opens," *Palante* 4, no. 11 (1972): 6.

[45] Women's Union, "FBI and City Threaten to Close Down Day Care Center," *Palante* 4, no. 19 (1972): 6.

[46] Lydia Silva, "Why a Women's Union," *Palante* 4, no. 8 (1972): 6.

[47] Juan González, "On Our Errors," *Palante* 4, no. 4 (1972): 12.

[48] González, "On Our Errors," 12.

[49] Central Committee, "Communiqué," 21.

[50] Young Lords Party Central Committee, "Faction Leaves Young Lords Party," *Palante* 4, no. 12 (1972), special edition.

[51] Puerto Rican Revolutionary Workers Organization (PRRWO), "Resolutions and Speeches," First Party Congress, 1972, 31.

[52] PRRWO, "Resolutions and Speeches," 14.

[53] Juan González Papers, Box 29, Folders 10 and 11, Center for Puerto Rican Studies Library and Archives at Hunter College, New York City.

[54] Juan González Papers, Box 29, Folders 10 and 11, Center for Puerto Rican Studies Library and Archives at Hunter College, New York City.

[55] PRRWO, "Resolutions and Speeches," 2.

[56] PRRWO, "Resolutions and Speeches," 32.

[57] Morales, *Through the Eyes of Rebel Women*, 118–23.

PART V. RECKONING WITH THE PAST

[1] Eduardo Galeano, *Open Veins of Latin America: Five Centuries of the Pillage of a Continent* (New York: Monthly Review Press, 1973), 267.

CHAPTER 14. STATE SURVEILLANCE, POLICE VIOLENCE, AND THE ENEMY WITHIN

[1] Brian Glick, preface to *The COINTELPRO Papers: Documents from the FBI's Secret Wars against Dissent in the United States*, by Ward Churchill and Jim Vander Wall (Boston: South End Press, 1990), xv.

[2] Carmin Maffea, "The Fight to Abolish the Police Is the Fight to Abolish Capitalism," Left Voice, June 10, 2020, https://www.leftvoice.org/the-fight-to-abolish-the-police-is-the-fight-to-abolish-capitalism/.

[3] Aryeh Neier, "Surveillance by the FBI," *Index on Censorship* 10, no. 2 (April 1981): 44, https://journals.sagepub.com/toc/ioca/10/2.

[4] Alex Zambito, "The FBI's War on the Left: A Short History of COINTELPRO," Midwestern Marx, October 4, 2020, https://www.midwesternmarx.com/articles/the-fbis-war-on-the-left-a-short-history-of-cointelpro-by-alex-zambito.

[5] Ward Churchill and Jim Vander Wall, *The COINTELPRO Papers: Documents from the FBI's Secret Wars against Dissent in the United States* (Boston: South End Press, 1990), 209.

[6] "Black Panther Greatest Threat to U.S. Security," *Desert Sun* (Palm Springs, CA), July 16, 1969, at the California Digital Newspaper Collection, https://cdnc.ucr.edu/?a=d&d=DS19690716.2.89&e=-------en--20--1--txt-txIN--------1.

[7] Nina Renata Aron, "When the Black Justice Movement Got Too Powerful, the FBI Got Scared and Got Ugly," Medium, February 9, 2017, https://timeline.com/black-justice-fbi-scared-ebcf2986515c.

[8] Aron, "When the Black Justice Movement Got Too Powerful."

[9] Zambito, "The FBI's War on the Left."

[10] "Police Kill Two Members of the Black Panther Party," History, November 13, 2009; last modified December 1, 2021, https://www.history.com/this-day-in-history/police-kill-two-members-of-the-black-panther-party.

[11] Staudenmaier, "Puerto Rican Independence Movement," 2769.

[12] César Ayala, "Political Persecution in Puerto Rico: Uncovering Secret Files," *Against the Current*, no. 85 (March–April 20000), https://againstthecurrent.org/atc085/p1685/.

[13] Churchill and Vander Wall, *The COINTELPRO Papers*, 69.

[14] "The Basics on COINTELPRO and How to Counter It," Real People's Media, March 10, 2020, https://realpeoples.media/the-basics-on-cointelpro-and-how-to-counter-it/.

[15] Glick, preface to *The COINTELPRO Papers*, x.

[16] Ryan Wong, "The Long 1960s, Seen through NYPD Surveillance Photographs," Hyperallergic, December 8, 2017, https://hyperallergic.com/403347/the-long-1960s-seen-through-nypd-surveillance-photographs/.

[17] Kristian Williams, *Our Enemies in Blue: Police and Power in America* (Cambridge, MA: South End Press, 2007), 155.

[18] Marilynn S. Johnson, "Challenging Police Repression: Federal Activism and Local Reform in New York City," in *Uniform Behavior: Police Localism and National Politics*, ed. Stacy K. McGoldrick and Andrea McArdle (New York: Palgrave Macmillan, 2006), 86.

[19] Sherry Wolf, "Spies, Lies, and War: Lessons of COINTELPRO," *International Socialist Review*, September–October 2006, at Third World Traveler, https://thirdworldtraveler.com/FBI/Lessons_COINTELPRO.html.

[20] Chisun Lee, "Why the NYPD Is Fighting for the Right to Spy on You," *Village Voice*, December 18, 2002, 33.

[21] Churchill and Vander Wall, *The COINTELPRO Papers*, 69.

[22] Kevin Zeese and Margaret Flowers, "Police Violence and Racism Have Always Been Tools of Capitalism," Countercurrents, June 22, 2020, https://countercurrents.org/2020/06/police-violence-and-racism-have-always-been-tools-of-capitalism/.

[23] YLP Defense Ministry, "Beware of What You Say (Bugging)," *Palante* 3, no. 3 (1971): 10.

[24] Neier, "Surveillance by the FBI," 45.

[25] This information was obtained from various Freedom of Information Act files dated from December 1968 to December 20, 1972.

[26] Hernan Flores, "Repression against the Young Lords," *Palante* 3, no. 3 (1971): 9.

[27] "Handschu V. Special Services Division (Challenging NYPD Surveillance Practices Targeting Political Groups)," New York Civil Liberties Union, https://www.nyclu.org/en/cases/handschu-v-special-services-division-challenging-nypd-surveillance-practices-targeting.

[28] Josmar Trujillo, "No Backspace: NY's Rules for Policing Political Activity Still Need Tightening," *City Limits*, March 17, 2017, https://citylimits.org/2017/03/17/no-backspace-nys-rules-for-policing-political-activity-still-need-tightening/.

[29] Joseph Goldstein, "Old New York Police Surveillance Is Found, Forcing Big Brother Out of Hiding," *New York Times*, June 16, 2016, https://www.nytimes.com/2016/06/17/nyregion/old-new-york-police-surveillance-is-found-forcing-big-brother-out-of-hiding.html?searchResultPosition=3.

CHAPTER 15. "THE PAST DOES NOT EXIST INDEPENDENTLY FROM THE PRESENT"

[1] Romay Guerra, "New World Coming: Race in Socialist Cuba." YouTube video, https://www.youtube.com/watch?v=5jJQBtPTPks

[2] J. Nelson, "Abortions under Community Control," 157.

[3] Sylvia Walby, "Theorising Patriarchy," *Sociology* 23, no. 2 (May 1989): 214, https://www.jstor.org/stable/42853921.

[4] Soares, "Joy, Rage, and Activism," 947.

[5] Rose M. Brewer, "Black Radical Theory and Practice: Gender, Race, and Class," *Socialism and Democracy* 17, no. 2 (Winter–Spring 2003), ttps://sdonline.org/issue/33/black-radical-theory-and-practice-gender-race-and-class.

[6] "Women at the Core of the Fight against COVID-19 Crisis," Organisation for Economic Co-operation and Development, April 1, 2020, https://www.oecd.org/coronavirus/policy-responses/women-at-the-core-of-the-fight-against-covid-19-crisis-553a8269/.

[7] Kate Power, "The COVID-19 Pandemic Has Increased the Care Burden of Women and Families," *Sustainability: Science, Practice and Policy* 16, no. 1 (2020), https://www.tandfonline.com/doi/full/10.1080/15487733.2020.1776561.

[8] Justin Fox and Elaine He, "The Pandemic Was Historically Bad for Working-Class Women," *Bloomberg*, March 30, 2021, https://www.bloomberg.com/opinion/articles/2021-03-30/covid-19-job-losses-were-historic-for-black-and-hispanic-women.

[9] Rick W. A. Smith, "How Imperialism Gave Us 2020," *Sapiens*, February 16, 2021, https://www.sapiens.org/culture/imperialism-2020/.

[10] Edna Acosta-Belén and Christine E. Bose, "From Structural Subordination to Empowerment: Women and Development in Third World Contexts," Gender and Society 4, no. 3 (1990): 300, doi:10.1177/089124390004003003.

[11] Natália M. De Souza and Lara M. Rodrigues Selis, "Gender violence and feminist resistance in Latin America," International Feminist Journal of Politics 24, no. 1 (2022): 7, doi:10.1080/14616742.2021.2019483.

[12] Juan C. Dávila and Osvaldo Budet, "Organizing to End Gender-Based Violence in PR," When We Fight, We Win, podcast audio, https://www.whenwefightwewin.com/listen/season-2-episode-2-estadodeemergencia-organizing-to-end-gender-based-violence-in-pr/.

[13] Marisol LeBrón, "Where Were You When We Were Being Killed? How Puerto Rican Feminists Help Us Understand Policing and State Violence," Society and Space, October 1, 2020, https://www.societyandspace.org/articles/where-were-you-when-we-were-being-killed-how-puerto-rican-feminists-help-us-understand-policing-and-state-violence.

[14] Kristine Liao, "6 Ways Young People Stepped Up to Make the World a Better Place in 2020," Global Citizen, December 24, 2020, https://www.globalcitizen.org/en/content/2020-youth-activism/.

[15] Geoff Gilliard, "New Research Reveals Power of Women's Movements over the Past 50 Years - SFU News - Simon Fraser University," Simon Fraser University, last modified March 6, 2020, https://www.sfu.ca/sfunews/stories/2020/03/new-research-reveals-power-of-women-s-movements-over-the-past-50.html.

[16] Carin Zissis et al., "Explainer: Abortion Rights in Latin America," Americas Society/Council of the Americas, last modified June 28, 2022, https://www.as-coa.org/articles/explainer-abortion-rights-latin-america.

[17] Erika Guevara Rosas, "From Mobilization to Solidarity: The Power of Feminist Struggles in Latin America," openDemocracy, December 2, 2021, https://www.opendemocracy.net/en/north-africa-west-asia/from-mobilization-to-solidarity-the-power-of-feminist-struggles-in-latin-america/.

INDEX

Bold page numbers refer to illustrations

Workers' Federation, people's organization of the YLP, 141, 161, 162

ABOUT THE AUTHOR

I ris Morales is a longtime activist, educator, media producer, and author. Over several decades, she has been involved in movements for
social justice and human rights with a focus on economic and racial
justice, women's rights, and the decolonization of Puerto Rico. Cur-
rently, she serves on the advisory board of the *Instituto de Formación
Política* of Mijente, a political home for Latinx people who seek racial,
economic, gender, and climate justice.

Since the 1980s, Morales has created programs at the intersection of
social justice and media as a tool for change and has founded several organizations dedicated to youth media education. As founder and editor
of Red Sugarcane Press, Morales brings her love of community and history to produce books and projects about the experiences of Black, Indigenous, and people of color in the Americas. Her anthologies include
Voices from Puerto Rico: Post-Hurricane María, inspired by her trip to
Puerto Rico after Hurricane Maria to assist with the launch of a fund to
bring resources and financial support to grassroots communities. This
bilingual collection of writings from activists and artists brings attention
to local organizing efforts. *Latinas: Struggles & Protests in 21st Century
USA* is a collection of poetry and prose reflecting on women's lived experiences in the United States and the ways that Latinas advance gender
justice.

During the 1960s and 1970s, Morales was a leading member of the
New York Young Lords, serving as deputy minister of education, cofounder of its Women's Caucus and Women's Union, and coleader of
the Philadelphia chapter. Morales brings a feminist perspective to documenting the organization's challenges, setbacks, and accomplishments.
She is the producer, writer, and codirector of the award-winning documentary, *¡Palante, Siempre Palante!,* which was broadcast on public television in 1996, and continues to be screened in classrooms and community venues across the United States and the Caribbean.

A native New Yorker, Morales holds a JD degree from New York
University School of Law and an M.F.A in Integrated Media Arts from
Hunter College.

About Red Sugarcane Press

Red Sugarcane Press, Inc. is an independent press dedicated to the history and culture of Puerto Rican, Black, Indigenous, and people of color in the Americas. It aims to amplify the voices of Indigenous and African peoples and their descendants who from enslavement to the present have triumphed through the courage and tenacity of many generations.

Red Sugarcane Press publishes well-known and emerging writers, artists, and activists whose works break new ground. The books and related projects are collaborations whose perspectives and artistic styles broaden our knowledge, inform, and entertain. Their radical imaginations and distinct voices encourage discussion and inspire action for a more just world.

Current publications include a variety of genres, poetry collections, plays, political histories, children's stories, and anthologies; several are bilingual in English and Spanish. Books are sold on the Internet in both print and e-book versions available on multiple platforms to individuals, bookstores, and libraries.

www.RedSugarcanePress.com